# MURDERED INNOCENTS

# COREY MITCHELL

**PINNACLE BOOKS**
Kensington Publishing Corp.
http://www.kensingtonbooks.com

For Audra,
A great teacher, a best friend, a wonderful wife

# PROLOGUE

*Friday, December 6, 1991*
*Hillside Center, West Anderson Lane*
*Austin, Texas*
*11:47 p.m.*

*Smoke.*

Austin police officer Troy Gay saw the smoke rising from the strip center mall in North Austin just off MoPac Freeway. Officer Gay had served as a police officer since 1987; however, he had just begun to work in Austin one month earlier.

Officer Gay was working an overtime DWI assignment on this blustery Friday night. He drove his marked police cruiser around the Shoal Creek area, east on Anderson Lane. It was a thriving area with several shops and restaurants, not to mention the expansive Northcross Mall, which was teeming with teenagers.

The smoke began to rise from the area of the Hillside Center strip center. Hillside was typical of the strip center malls that were taking over Texas towns like the bubonic plague as it swept through medieval country-sides during the Dark Ages.

Officer Gay drove up Anderson Lane to Rockwood Lane and saw the smoke billowing up from behind the buildings. He circled his cruiser around to the back side of the stores down a dark alley. As he rounded the corner, he slowed the vehicle down so he could make sure he spotted the location of the fire. It did not take long before he saw flames spew out of the middle of a set of metal double doors. The yellowish orange flames flicked out of the crack in the door like the tongue of a demon.

At the same time, the doors of the building next to the fire opened up. A man peered out and saw Officer Gay. Jorge Barney, owner of the Party House Depot, asked Officer Gay what was going on.

"Sir, I need for you to grab your belongings and get out of there," Gay ordered.

Barney complied and retreated back inside his store.

Officer Gay popped the gear of his patrol car in reverse and backed up out of the alleyway. He headed for the front of the stores to determine which business was on fire. He pulled around front and scanned the stores. There was a copier shop, a women's clothing store, a pizzeria, and the Party House Depot. He noticed smoke poring out of the Party House Depot. He also noticed it poring out of the business next door: I Can't Believe It's Yogurt.

Gay grabbed his radio microphone and contacted dispatch. He spoke calmly. "We have a fire in a small business at the corner of Burnet and Anderson Lane."

One problem.

Officer Gay mistakenly gave the wrong address.

Officer Dennis Smith, driving a different patrol car, also spotted the smoke. He radioed in the correct location of the fire. Officer Smith turned his vehicle around and made a beeline for the strip center.

Officers Gay and Smith exited their vehicles. They walked around back into the alleyway. This time, Gay noted, the flames had stopped. Something peculiar, however, caught his eye. Water began to gush out of the bottom of the double doors. This did not make any sense as the Austin Fire Department (AFD) firefighters had not yet arrived at the scene. Unbeknownst to Officer Gay, a PVC water pipe burst from the yogurt shop ceiling because of the intense heat. A torrent of water rushed out of the pipe, onto the floor, and out the back door. The two officers decided to head back to the front of the store and wait for the firefighters.

The officers cleared the area in front of the yogurt shop. They asked Barney to move his car. A space was cleared for fire engine #8, driven by Henri LaCaille, and captained by Lieutenant Rene Hector Garza. Firefighter David Deveau was the designated tailboard man. The lumbering candy-apple-red fire truck pulled directly in front of the entrance to the yogurt shop. Lieutenant Garza and firefighter Deveau leaped from the truck and immediately suited up. Officers Gay and Smith made sure that all of the nearby businesses were cleared so no one would get hurt.

It appeared to be a routine fire call.

Engine 8's job, according to Garza, was "to make entry, find the fire, and put it out with our water that we carry and hoses."

"Deveau, I want you to remove the rack line," Garza instructed his charge. The rack line is a 1¾-inch hose line that is attached to the fire truck. Deveau did as he was told. He was ready for the attack line on the fire. Suited up with handy talkies (handheld radios), hand lights, flame-retardant jackets, protective face pieces, and air packs, the two men were prepared to enter the store.

Gray smoke seeped out the front door. Garza realized that the fire was still burning. He noticed the shop windows were covered with black soot. The firemen approached the front door. Garza's motto was: "You try before you pry." He walked up to the front door, grasped the door handle, and pulled. It did not open. He was forced to pry it open. A wave of smoke greeted the two firefighters. Garza glanced up at the ceiling at the front of the store. Smoke scampered across the ceiling like Linda Blair's deleted Spider Crawl scene from *The Exorcist*. Slowly his eyes adjusted to the view in front of him. It appeared as if there were several dining tables with wooden chairs stacked on top of them. This was the dining-room area of the yogurt shop.

Garza and Deveau got down on their bellies and began to crawl through the front of the store. Being low to the ground provided better visibility in the heavily smoke-filled room. Deveau began to charge the water hose. As the water flowed, he led the way to the back of the store. Garza attached himself to Deveau's hip. Neither man could see more than a few inches in front of them. The billowing smoke practically blinded their path. Even the hand lights they carried provided little assistance.

Garza and Deveau inched their way up to the counter. They did not see any flames. They worked their way along the counter until they reached the right-hand side. They found themselves in a small hallway that went from the counter to the kitchen, located in back of the store.

They now saw the fire.

Garza noticed flames whipping above a large walk-in cooler, which was used to store yogurt. The two firefighters sloshed through the water on the floor. Garza pointed out the hot spot to Deveau, who stood up and opened the nozzle of the fire hose. Instead of a forceful rush of fluid, water merely dribbled out.

Garza tapped Deveau on the shoulder again. He signaled with his hands and said, "I'm going back outside." Deveau understood and nodded. Garza headed back out so he could increase the water pressure. He grabbed onto the hose and used it as a guide through the dense smoke. Once at the entrance, he signaled to LaCaille to increase the water pressure. Garza immediately headed back inside to assist Deveau. The two men began to "knock out" the fire (douse it with water), which caused steam, which then further doused the flames. Within one to two minutes, the firefighters had the conflagration under control. Only a few glowing embers remained.

Garza needed to ventilate the room. The combination of smoke, steam, and darkness created a claustrophobic enclosure. Neither man could see. Garza ran his gloved hands along the wall searching for a door or window to open. He felt something and began to reach for it when Deveau grabbed his shoulder. Using his hand light, Deveau directed the lieutenant's eyes to the ground. He pointed with his other hand to something that looked familiar.

"Is that a foot?" Deveau shouted through his protective mask.

"Yeah, I think it's a foot," replied an anxious yet composed Garza. "I want to take a closer look."

Garza stepped back and crouched down for a more thorough inspection. As he scooted backward, he bumped into something. He looked back and down. He could not make it out at first. Once he shone his hand light, he realized what he had bumped into.

It was an arm.

Garza realized it was from a different person. It was the body of a young girl. She lay flat on her stomach, with her right arm underneath her chest, clutching the air with her right hand. She was completely naked and facedown in more than an inch of mucky water. A cash register drawer lay beside her head.

Steeling himself, Garza looked up at Deveau and shouted through his face piece, "Stay put! I'm gonna get some more help!"

Deveau gave him the thumbs-up and watched as his boss went for more help. He stood alone in the smoke-filled, pitch-black room, with two dead bodies at his feet.

Garza made it outside, scuttled over to the fire truck, and got on the radio. He knew something was not right. He walked over to the battalion chief, who assumed control while the men were inside the building.

"Something's wrong. We've got two victims. Both of them are naked. One is completely burned," Garza informed the chief. "I don't think we should do anything. Something is wrong here."

Firefighter LaCaille stepped up. "I'm ready to go in, sir!"

"No, I don't think you should," Garza warned his charge. "Something's not right."

Garza went back in the store. He slowly made his way to the back kitchen area, using the hose to guide him. As he came upon Deveau, he noticed a tiny light escaping from within the acrid smoke. It came from the back double doors. The room still needed to be ventilated, so he headed toward the doors, leaned his shoulder against one of them, and it opened easily. As he turned around, he saw the burned body within inches of his feet. As the smoke rushed out of the building, the scene became clearer.

It was worse than he imagined.

A second charred corpse stared back at him. The eyes were open, but clouded with a dark, milky sheen. An upside-down smile like that of a possessed clown stared back at him. It was the head of another body. It appeared to be positioned underneath the first charred body. The charred body was unrecognizable as a specific person. The lower torso was distinguishable; however, it appeared to have suffered charring and rupturing, or splitting, due to the intense heat from the flames. Both charred bodies were burned beyond recognition. The third body appeared to be completely nude as well.

Garza and Deveau both got a better look at the two charred bodies. They appeared to be female. Not only were they nearly completely burned, but their hands were bound behind their backs. One of the bodies was draped over the other at a forty-five-degree angle. The legs of each female were spread open. Their backsides lay upon the hard, messy floor. The fire did not burn beneath them and left the two females with undamaged flesh on their backsides. They appeared to have gags tied over their mouths.

Garza surveyed the scene. He had never seen anything like it.

But it was not over.

As the smoke dissipated, fourth body came into focus. Twelve inches away from the stacked bodies lay a third charred body on its side, right next to a metal rack shelf that lined the east sidewall. A metal ceiling rod rested in between the corpse's legs. Once Garza got closer, he shone his hand light on what was once a human face. Now it was simply a mixture of black and blood.

At that point, Garza exited the yogurt shop. He stepped through the metal double doors and outside into the back alley. A fire truck had arrived in the back and spotlighted the inside of the store with bright klieg lights. Garza would not return.

Inside the shop, Deveau's face piece alarm screeched, which signaled that he was low on air. He waited until another firefighter entered the scene. Robert Kimmons came in to replace him. Deveau handed the hose to Kimmons and exited through the front entrance. When he stepped out, he was surprised to see almost twenty firefighters on the premises.

Deveau restocked with a new air bottle and headed back into the shop. By the time he returned, there were three more firefighters ready to take his place. Instead of adding to the crowded scene, he turned around and went back outside to converse with Lieutenant Garza. The two men who discovered the bodies were reassigned to clear smoke out of the adjoining businesses.

Back inside, firefighter Kimmons manned the hose and continued to knock down flare-ups. As he finished, he walked over to the pile of bodies in the back of the shop. He leaned in to take a closer look. He gasped as he saw something shiny positioned between the legs of one of the bodies. He peered even closer and saw what he believed was an ice-cream scoop with a retractable thumb mechanism used to release the ice cream. He believed the handle was sticking out and that the metallic scoop was shoved inside the corpse's vagina. Kimmons recoiled and stepped back. He turned to leave and saw three or four more people enter the front entrance of the yogurt shop. They appeared to be firefighters and emergency medical service (EMS) technicians.

"Hey, guys, we need to be careful in there. We've got multiple bodies," Kimmons instructed. "We want to keep it as clean as possible."

The other men nonchalantly acknowledged his presence. Kimmons left through the front entrance of the shop while the group of men headed to the pyre.

As Kimmons walked out, he spotted Sergeant John Jones, of the Austin Police Department (APD). The short, portly African American officer was followed by a female television newsreader and a television cameraman from the Austin CBS affiliate, Channel 7. Just minutes earlier, Jones was called to the scene by police dispatch. At first, the report stated that a robbery had occurred and that there was a fire. Three bodies were discovered. Jones later stated that after he drove about one mile, dispatch called again. A fourth body was found.

Sergeant Jones spoke with the battalion chief and then ambled through the yogurt shop front entrance. By the time he arrived in the back kitchen and office area, the firefighters had the place entirely lit up. Jones had no problem seeing the aftermath. He described it as "wholesale carnage."

"I looked in there," he recalled in a slight Southern accent, "and said, 'Oh, my Gawd. . . .'"

Sergeant Jones learned the name of two teenage girls who worked in the yogurt shop. Jennifer Harbison, seventeen, and her best friend, Eliza Thomas, also seventeen, who lived just a few blocks from the store. He had no idea who the other two girls were.

Jones appeared horror-struck by the chaos before him.

"It was like no other crime scene in history."

He had no idea.

# PART I
# THE GIRLS

# CHAPTER 1

Jennifer and Sarah Harbison were the precocious daughters of Mike and Barbara Harbison. Their parents were high-school sweethearts from the small town of Hooks, Texas. Mike and Barbara graduated from high school and married one year later on Independence Day, July 4, 1970.

They were "babies," Barbara Harbison said of the couple. She described herself as the more "loosey-goosey liberal type," while Mike was definitely more small-town and conservative. She added that "they were so poor that they did not even have a car between them. We had to get a loan just to get enough money for a down payment on a car."

Barbara longed to spread her wings and escape the small-town mentality. She was ready to assert her independence along with Mike. One year to the day after they were married, on July 4, 1971, the couple packed up and moved to Austin. Barbara immediately found work at a Casual Corner store, located in Highland Mall. She worked there for three months before switching to a job at the old Capital National Bank in downtown Austin.

In less than three years, Barbara became pregnant. On May 9, 1974, she gave birth to a tiny baby girl they named Jennifer. Mike then decided they would be better off back home in Hooks. Again the Harbisons packed their bags and moved halfway across the state of Texas. Within less than 2½ years, on October 28, 1976, Barbara gave birth to another daughter, whom they named Sarah.

The serenity, however, did not last.

Barbara was still searching for something that the town of Hooks could not offer. On May 14, 1979, she packed her bags and took the two girls with her back to Austin. She knew the only independence she could find existed in the Texas state capital.

"When I left Mike, I felt like I could do anything," Barbara exclaimed.

Barbara soon realized she could not do it all. She talked about the responsibility of feeding her daughters, keeping clothes on their backs, and providing a roof over their heads.

"It's much harder than people acknowledge. It was much harder for me."

Later that year, one specific group of people helped out the young mother. Child, Inc. took Barbara Harbison and her two daughters under their protective wing. Child, Inc., a government-funded program, provides early education for children whose parents earn less than the poverty level. Jennifer was five years old and starting kindergarten. Barbara had transportation issues because kindergarten only provided a half-day program and she was unable to pick her daughter up from school. She also could not get Jennifer into a day care program. A friend informed her about Child, Inc., but she resisted at first. Eventually she relented and asked for help. Child, Inc. accepted Jennifer. They later accepted Sarah. The assistance from Child, Inc. allowed Barbara to work, save money, and raise her daughters properly.

The following year, in 1980, Barbara met a young Italian man by the name of Francis "Skip" Suraci. The couple married that same year. Barbara stated that "he didn't really want to get married." However, she considered herself and her two daughters to be "quite a catch." Skip relented.

According to Barbara, Skip was "a little harsh with the girls. Stern." He was "a bit of an outsider in the family." Yet, somehow, the couple managed to make their relationship work.

Barbara recalled the precociousness of her youngest daughter, Sarah. When she was in the fourth grade, she informed her mother, "Mom, I don't know everything you think I know." Barbara was stunned. She truly believed her daughters were the most intelligent children in the world.

As the girls grew, they became involved in a multitude of fun experiences. They loved the outdoors, they loved to playfully pick on each other and their mother, and they loved music. Both Mike Harbison and Skip Suraci loved to sing, so the girls grew up with a deep appreciation for music. Both girls would often sing around the house. They played musical instruments as well. Jennifer learned to play the viola in fourth grade. Sarah would also learn an instrument in fourth grade, the alto saxophone. She learned it in her music class at the Saint Louis Catholic School, located off Anderson Lane in North Austin. Both sisters enrolled in the private school in 1986.

The girls grew into beautiful young ladies. Jennifer, all eighty-six pounds of her, stood five feet two, and practically disappeared when she turned sideways. Her mother claimed that she was a fireball of energy and called her "a skinny little thing." She added that Jennifer "lived off chips and soda. She had terrible health. She never slept at night. Too much caffeine. She had a hard time getting up in the morning." Her mother also described her as "wound up real tight." Jennifer hardly ever ate, not because she was anorexic or bulimic, but because she was so energetic and active.

Sarah also stood five feet two and was the heavier of the sisters. Of course, anyone standing next to Jennifer would have been considered heavier. Sarah grew into a lovely young woman with flawless peaches-and-cream skin and big, thick blond Texas hair. Sarah was the more conservative of the two girls. She kept in shape and ate a healthy diet all the time. She was the quieter of the two girls, but she was known for her witty sense of humor.

"Sarah was a serious comedian," her mother said. "She would watch any comedian on videotape. She was studying punch lines, pauses, and timing. She used to love to cut up."

Both girls excelled in their studies. Honors classes were the norm. They were also involved in a multitude of scholastic extracurricular activities. Jennifer served as a team manager for the Lanier High School Vikettes drill team for two years. She told her mother that when she first started, the older girls did not trust her. Eventually they came to rely on her, but when it was Jennifer's turn to be offered a position on the team, she turned it down. Her mother asked her why after she spent so much time helping out.

"I've already conquered that," Jennifer replied, referring to winning the trust of the older girls.

Sarah was the more athletic of the two girls. She was proficient at volleyball and basketball. She also participated as an Extra Gold cheerleader her freshman year.

As they got older, the girls' attentions turned toward animals, boys, and music. Country on all three counts.

They loved to listen to country music. "They were

way into Willie," Barbara recounted, referring to Austin native and country music legend Willie Nelson. The girls also found joy in singing songs by George Strait and Garth Brooks.

The sisters also liked the older boys at Lanier High School, especially the ones in the Future Farmers of America (FFA). "Older boys in blue jeans," their mother recalled with a laugh. "That was a plus right there for Jennifer."

The girls, however, were interested in more than just cowboys. Both girls shone in their agricultural endeavors. Jennifer served as the school's agricultural club president her junior and senior year in high school.

"She enjoyed being part of the team. I also believe the girls enjoyed ag because it was something I had no interest in. It was a way for them to assert their independence from me."

The girls learned responsibility in their agricultural courses. They would head over to the FFA farm every day before and after school to care and feed their animals.

Jennifer and Sarah both thrived on competition. Their mother recalled one FFA meet where both sisters showed off their prize lambs. The girls were positioned in opposite brackets. Each girl progressed to the next round, beating each prospective opponent, until they both won their brackets and faced off against each other.

Jennifer also excelled in a national horticultural competition through FFA that took place in Kansas City. She placed eighth in the country, but was more excited about getting to see snow and ice for the first time.

Jennifer's boyfriend, Sam Buchanan, was also a senior at Lanier High School. The stocky blond cowboy was a member of FFA and played baseball for the Lanier Vikings during his first three years of high school. Everyone on the baseball team fell in love with Jennifer.

Even head coach Ed Sanders loved having Jennifer around. She became the team's unofficial mascot.

Jennifer Harbison's best friend was the olive-complected, dark-haired Eliza Thomas. Eliza was born on May 16, 1974, one week after Jennifer was born. Eliza's parents, James and Maria Thomas, divorced when she was little. Her father, a social worker, remarried Norma Fowler, an associate professor of botany from the University of Texas. Eliza, Maria Thomas, and Eliza's younger sister, Sonora, all lived together in a small house off Skylark Lane, less than one-half mile from I Can't Believe It's Yogurt.

Eliza started working in the yogurt shop in late 1990. Several months later, she helped Jennifer get a job there. Eliza worked at the yogurt shop so she could buy and then later maintain a dilapidated green 1971 Karmann Ghia. The car was in a constant state of disrepair. One of her friends described her car as looking like an egg and that it was "junky."

Jennifer used to tell her mother that Eliza was "the most beautiful girl" she ever knew. With her long brown hair and brown almond-shaped eyes, Eliza had an exotic look to her. Despite her appearance, she thrived in several nontraditional female fields, such as welding and small-engine repair. Useful for the Karmann Ghia.

Eliza succeeded in the world of agriculture as well. She transferred from nearby McCallum High School in Austin to Lanier High School after her junior year so she could join the Lanier FFA chapter and be with Jennifer.

Eliza would also venture over to the Lanier FFA farm, located off Lamar Boulevard and Ferguson Drive, approximately two miles away from campus. There she took care of her eight-hundred-pound prize pig, Stoney, which made auction at the Travis County Junior Livestock Show in the spring of 1991.

At home, Eliza had her own personal menagerie-in-the-making. She kept three gray crawfish in a pan beside her bed. She also owned a pair of "ugly rats."

Eliza also loved country music and preferred Willie Nelson. She also spent her spare time, what little there was, reading books. Her mother said that she would often have two or three books going at the same time. Her mother was convinced that Eliza would eventually become a writer.

Eliza had other aspirations as well. She wanted to become a veterinarian. Her goal was to attend Texas A&M University and its internationally renowned agricultural program. She dreamed of earning a degree, becoming a licensed vet, and owning a ranch so she could take care of even more animals when she came home from work.

Eliza, however, was not ready to leave home just yet. She let her mother know that she wanted to stay with her for a couple more years before she went off to Texas A&M. She did not want her mother to be lonely. She decided, instead, to attend Austin Community College for a couple of years. Maria Thomas was elated.

Sarah Harbison's best friend was thirteen-year-old Burnet Middle School eighth-grader Amy Ayers. Amy was the second child of Bob and Pam Ayers, who had an older son, Shawn. Amy was born on January 31, 1978. She attended Wooten Elementary School in Austin. It was apparent from an early age that Amy would be an achiever in school.

Burnet Middle School principal James Wilson described Amy as the epitome of the good student: "A good student is one who makes good grades, does well in class, has lots of friends, and participates in extracurricular activities." Amy did all of those things. She was a member of the Aim High team, a member of the yearbook staff, and she received two academic achievement awards. Amy also received the Outstanding Student Award at Burnet.

Just like Sarah, Jennifer, and Eliza, Amy had a passion for animals. Like many young girls, she had a special place in her heart for horses. Encouraged by her father, a polite, honest-to-goodness cowboy, Amy began showing quarter horses when she was only three years old.

Amy was probably the most country out of all four of the girls. As she grew older, she inhabited the role of the all-American country girl. From her boots to her blue jeans to her preference in music, Amy was pure country.

The quiet, reserved young girl, who took after her mother in that regard, was also very popular. Her brother, Shawn, had been a member of the FFA, which inspired her to get involved in the organization at an early age. She became a junior member of the Lanier chapter during the third grade. She was later nominated as the vice president of the Junior FFA.

Amy was hugely successful in competition. She showed hogs in competition at the Travis County Junior Livestock Show for five years. One year, she won the Showmanship Award. She also participated in the Livestock Show Arts and Crafts Fair, where she won the Grand Champion Award at the Travis County Fair for her needlepoint doorstop.

Not only did her participation in FFA bring Amy closer to animals, it brought her closer to her best friend, Sarah Harbison. Despite their age difference, which was considered a big deal for teenagers, the two girls got along wonderfully. Amy confided in Sarah her dream to become a veterinarian and to own a ranch, just like Eliza.

All four girls became the best of friends. They would always spend time together, in school and out of school. They would spend the night at each other's houses, go to competitions together, spend time at the FFA farm, go shopping together.

You name it, they did it.

It was a common sight to see the bright, smiling faces of Jennifer and Sarah Harbison, Eliza Thomas, and Amy Ayers together.

Faces that lit up rooms and barns wherever they went.

# CHAPTER 2

December 6, 1991
Austin, Texas
4:00 P.M.

It seemed like another ordinary day. All four girls went to school. When she got home, Sarah immediately called Amy and invited her over to spend the night. Jennifer would pick Amy up and take the two girls to Northcross Mall that night. The girls would gallivant around the mall while Jennifer worked at I Can't Believe It's Yogurt. Before her shift was up, Jennifer would pick up the two girls, bring them back to the shop, and have them help close up. Amy readily agreed and began to pick out her clothes for the evening.

Amy grabbed her beige tote bag. She stuffed the bag with more clothes for the sleepover. She threw on her favorite outfit: turquoise Wrangler jeans, her brother's dark brown leather bomber jacket, her ever-present cowboy boots, a heart-shaped belt buckle that belonged to her mother, a pair of gold shrimp earrings, and three friendship bracelets. She was ready for a fun night with her best friends.

Sarah sat on the couch in her home. Her mother walked in after a draining day at work at the bank and saw the huge smile on her daughter's face.

"So what are you smiling so big about?"

"I just spoke with Amy. We're gonna go to the mall tonight," Sarah replied as she peeled an orange. "I think we're gonna see a movie."

"How are you gonna get there? Because I'm just exhausted. I really don't want to take y'all up there. I'm sorry. Maybe you can ask Jennifer to take y'all."

"Jennifer offered to take us."

A day like any other in the Suraci household.

Sometime between 6:15 and 6:30 P.M., Jennifer showed up. She had returned from her boyfriend Sam Buchanan's house. Sam's grandfather Lynn Irwin had passed away a few days earlier. Sam missed school that day to act as a pallbearer at his grandfather's funeral. Jennifer stopped by after she dropped off her sister from school. She was there to comfort him. When she arrived at her home, she bounded through the front door, yelled out hello to her mom and sister, and headed for her bedroom to change. The tiny, eighty-six-pound Jennifer pulled on her size-zero pair of blue jeans, her black high-top tennis shoes, and an I Can't Believe It's Yogurt Izod-style shirt. She yelled out to Sarah to make sure she was ready to go.

Sarah was dressed in her customary Western garb. She wore a pair of Rocky Mountain blue jeans, a pair of pull-on Ropers boots, and a black Western-cut jacket with an extravagant Aztec symbol on the back. The two sisters smiled, hugged, and gave their Mom a kiss good-bye.

Jennifer and Sarah headed out of the house, giggling as they went. They jumped into Jennifer's tiny Chevy S10 pickup truck, a gift from her father, and headed to Ohlen Road to pick up Amy. Next stop was a family friend's house, because Jennifer needed to fill out an application to run for "Queen of the FFA." She and Eliza agreed that they would both run. Jennifer also left her wallet at another friend's house so she went and picked that up too.

Jennifer dropped off the two younger girls at Northcross Mall and headed over to the yogurt shop. She saw Eliza's Karmann Ghia. She knew her best friend would be glad to see her. Eliza had been on the clock since 5:00 P.M. when the day shift left. Jennifer was supposed to be at work by 7:00 P.M. She was ten minutes late.

Eliza Thomas spent that Friday morning getting ready by talking to her mother.

"Mom, can you go with me after school today and help me with Stoney?" Her pig was recently diagnosed with a disease and required two shots a day and tiny Eliza could not inject him by herself.

Therefore, Maria Thomas went with her daughter to the pen before school. Unfortunately, she could not help her daughter administer the shot. Eliza, instead, had one of her FFA buddies help her out while Maria cleaned up the pigpen.

Eliza headed off for school. Her mother headed off to work.

Eliza went to her classes for the day and then returned home so she could change clothes for work. She threw on a pair of blue jeans, some white high-top tennis shoes, her I Can't Believe It's Yogurt Izod-style shirt, and pulled her hair up in a scrunchy. She arrived at the store just before 5:00 P.M. She was ready to work her Friday-night shift until 11:00 P.M. with her best friend, Jennifer. Fridays were always fun because they usually stayed busy. Several of their friends and fellow teenagers would saunter over to get yogurt after coming out of the movie theaters at Northcross Mall. There were also several older customers who came from the nearby art house, the Village Cinema, located just two blocks north on Anderson Lane. It had been slower lately, however, due to the slightly colder weather.

Eliza always enjoyed working with Jennifer. The time seemed to pass much more quickly when they were together.

Eliza spoke with members of the daytime shift at the yogurt shop, then headed back to the office to pick up her cash register drawer. She opened the office and found it along with her usual allotted $87.50 in cash and coins. She signed off for the register and returned to the area behind the serving counter. She was ready to take over.

She was all by herself.

Two hours later, Jennifer showed up. She informed Eliza of her plans to pick up Sarah and Amy before closing time and bring them back to the shop. Sarah and Amy occasionally helped the girls out with the cleaning, which made everything go much faster. The two older girls were excited because they could get out earlier.

Two hours later, around 9:00 or 9:30 P.M., Maria Thomas paid the girls a surprise visit. She stopped by to chat with her daughter. There were only a few customers in the shop at the time, so Eliza came out from behind the counter and sat with her mother at a dining table. They chatted about Eliza's classes and how work was going. Approximately ten or fifteen minutes later, two giggling young girls came in through the front entrance of the yogurt shop. One of the girls held a cardboard box in her hands. It smelled of pizza. Eliza looked up and instantly recognized the girls. She waved them over.

"Hey, guys, I want you to meet my mother. Mom, this is Sarah, Jennifer's little sister, and her best friend, Amy."

It was the first time that Maria Thomas had met either girl. They exchanged pleasantries. As they spoke, a gentleman entered the restaurant. He strode toward the counter but did not step up to the register. Eliza looked up at the man. She recognized Dearl Croft, whom she and her mother met while working out at HQ Fitness. Croft engaged the table of young ladies.

It was almost 10:00 P.M.

Jovial conversation filled the empty dining room.

Soon the door opened and two more customers entered the store. Croft excused himself and headed toward the counter that Eliza manned. Croft walked up to the ordering area and stood behind a young man in a green fatigue army jacket. Croft noticed the male stood almost six feet tall and was of slender build. Instead of walking up to the cash register, however, he stood a foot or so behind the young man. Croft scanned the menu board and its wide selection of frozen concoctions.

Suddenly the young man turned around and in a deep voice said, "Are you driving that car outside with the lights on top?"

Croft was a former military police officer and owner of Longhorn Security. He, indeed, drove such a vehicle.

"Yes, I am," he replied.

"Are you police or security? What are you?" the teenage boy asked.

"I own a security company," Croft answered. At the same time, Jennifer brought two yogurt servings to the register. She placed them next to Eliza. The couple that ordered took their desserts and left the store.

Jennifer made eye contact with the boy and said, "C'mon up here," motioning toward the counter so Eliza could take his order. Instead, the boy turned to Croft and said, "You go ahead on."

"No, you go ahead, because you was here before I was." He smiled when he replied.

"Well, you just go ahead," the boy insisted, "and go ahead of me."

Again Croft declined. "No. You were here before me. Go ahead." It turned into a demented "Chip and Dale" routine. Both men kept going back and forth as to who should have their order taken next. Finally Croft looked up at Jennifer and stated "Go ahead and wait on him. He was here before I was."

Jennifer nodded and looked back at the young man. "What do you want?" she asked politely. "Come up here," she said as she wiggled her finger toward the counter. "What do you want?"

The boy looked up at the menu again. "I will take a cold drink."

"All we have is Sprite."

"That's okay."

Jennifer poured the boy's drink, placed it in a paper sack, and walked it down to the register. She walked back to take Croft's order. She and Croft exchanged knowing glances and quietly chuckled. Croft heard the boy speak loudly to Eliza. He had no idea what he said to her.

Quickly the young man scurried past Croft down the hallway and past the counter. The young man looked up at Jennifer and motioned toward the back, signaling his need to use the rest room.

"Where's he going?" Croft asked Jennifer.

"He has to go to the rest room."

"I didn't know you had a rest room back there."

Jennifer laughed, as she was wont to do, and told him, "Well, it's not open to the public, but he said he had to go, so I let him back there." Jennifer took Croft's order of three cups of yogurt and slid it down to Eliza.

Croft's suspicions were raised. Instead of leaving the shop, he decided to bide his time and see what the kid was up to. He chatted with Maria Thomas some more, all the while keeping an eye out for the boy. He stepped back up to the counter and asked Jennifer for a sample of the strawberry yogurt. Then he tried the chocolate.

Still, no boy.

Finally Croft decided to leave, even though the boy did not return. Croft nodded toward the ladies, said his good-byes, and exited the yogurt shop.

He would never see his "yogurt girl" again.

Maria Thomas said her good-byes and walked out the front door.

Eliza received another surprise that night. Her father, James Thomas, also popped into the yogurt shop to visit his daughter. He had returned from a graduate-student party north of the yogurt shop. He and his wife, Norma Fowler, arrived sometime after 10:00 P.M.

Eliza introduced her father to Jennifer. It was the first time they met. James Thomas talked to his daughter about how things were going. He also spoke with Jennifer about an economics class she was taking. After about twenty minutes or so, James Thomas and his wife said their good-byes.

At 10:30 P.M., the girls started to clean the trays that lay in front of the yogurt machines. The ladles were removed from the toppings, which were used by the customers. Then each of the toppings—sixteen in all—were dumped into a large bucket. They were also required to empty all of the trash cans inside the store, then place the trash bags beside the back door. These chores were usually taken care of before closing so as to expedite the cleaning process.

The last customer was served at 10:45 P.M.

When the clock struck 11:00 P.M., the girls locked the front door and left the key in the lock. They did that so they would not lose the key while they cleaned the store. They swept and mopped the floors and hoisted chairs on top of the dining-room tables. One of the girls would put away the fruit toppings. Next up, they would empty the yogurt machines. The remaining yogurt was dumped into a five-gallon bucket, which was transported into the walk-in cooler. The fruit toppings were also placed in the cooler. Dry toppings were stored under the serving counter.

Eliza took the ice scoop from the ice-making machine and placed it in the back sink. Jennifer set up to count the night's earnings on a metal table in the back.

The time was around 11:15 P.M. Amy and Sarah sat in the front dining area chatting merrily, oblivious. As Eliza finished rinsing the silver ice scoop, she heard movement in the back of the store. She looked up and saw the metal double doors opening. A man crept inside. She was surprised by the intrusion.

"Hey, you! What are you doing?" Eliza queried. "You don't belong here."

# CHAPTER 3

*Saturday, December 7, 1991*
*I Can't Believe It's Yogurt*
*12:05 A.M.*

Austin police sergeant John Jones exited the scene of carnage inside the yogurt shop. Flanked by two television station personnel, Jones attempted to make sense of the situation before him. The nineteen-year veteran officer never witnessed an atrocity of such magnitude in the relatively quiet city of Austin.

One of the most important people on the scene was arson investigator Melvin Stahl. The nineteen-year fire department veteran was called on to determine the origin and cause of the fire. Stahl described his responsibility as a "process of elimination." His job was to dig through the fire scene and locate any burn patterns. These consist of "pour patterns," or patterns that appear where a flammable liquid is dripped onto floors or walls. He would also look for different types of metal and determine their melting point, which let him know how hot the fire may have been.

Austin arson investigators are not called to every fire. Usually they are called in cases of undeterminable causes of fire, a large loss of property fire, any multiple fires, or any fire fatality. Several arson investigators arrived at the Hillside Center that evening. Melvin Stahl was the first on the scene. He spotted Sergeant Jones and approached him. He asked if he could enter the shop and take photographs. Jones assented and Stahl proceeded inside. He believed photographing the scene as soon as he walked through the doors was necessary, because crime scenes may be altered due to disturbances caused by those who work the scene. After taking some photos, Stahl returned outside and ran into Jones who informed him that Alcohol, Tobacco, and Firearms (ATF) agent Charles "Chuck" Meyer had been contacted, as well as the Texas Department of Public Safety (DPS) crime lab. ATF is called to a fire when there are fatalities involved. At the time, DPS was solely responsible for processing homicide crime scenes. The decision was made to not remove the bodies of the four girls until DPS arrived. Stahl reentered the yogurt shop and took more photographs.

After he finished photographing the layout of the store, Stahl drew a sketch of the fire scene. He also conducted interviews with various firefighters and police officers. He even escorted the EMS personnel to the back of the shop where the bodies were located. One of the EMS technicians leaned in and took a close look at the body of Amy Ayers. Without touching her in any way, he pronounced her DOS—dead on scene. The technician walked over to the three bodies of Sarah Harbison, Eliza Thomas, and Jennifer Harbison. Again, without hesitation, he pronounced the girls DOS.

The EMS technicians' jobs were done.

When they left, Stahl resumed taking pictures. He

did not want to start working on the fire scene until DPS arrived and dealt with the bodies and trace evidence.

Stahl would wait a long time.

# CHAPTER 4

*December 7, 1991*
*I Can't Believe It's Yogurt*
*4:00 A.M.*

Four hours after they were contacted for one of the worst mass murders in Austin's history, three DPS officials showed up. According to criminalist Irma Rios, the reason they arrived so late is that she had to piece together a team late at night going into a weekend.

Not an easy task, especially during the holiday season.

Thirty-year-old Rios, a seven-year employee of DPS, headed the team. She was assisted by latent-print examiner Rachel Riffe and photographer Mike Holle. It was Rios's duty to search for and locate evidence and determine the origin of that evidence, if possible. Riffe would lift any usable fingerprints. Holle would photograph the victims, the crime scene itself, and any other activity in the room.

Rios had almost no experience with arson homicides. She had only processed one scene prior to that night, according to her own testimony. Rios noted several officers on the scene, including Jones, Detective Mike Huckabay, Lieutenant Andy Waters, and Sergeant Jesse Vasquez. As she entered the back portion of the shop, she also noted that several firefighters were present. Many of them were hanging outside the open double doors. Some were still traipsing through the scene.

Rios began to search for evidence.

She instantly noted the damage wrought by the fire.

"There was so much devastation," Rios explained. A plastic phone that was mounted on a wall in the kitchen melted but remained in place. Several utensils above the washing sink were melted. She noted the nude body of thirteen-year-old Amy Ayers. Her corpse lay facedown in almost an inch of water saturated with soot. Rios made notation of the three severely burned corpses farther back. She wrote that they were nude too. As the DPS officials looked closer, they found various articles of clothing: a pink sweater, black Reebok tennis shoes, and some cowgirl boots.

Mike Holle was responsible for photographing the victims. He took numerous shots of the girls. Many of the pictures show the fourth body, which rested almost underneath two metal shelves next to the walk-in cooler. The body belonged to Jennifer Harbison. Less than two feet away lay the body of her sister, Sarah, whose bound body was draped across the body of Eliza Thomas. Between Sarah's legs lay a metal ice scoop, what firefighter Kimmons mistook for an ice-cream scoop. The burned, naked girls' bodies resembled a lunatic game of pickup sticks. Holle snapped the pictures.

Rios collected what little evidence she could. The dousing of the fire and the broken water pipe may have washed out potential evidence. She went with what was available.

She moved in toward the bodies.

Rios noticed stains on the body of Amy Ayers. As she approached the youngest girl's noncharred corpse, she noted what appeared to be a gag around her neck. Amy also lay on top of a knotted-up blouse. Rios's attention returned to the stains—they appeared to be blood drops on Amy's left leg. There were a few more drops on her left shoulder. Rios pulled out her swabbing material to gather the evidence. The blood was difficult to remove. It stuck to the girl's skin. Rios hunkered down and swabbed hard with her damp cotton Q-Tip. Some of Amy's skin came off in the process.

After gathering the blood, Rios examined the rectal and genital areas of Amy's corpse. She was looking for traces of acid phosphatase, an enzyme found in various body fluids, including semen. She inserted a Q-Tip into Amy's rectum. She then swabbed the vaginal area of the victim. The presumptive test for the rectum turned out negative. She saved the vaginal swabs for testing later in the DPS laboratory.

Rios moved on to the pile of girls. She detailed the restraints used on each of the girls. She also conducted enzyme tests on the three bodies. All of the rectal tests for the girls were negative. The only additional vaginal swab test conducted on the scene was on Sarah. It, too, came back negative. There was, however, a strange glop of mucus that floated underneath Sarah's crotch. Rios collected it with a Q-Tip and deposited it along with the other vaginal samples for later lab work.

When the DPS unit finished its work, they turned the bodies over to the medical examiner (ME). Rios could not recall how long she spent inside the yogurt shop.

After the bodies were removed, Rios and her team continued to look for pertinent evidence. She collected shoes, clothes, and various bloodstains around the room. Such a search and gathering is normally conducted using a grid search, or poring over the crime scene, inch by inch, in areas marked off as grids so that the officers can keep track of their findings and know what areas they have covered. Rios did not conduct a grid search, but rather something she called "U shaped." She did, however, discover a fired slug as she sifted through the debris. Also, another DPS lab technician at the scene discovered the shell casing for the slug.

The DPS team removed the ceiling tiles that were melted and had fallen down on top of the bodies. The tiles felt like mush in their hands.

Rios exited through the back double doors when she noticed a Dumpster. She asked one of the police officers to take a look inside. The officer grabbed only the top layer of trash, peered under, and saw nothing.

After several hours, the DPS officials left the scene.

Rios felt confident that she and her team did an extensive and thorough job.

# CHAPTER 5

*December 7, 1991*
*Town North Nissan Dealership*
*North Austin*

Robbins Academy student Maurice Pierce and his buddy Forrest Welborn, a McCallum High School freshman, sneaked onto the Town North Nissan Dealership car lot at Lamar Boulevard and Highway 183, just off Mopac. It was located about three miles from the yogurt shop. The delinquents were looking for some wheels so they could get out of town.

Pierce spotted a brand-new gold Pathfinder.

Later that night, he and Welborn, along with their buddies Robert Springsteen IV and Michael Scott, took the SUV out for a spin. A little hell-raising, a little drinking, and a little gunplay were in order, followed by a trip to San Antonio.

All harmless fun as far as they were concerned.

# CHAPTER 6

Austin, Texas. The capital of the third most populous state in the United States. Home to the University of Texas, the Texas Longhorns, and a thriving liberal bastion populated with hippies, musicians, and politicians. Before 1991, Austin was a sleepy little college town with barely a hint of crime or pervasive violence. It was a quiet haven away from the hustle and bustle of other metropolitan meccas of Texas: Dallas, Houston, and San Antonio.

Students from all over the world attend the highly respected educational institution. Several don't leave after graduation. Many people fall in love with the sleepy city.

In 1991, however, times were a bit tougher with the aftermath of the real estate bust of the late 1980s still lingering in the air like the smoke from a Texas Aggie bonfire. The Gulf War raised blood levels between collegiate liberals and neocon politicos who patrolled Congress Avenue. Also, the tragedy of guitarist Stevie Ray Vaughan's 1990 helicopter death continued to cast a pall over the city known for its live-music scene.

But Austinites do not stay down for long. In fact, in August 1991, the city council officially named Austin the "Live Music Capital of the World." The economy was also slowly rebounding, in part due to the controversy over the city's favorite watering hole, Barton Springs. In 1990, the Save Our Springs (SOS) Coalition fought to prevent Freeport McMoRan, an international mining company out of New Orleans, from erecting a planned urban development of more than four thousand acres directly adjacent to the creek. The fight was successful. It opened the door for a new economic boom in the state's capital.

There was another, important, attractive quality about Austin: low crime rates.

Or so people thought.

In reality, Texas was considered to be one of the most dangerous states in the country in 1990 and 1991. According to the Criminal Justice Policy Council, six Texas cities—Austin, Houston, Dallas, San Antonio, El Paso, and Fort Worth—were among the top fourteen most dangerous cities in the United States.

Austin scored the fourth-worst crime ranking in Texas in 1990. The major reason was due to property crimes, where it ranked fourth overall. Its violent-crime ranking was seventh with only forty-six homicides committed that year. There were 280 reported rapes, 1,461 robberies, and 1,539 assaults. Not too bad for a city with nearly half a million residents.

These lower violent-crime totals, however, do not mask the fact that Austin has a very spectacular history of violence.

Many people are familiar with the 1966 University of Texas Tower massacre perpetrated by former college student Charles Whitman. The sniper has been immortalized in several media, including a book, *A Sniper in the Tower*, by Gary M. Lavergne, a television movie entitled *The Deadly Tower*, an independent film entitled *The Delicate Art of the Rifle*, and in song with Kinky Friedman's "The Ballad of Charles Whitman." He is even admired for his handiwork in the Stanley Kubrick 1987 film *Full Metal Jacket* by Gunny Sergeant Hartman who talks about "what one motivated Marine and his rifle can do."

There are several cases, however, that have not been splashed all over the headlines, but they did spill blood on the Austin concrete.

One of the most notorious cases took place in downtown Austin from 1884 and 1885. A serial killer known as the "Servant Girl Annihilator" hacked up eight women, most of them black servants, with an ax. The murders predated the more infamous "Jack the Ripper" killings by three years. In both cases, no killer has ever been found.

Eighty years later, on July 18, 1965—one year before Charles Whitman went ballistic—James Cross Jr. committed a multiple murder in an apartment on Manor Road. Cross raped and strangled two University of Texas Chi Omega sorority members, Shirley Stark and Susan Rigsby. When he was finished, he stuffed their bodies into a closet and invited his girlfriend over for a dinner rendezvous.

In 1974, two young Mormon missionaries, Mark Fischer and Gary Darley, were dismembered with a band saw in a taxidermy shop. The killer, Robert Kleasen, was convicted, but he was then released from prison three years later after it was determined that evidence against him was seized by police illegally.

In 1984, Henry Lee Lucas, drifter and alleged serial killer of more than three hundred people, was convicted in the "Orange Socks" case of a girl whose body was found in Georgetown, just north of Austin, in 1979. The classic independent horror film *Henry: Portrait of a Serial Killer* is loosely based on Lucas and his buddy Ottis Toole's murderous misdeeds. Most of Lucas's confessions turned out to be bunk. Apparently, several police organizations used Lucas to clear out a bevy of unsolved murders.

On October 4, 1983, another unsolved quadruple arson murder occurred. Jesus Gomez, sixty-nine, Louise Nash, sixty-seven, Frances Reyes, forty-five, and Natalio Rodriguez, sixty, were killed while they slept inside a boarding house East Second Street in East Austin. Some unknown killer or killers tossed a flammable accelerant into two rooms and lit them on fire. Many people believed the case went unsolved because no one in the Austin Police Department cared about the victims, who were low-income Hispanics.

In 1989, twenty-one-year-old University of Texas premed student Mark Kilroy disappeared while on a spring break trip to Matamoros, Mexico. One month later, his body, along with thirteen others, was unearthed from a shallow grave on a ranch called Rancho Santa Elena. Adolfo de Jesus Constanzo, a charismatic religious fanatic, sacrificed young people as an occult offering for protection during his drug-smuggling escapades. Kilroy was one of his victims. The case was also commemorated in music in a *corrido* known as "Tragedy in Matamoros," by the group Suspiros de Salamanca.

Another tragedy occurred two years later, almost seventy miles north of Austin. On October 16, 1991, Belton, Texas resident-cum-musician-with-a-messianic-complex George Hennard rammed his Ford Ranger pickup truck through a large glass window of a Luby's Cafeteria, jumped out of the vehicle armed with two semiautomatic weapons, and began firing indiscriminately at the diners. After he killed twenty-two patrons, in the process becoming the most prolific mass murderer in the history of the United States, Hennard hid in the bathroom alcove and turned the gun on himself. A twenty-third victim died later in the hospital.

The Luby's massacre occurred seven weeks before the yogurt shop murders.

Something about the yogurt shop murders, however, touched Austinites more so than all of the other previous crimes. People were already on edge because of the Luby's tragedy, but it was something more. Most pointed to the youth and innocence of the girls. Others cited the fact that the killer or killers had not been discovered immediately.

The only certainty was that the city of Austin changed forever.

# CHAPTER 7

In the beginning, the "Yogurt Shop Murders" task force worked out of the main APD headquarters located at Interstate 35 and Eighth Street in downtown Austin. Senior sergeant Hector Polanco was named the supervisor over the case, Sergeant John Jones was the case agent, and Detective Mike Huckabay was lead investigator. Jones was responsible for keeping the case in order and directing the flow of the case. Huckabay did all of the interviewing of the major suspects and handled all of the leads.

Fifteen-year veteran Detective Mike Huckabay was Jones's right-hand man in the task force. Huckabay grew up in Odessa, Texas, with three brothers and a sister. He claimed to have experienced a rough childhood due to a father who drank too much and bounced around from job to job. According to Huckabay, there was a lot of "fussing, fighting, and feuding going on."

To deal with the stress of home, Huckabay developed a love for work. His first job at the young age of eleven was selling peaches for his grandmother. He also had his own paper route and later worked in a grocery store.

Huckabay attended Odessa Permian High School and played football for the Panthers, the team featured in H. G. Bissinger's book, *Friday Night Lights*, about the legendary high-school football team. "Our mascot's name was 'Mojo,' which is a mystique," claimed Huckabay. "I can't tell you what it means because it is a secret. Only the football players on the team knew what it meant."

After Huckabay graduated from high school, he joined the U.S. Army, fought in Vietnam, and came home because of a war injury. He received two Purple Hearts and a Bronze Medal for Valor for his efforts.

After the war, Huckabay answered an advertisement in the paper for a position with the Austin Police Department. He got married, worked full-time for the police, and attended college at night at St. Edward's University, where he received a degree in criminal justice.

Huckabay was the father of two sons, but he was also recently divorced. Despite the stress of a failed marriage, he was known throughout the police department for his genial sense of humor.

Huckabay was not, however, in a laughing mood. He was peeved at how much "holdback" information had leaked out in the yogurt shop case.

Holdback information is information that police officers choose not to leak to the press or public. They hold it back in an effort to discern which confessions are false and which ring true. Only the killer or killers would know this holdback information.

Usually it is something key or unusual.

Like the stacking of bodies in a pile or an ice scoop inserted into a victim's orifice. Huckabay noticed a recurring theme with several of the tipsters that called in. They usually mentioned such supposedly secret information. The detective suspected a leak from within the police department. Others believed the information came from one of the EMS technicians on the scene that night.

However it leaked, there was no doubt it was out there. It would be a challenge for Huckabay and Jones to keep the holdback information under control.

# CHAPTER 8

*Monday, December 9, 1991*
*Travis County 299th District Court*
*Austin, Texas*

One of the efforts undertaken to keep information from leaking out was highly unusual in the history of Austin. Travis County assistant district attorney (ADA) Robert Smith asked Judge Jon Wisser to seal the autopsy reports of the four girls. ADA Buddy Meyer claimed the request was made because the release of certain information about the murders could "jeopardize the investigation. It's not necessary in every case, but in this case it is."

Travis County ME Robert Bayardo, who did not perform the autopsies because he was out of town on vacation, was surprised. It was the first such request in the fourteen years he headed up the medical examiner's office.

Judge Wisser agreed to Smith's request and signed a motion to seal the reports. "The district attorney came over and asked me to do it because the details were essential to their investigation." He justified the order by stating that, "Whenever you arrest someone and they decide to give a confession, you have to have stuff that no one other than the one confessing knows about."

Meyer later declared that the autopsies would remain sealed until someone was arrested for the murders.

# CHAPTER 9

*December 9, 1991*
*Lanier High School and Burnet Middle School*
*Austin, Texas*

A stunned silence hung over Lanier High School. Three of the school's brightest stars had been taken away. Jennifer, Sarah, and Eliza were dearly loved by their classmates. They were already sorely missed. Most everyone on campus walked around in a daze. Class was the last thing on the kids' minds. The teachers' too.

"A death from sickness or an accident, we could understand," Vice Principal Georgia Johnson told the *Austin American-Statesman*, "but this we can't understand. Nobody has an answer as to why."

Student council president Shauna Kunkel expressed similar sentiments. "Everybody's still pretty much in shock. There's a lot of denial. Nobody wants to think this happened." She finished by saying, "Everybody is hurting."

To help alleviate some of the hurt, Lanier High

School brought in a dozen counselors for the students. As one walked the halls that day, one could see groups of girls huddled together sharing tears. Some of the boys were crying too.

In addition to the tears, rage coursed through the school's veins. It had been over two days since the girls were murdered and the killer or killers had not been caught.

"There is anger that there is a person or people out there," wrote Amy Hettenhausen, editor of the Lanier High School newspaper, the *Runeskrift*, "who may never get caught. May never have to pay."

Other students grieved in a different way. About sixty students headed over to the yogurt shop during their lunch hour. A pallor of disbelief existed that was even stronger than what was felt at school.

Betty Phillips, an Austin Independent School District coordinator of Student Intervention Services, summed it up best: "Their feelings are what you would expect. There is just shock, horror, and indignation."

Counselors were available at Burnet Middle School to help students deal with the death of one of its most popular students, Amy Ayers. Principal James Wilson proudly stated that "we were able to isolate and identify those kids, and nurture them, and counsel them. To be there and listen."

Some mourners turned to a higher power for an explanation.

# CHAPTER 10

*Tuesday, December 10, 1991*
*St. Louis Catholic Church*
*Austin, Texas*

Jennifer Harbison attended St. Louis Catholic School, located on Burnet Road, from seventh to eighth grade. Her sister, Sarah, attended from fourth to eighth grade. Despite being located off a bustling cross street, the school has a quiet ambience that seems sequestered away from the worries of modern life. It is tucked comfortably behind a large church with ornate stained-glass windows that beckon one to enter and seek a greater purpose.

The church and school are located less than one mile away from the Hillside Center, one mile away from I Can't Believe It's Yogurt. The church is easily spotted from the back side of nearby Northcross Mall, the local-hangout for teenagers on the north side of Austin.

The gathering on this day, however, would not be filled with laughter and smart-aleck comments. There would be no horsing around and spying on pretty girls.

The occasion was marked, rather, with tears and hugs, wails, and words of strength.

Nearly fifteen hundred people of all ages, predominately students, pressed together inside the cavernous chapel. Lanier High School was closed early so students and faculty could attend the services. Three Lanier school buses provided transportation from the campus on Peyton Gin Road to the church.

The entrance to the church was filled with students wearing their denim FFA jackets. Students from as far away as Midland and Manor came to take part in the ceremony. Each wooden pew was filled to capacity, both in front of the altar and to its side. People knelt in between the aisles. Nearly five hundred more people were unable to get inside the church. Instead of leaving, however, they remained outside.

Those who were inside witnessed four white caskets brought to the altar by pallbearers, themselves just kids. Most were fellow FFA members. Once the caskets were placed on the altar, several bouquets of flowers were gracefully placed upon them. Some of the pallbearers removed their jackets and draped them across the caskets. The front corner of the altar was adorned with a large golden eagle, which seemed to be watching over the girls.

According to Judy Bonham, an administrator at the church, her daughter Elizabeth was good friends with Sarah Harbison. Sarah taught Elizabeth how to play basketball earlier that year. Elizabeth spent the entire weekend after her friend's death in denial. Her mother stated that Elizabeth kept repeating, "This doesn't happen to someone her age. She's too young." She could not bring herself to cry during the entire weekend.

Judy Bonham stood quietly in the church before the ceremony when a friend tugged at her blouse. The friend motioned toward the altar where Bonham witnessed her daughter draped over Sarah's coffin. Elizabeth was sobbing vigorously while hugging her friend's final resting vessel. Bonham instinctively moved to comfort her daughter but was held back.

"Let her cry," her friend said.

Judy Bonham stopped and watched her daughter. She could not help but shed several tears as well.

The Reverend Kirby Garner conducted mass for the girls.

"There are no words to express the pain and hurt we all feel," he told the hushed crowd. "We've been robbed. Someone we love dearly has been taken away from us." His quiet voice barely rose over the sobs and words of comfort that were being whispered.

The families of the four girls sat in the front pews. They attempted to remain stoic, but the events proved to be too overwhelming. Reverend Garner addressed the families on behalf of all Austinites when he comforted them by saying, "We offer our deepest sympathy. We share in your pain. We share in your loss."

Reverend Garner turned to the gathering at large. "These young women were filled with joy and with life. They were the kind of young girls you would hold up as an example to the community." He continued, "Each life is short. We all live between the bookends of time." Again he turned to the girls' families and stated, "Their short chapters had just begun, and they ended too soon. But they live on in our hearts."

Reverend Garner attempted to quell the sobs by speaking about various emotions that Austin citizens expressed about the murders. "Questions. So many questions.

"You want to know how I feel?" he asked the congregation. "I feel shock. I feel anger. I feel rage and frustration and pain. I feel helplessness and I feel loss."

Several in attendance nodded their heads in agreement.

"When we point that finger at the culprit," Garner continued, "three fingers are pointing back at us—the individual, the community, and society."

Reverend Garner concluded: "Look at that world. Look at our city. Prejudice, injustice, misunderstanding, discrimination, hunger, and violence. Our 'tribute' to these four exceptional young women and our 'response' to God is to work for the end of those things. To work for the day when all people can live as brothers and sisters."

After the ceremony, the caskets that contained the bodies of Amy Ayers, Sarah Harbison, and Jennifer Harbison were transferred north on Interstate 35 to the Capital Memorial Gardens cemetery in Pflugerville, Texas, just outside of Austin.

In the limo ride from the church to the cemetery, Barbara Suraci said to her husband, "Skip, let's do it again. Let's have more babies." Much to her chagrin, Skip answered, "We'll think about it." It was not what she wanted to hear.

The families arrived at the cemetery. All three girls were buried side by side by side. Their grave sites have one large plaque that contains all three of their names and dates of birth and death. Next to the raised dates are flip-up cameo-shaped photo holders with acrylic likenesses of the girls. A concrete bench lies directly west of the grave markers and is engraved with the words "Our Girls."

Barbara Suraci recalled an eerily prophetic moment with her daughter Sarah. The two were riding home in her car and listening to Garth Brooks sing his hit song "The Dance," on the car radio. Sarah suddenly turned and said, "Mother, if I die young, I want you to play this song at my funeral." Her mother, of course, could not believe her daughter would say such a thing. Now she complied with her daughter's wishes. "The Dance" was played at the graveside ceremony. They played another Garth Brooks song, "If Tomorrow Never Comes," for Jennifer, "Seven Spanish Angels" by Willie Nelson, for Eliza, and "Baby Blue" by George Strait, for Amy.

At the end of the graveside services, Dan Aguilera, a classmate of Jennifer's and Eliza's at Lanier, walked away from the crowd. He stopped, turned back toward them, pulled out his trumpet, and began to play "Amazing Grace." Weeping could be heard amidst the plaintiff wails of his playing as the crowd dispersed.

Eliza Thomas was not buried with her best friend, Jennifer. Her family elected to have her buried in Austin Memorial Park cemetery that same day. She is buried next to the future grave sites of her grandparents James and Sherry Thomas. According to Evelyn Williams, an employee of the Cook-Walden Capital Parks Funeral Home, the Thomases allegedly regretted the decision to bury Eliza alone, away from her friends, her other family.

The same day the girls were laid to rest, the local newspaper, the *Austin American-Statesman*, reported the most detailed information about the murders yet. Reporter Kerry Haglund wrote that a DPS dispatcher informed her that an Austin police teletype report listed several unknown pieces of information about the crime scene:

- Sexual assault had not been ruled out.
- No known witnesses had been located.
- A small-caliber weapon had been used.
- The girls had been tied up with material found at the store.
- The fire had been started with material from the store.
- No sign of forced entry was found.

Haglund also spoke with Austin homicide lieutenant Andy Waters. He stated that the killers started the blaze to cover up any evidence. "Apparently, the offenders believed they would obliterate the evidence, but they were not successful." He also informed Haglund that tips were pouring in; however, the police had not determined any suspects at the time.

"We are confident that we will solve these murders," exclaimed Waters, "but it may take some time."

# CHAPTER 11

*Saturday, December 14, 1991*
*Northcross Mall*
*Austin, Texas*

Maurice Pierce, who had stolen a Nissan Pathfinder the previous weekend, was in trouble again. This time, it involved something much more serious. The short and stocky teenager with the long dirty blond mullet was arrested for carrying a .22-caliber revolver inside Northcross Mall. The gun was tucked in the waistband of his pants. He was placed under arrest and taken downtown to the APD headquarters on Eighth Street.

According to Mike Huckabay, Hector Polanco and Rodney Bryant, of Youth Services, interviewed Maurice Pierce. Polanco did not know everything about the case and Bryant was a fill-in while Huckabay and Detective Bruce Boardman were called out to a bank robbery and murder-suicide.

Pierce claimed in the interview with Polanco and Bryant that he lent the gun to his good buddy Forrest Welborn. He also made a startling claim—the gun had been used during the yogurt shop murders. Pierce spoke about different aspects of the crime scene that Welborn supposedly relayed to him.

According to Huckabay, Pierce told Polanco and Bryant: "'I didn't do it, but I know who did.' He then starts naming names." Huckabay added that Pierce checked off a list of crime scene details inside the yogurt shop. "Everything he told them that he was told by this other person," Huckabay stated, "was factual."

The police decided to hook Pierce up with a wire and have him speak with Welborn. The intent was to implicate the fifteen-year-old in the murders. Pierce met with Welborn and attempted to steer the conversation in the direction of the yogurt shop case. Welborn, however, did not bite. He seemed befuddled by the questions that Pierce asked him. He had no idea what Pierce was talking about.

The police believed Welborn. They wrote him off as a suspect.

The police did not believe a single word out of Pierce's mouth. They sensed he was just an obnoxious braggart looking for attention. Pierce was released and marked off the potential suspect list.

It was a list that would continue to grow and grow.

*December 15, 1991*

Maurice Pierce's two other buddies, Robert Springsteen and Michael Scott, were called in for questioning. They were also his Pathfinder joyriding pals.

In addition to Welborn, Pierce implicated Springsteen and Scott in the yogurt shop murders. Detective Bruce Boardman decided to bring them in, but only as witnesses.

At approximately 2:00 P.M., Boardman interviewed Springsteen. He took notes as he questioned the young man.

According to those notes, Springsteen said he spent most of his day at Northcross Mall. He claimed he left there around 1:30 or 1:45 A.M., after the midnight movie ended. He later learned of the murders from someone named "Mace." He also believed that Scott dated one of the girls who was murdered.

Springsteen claimed that he and Scott went to a party after they left the mall. They returned home at 3:30 in the morning.

Boardman spoke with Springsteen for nearly two hours. He spoke with Scott for almost the same amount of time.

He let both boys go.

# CHAPTER 12

*Wednesday, December 25, 1991*
*3000 Block of Tamarack Trail—Suraci Household*
*Austin, Texas*

The bustling two-story home was quiet, but not silent. No longer were there playful squeals of delight for Christmas. No more bouts of laughter ringing through the hallways. Skip and Barbara Suraci, the parents of Jennifer and Sarah Harbison, spent their first Christmas at home without their two precious daughters.

They were, however, surrounded by other people.

A couple stopped by their house to help ease the Suracis' pain. They had just lost their daughter to murder as well. She was killed by her boyfriend.

"I'm not sure if they came to help us," Barbara Suraci would later say, "or vice versa, but it didn't matter. They just came to touch base with us.

"People were coming in checking on us. People were worrying about us, but it was really too soon for anyone to worry about us. I was in so much shock. I was glazed over."

The girls' mother spoke about a Christmas tree that the sisters would never see. "I had ordered a live tree to be delivered to the house and it got there the week after they were killed, and I said to Skip, 'I know this is really weird, but I want you to put that tree up.'" Suraci would not decorate it, but she wanted it up. It was surrounded by dozens of poinsettias sent from well-wishers from around the country. The family received literally thousands of flowers.

"It was so void," Suraci said of the Christmas tree, "it was almost scary."

Another void was felt by Eliza Thomas's grandfather, James Thomas, who wrote an article in that day's newspaper about the murders. Thomas also wrote about the pain of Pearl Harbor and about learning of the death of a good friend who was killed by enemy tank fire in World War II, just days shy of his twenty-first birthday.

Thomas reiterated Reverend Garner's sermon that the girls' lives were short chapters that came to a too abrupt end.

Thomas's article extended beyond the yogurt shop murders to American society at large. He bemoaned poverty, drug abuse, and violence in culture. He wrote of a need to reject such tenets in American society, to eliminate bad choices from one's lifestyle.

He wrote of an Austin woman who purchased a bullhorn to use every time a drug dealer drove into her neighborhood. When she yelled, they left. "Austin and all communities all over America need to follow her example and say with a loud voice that we will not stand for drugs and all these shows that teach violence and disrespect for life." Thomas was determined to "turn around the public slide toward barbarism."

Barbara and Skip Suraci were doing their part to help stop the violence. Despite their pain and suffering, the couple, who lost all of their children, were determined to get involved. They participated in a group known as Project Help Us, which was formed after the murders to elicit citizen participation in helping to solve the crime. Skip was elected spokesperson. His first duty was to write a letter to the citizens of Austin asking for help. He requested that people turn on their automobile headlights during the day, display white ribbons for the girls, provide help for Child, Inc., and contact local television stations and newspapers and express their grief and anger over the crimes.

While activity helped keep the families' minds off the constant pain, that first Christmas would be the most painful of their lives. Through tears, however, Skip recalled a humorous story about Jennifer.

Just a few weeks before her murder, Jennifer served yogurt to Governor Ann Richards. "Jennifer came home that night and talked with her mother, as she often did," Suraci wistfully recalled. "She beamed, she laughed, and her mother asked, 'Did you charge her?' And she said, 'No. But I charged the friend who was with her.'"

Governor Richards later expressed her condolences for the loss of all four girls, including Jennifer. The governor went on television with the girls' families to make a public plea "to ask everyone in the community to assist our law enforcement officials in solving this crime."

# CHAPTER 13

*Sunday December 29, 1991*
*West Fifth Street car wash*
*Austin, Texas*

Colleen Reed, a petite, perky twenty-eight-year-old University of Texas graduate, finished soaping up her white convertible Mazda Miata. Simultaneously a large tan Ford Thunderbird pulled into another stall in the car wash. Inside were two men.

One of the men got out of the car to toss some trash into a receptacle. The other man headed in the direction of Colleen Reed. According to author Bob Stewart in his book, *No Remorse*, the man at the trash can heard a woman scream out, "Please! Not me. Not me!" He peeked around to see what the commotion was all about when he saw his buddy grasp Reed with an oversize hand and lift her several inches off the ground. His other hand held the defenseless girl's hands behind her back.

"Please, God, don't let this happen to me," Reed cried. She and her sister had discussed the girls who were killed in the yogurt shop. She prayed that nothing like that would happen to her.

"You're going with me," the large man commanded.

According to Stewart, Reed glanced over to the man at the trash can and begged, "Help me!" But the man did not help Reed. Instead, he threw her into the backseat of the Thunderbird. He jumped in the back next to her and pinned her down so she could not move. The large man calmly crawled into the driver's seat, quietly pulled out of the car wash, and proceeded to head out the wrong way down a one-way street. After nearly hitting several cars, the two men escaped with Colleen Reed.

"Please not me. Not me," she pleaded with her captors. "Help me."

# CHAPTER 14

*Friday, January 3, 1992*
*Yogurt Shop Task Force Headquarters*
*Anderson Lane*
*Austin, Texas*

After being swamped by hundreds of phone calls, tips, and confessions in just a matter of weeks, it was apparent that a larger team was needed.

It was also apparent that the case was too big to be worked out of "Main." Within weeks, a makeshift command center was set up on Anderson Lane in a rented office space next to Red Lobster, near I Can't Believe It's Yogurt. The inside was sparsely furnished with brown folding tables, large dry erase boards, and emerald green carpet. Boxes of tip information were stacked floor to ceiling. An open manila folder that contained photos of the four girls layered on top of pink construction paper was taped up on the inside frame of the door.

The task force offices were set up so that police could hopefully decipher the ass end of an armadillo from a hole in the wall—such as the boyfriend and girlfriend who confessed to the murders, yet knew nothing about the crime scene.

They first attracted attention when someone reported a tip to Sergeant Jones, saying a teenage girl gave a cryptic message that she saw "certain things" in the Hillside Center parking lot. Jones brought the girl into the interview room for questioning. The small room contained a round table, two chairs, and a coffeemaker. The door to the room had a misspelled plaque that said, VIDEO INTERVIEW—QUITE PLEASE.

At first, Jones's hopes were raised when the girlfriend hesitated for an extended period of time when asked for the name of her boyfriend. "We thought, 'Hey, maybe this it.'"

That would not be the case.

The girl spouted out nonsense. None of the information she gave matched the crime scene. She was wasting their time.

"They were telling us stuff that wasn't true," Jones stated, exasperated. "They were giving information that they had heard off the street. The killers have to tell us certain things that only the killers would know. That didn't happen in this case."

Jones wrote the couple off his growing list of suspects. Less than one month after the killings, Jones had already scratched off more than thirty-five potential suspects.

Jones never understood the bizarre confessions that came down the pike. He could not understand the psychological makeup of a person who clearly had no involvement in one of the state's most brutal crimes, but who would want to implicate himself with a confession.

"Confessions sound good," Jones lamented, "but that's not the standard by which charges are filed. If we have the right person, we will charge them."

Jones shrugged his shoulders and sighed. "A confession alone isn't enough to get a conviction."

One of Sergeant Jones's first orders of duty was to speak to Agent Ed Richards of the Federal Bureau of Investigation's Behavioral Science Unit (BSU). It was the first time in twenty years that anyone from the FBI's BSU helped in an Austin case. It was a rather fortuitous time to have their involvement. The BSU's profile had risen dramatically during the past year due to their appearance in the guise of Scott Glenn and Jodie Foster in the soon-to-be Academy Award–winning 1991 Best Picture, *The Silence of the Lambs*. The Jonathan Demme–directed film, based on a novel by Thomas Harris, struck a nerve with the moviegoing public when it was released in February 1991. The story centers on FBI agent Clarice Starling (Foster) and her endeavors to capture a serial killer named Jame "Buffalo Bill" Gumb (Ted Levine), who skins his female victims. By sitting down with world-famous serial killer, Hannibal "the Cannibal" Lecter (Anthony Hopkins), she learns the tricks of the trade so as to get into the mind of Buffalo Bill and capture him. Starling and Jack Crawford (Glenn) are members of BSU, renowned for its so-called science known as "profiling."

The term profiling describes a variety of methods used, based on an assessment of a crime scene and the patterns that lay therein, that may help investigators to determine the thought processes of a potential killer or killers.

With the success of *The Silence of the Lambs*, BSU's confidence was at an all-time high, despite the fact that profiling had never once been used to capture a single serial killer. Sergeant Jones also had confidence in Agent Richards. After all, how could he not trust a man who was a grandfather and reminded him of Santa Claus, with his big rosy red cheeks and snow-white hair?

Johnson also happened to be one of the first four

men to participate in BSU. He graduated in 1985. In the six years since he graduated, Richards studied more than four hundred violent crimes, including a 1980 unsolved murder in San Marcos, Texas, about thirty miles south of Austin. Richards helped local authorities sift through seventy-five suspects and narrow the field down to the killer, one Doil E. Lane.

San Marcos police captain Lisa Dvorak heaped mounds of praise on Richards: "We could not have found Lane without Richards's insight. Whenever you have a number of leads, it's like looking for a pin in a wheat field. Mr. Richards helped us narrow our scope."

Sergeant Jones met with Agent Richards that January. Based on information relayed to him by Jones, and a perusal of the crime scene photographs, Richards confidently created a profile of the killers in the yogurt shop murders. He informed Jones that he believed more than one person committed the crimes; they were probably white, but other ethnicities could not be ruled out; and they were probably in their late teens or early twenties. One person was the leader of the group.

Richards believed these things about the leader:

- He resented discipline and caused problems in school and at home.
- He was an underachiever in school.
- He probably did not complete high school.
- He angered easily.
- He used drugs and alcohol.
- He was an impulsive individual.
- He picked fights only when he could win.
- He needed his friends around when fighting another male.
- He was an unreliable employee at a menial job.
- He probably still lived with his parents.
- He probably had a criminal record.
- He may be abusive toward women.

• He seeks out women younger than he is.
• He frequented the area around the yogurt shop.

After Richards briefed Jones, he took a step back for a breather. "There's times I go home and cry after hammering and hammering and hammering cases all day long," Richards intoned. "I feel optimistic about this case, though. It's just a matter of time."

Sergeant Jones felt optimistic as well after he spoke with Richards. "We're real confident that this case will come to an end real soon," Jones announced beaming. "I don't think it's going to drag on very long. We're not dealing with a hopeless situation by any stretch of the imagination.

"It would be safe to say that apprehension is imminent."

# CHAPTER 15

Despite the profile provided by Ed Richards, Austin police detectives were still frustrated with their lack of progress. The number of worthless tips continued to increase. The large number of false confessions was driving Sergeant Jones and the task force crazy. One particular tip, however, seemed promising. Sergeant Jones decided to take action.

The name Clair Lavaye, an alleged High Priestess of an Austin Devil-worshiping cult, came across Jones's tip lines numerous times in connection with the murders. Lavaye was an alleged member of the People in Black, the unofficial name given to the Austin youth involved in the Goth and vampire scenes. The PIBs, as they came to be known, consisted of disaffected teenagers and college-age kids who wore lots of black, frequented dance clubs and punk rock bars, and overdosed on music by the Cure and Bauhaus.

Unusual looking to many people, they were basically harmless.

In March, the news program *48 Hours* broadcast the February 28, 1992, search and seizure of Lavaye's West

Campus duplex by Austin police. Officers Jones, Huckabay, Polanco, and several others made some interesting discoveries in Lavaye's crypt. Amongst the bloodied Christ figures and Lestat-influenced decor were hundreds of bones and a skull. The officers on the broadcast were certain that they were looking at a genuine human skull.

It wasn't.

It turned out to be a sculpted wax skull.

*Friday, January 31, 1992*
*Burnet Middle School*
*Austin, Texas*

Nearly 250 people, including Mayor Bruce Todd, gathered inside a courtyard at Amy Ayers's school. They were there to celebrate what would have been her fourteenth birthday. The school planted a fifteen-foot-high crepe myrtle tree in her honor. It was the perfect symbol of Amy's love of nature and life.

"She wasn't about dying," her father said. "She was about living. She was about happiness. She was about love."

Students of Burnet Middle School adorned the memorial tree with numerous white ribbons with messages of love and birthday wishes written in glitter. Less than a month later, a time capsule was buried beneath the tree and designated with a pink granite marker with the inscription AMY L. AYERS—A LIFE THAT SHOULD HAVE BEEN SPARED.

# CHAPTER 16

Another tip came in that sounded even more promising than the Clair Lavaye tip. A twenty-year-old African American drag queen by the name of Shawn Smith landed himself in jail on burglary charges. Smith, also known as "Buddha," was a flamboyant, homosexual club kid, according to his acquaintances Lori Ann Hoefling and Justin Vick.

Vick also stated that Buddha was a drug dealer. Another acquaintance, Craig Davis, considered Buddha to be "a loud, obnoxious kind of guy." Davis was not buddies with Buddha, but more of a fellow club scenester. Obviously, Buddha's "friends" did not think much of him.

He apparently did not think much of them either.

Buddha sat down with Sergeant Hector Polanco in the interview room of the homicide division. Sergeant Jones received a call at his home that Polanco was interviewing Smith and that Smith was naming names. Jones darted out of his home, headed directly for the police station, and hustled into the tiny interview room. Jones nodded toward Polanco and sat down with Smith. The young man apparently had some surprising news for the sergeant. He wanted to get something important off his chest. He was inside the yogurt shop on the night of the murders. Not only was he inside the shop, but he knew who killed the girls.

Buddha claimed he was awoken at 11:00 A.M. on December 6, 1991, by Davis and Vick. Buddha dragged his ass out of bed, got dressed, and eventually showed up at their duplex on Ohlen Road, near Lanier High School, around 1:00 P.M. When he arrived, he noticed that Davis was raving mad. He was screaming at the top of his lungs about some girl who had ripped him off.

"Dude, that fucking bitch is sticking it to me," Davis allegedly fumed. "I gave that fucking cunt two thousand dollars' worth of weed and she fucking ripped me off!" The girl, evidently, was supposed to take the marijuana and sell it to a Mexican man who lived in a nearby duplex.

"Dude, do you know of a way we can get even with her?" Davis asked.

"What exactly do you want to do, man?" Buddha answered a question with a question.

"Kill the bitch!" was Davis's reply.

Buddha stood there quietly in front of Davis. Vick and his blond-haired girlfriend, Hoefling, sat on the beaten-up couch. The couple nodded their heads in unison. Buddha was not quite sure what to make of the situation. He began to joke with Davis about how they could kill her. They began to discuss various methods of execution.

At the top of the list was a Colombian necktie— when a killer slits a victim's throat, reaches inside the gaping wound, grabs the victim's tongue, and yanks it out of the freshly bloody hole so that it dangles out. Next up, Chinese water torture followed by hog-tying their victim. Buddha laughed as they devised nefarious methods to slaughter this girl.

The bag of weed they smoked did not hurt either.

"So, you want to help us get even with Eliza?" Davis asked.

Buddha had no idea who Eliza was, nor did he want to know. He continued to laugh, but he could tell the tenor of the atmosphere had changed drastically. He looked into Davis's eyes and knew this was no joke. He remembered how Davis and Vick talked just a few months back about committing murder and getting away with it. He did not take them seriously. He assumed they were just fucking around.

This time was different.

Davis was pissed and a girl named Eliza was going to pay.

"I'm gonna grab my gun," Davis informed Buddha. "D'ya wanna come along and watch me scare this bitch?" he asked as he got up to retrieve his gun.

"Sure. Why not?" Buddha said.

He watched as Davis vanished into his bedroom. He looked over at Vick. He knew Justin was packing. He always carried a small revolver with him for "protection."

Davis walked back into the living room, looked at Buddha, and patted his waist through his T-shirt. "I have my gun." An outline of the automatic pistol was clearly visible inside the waistband of the skinny Davis's jeans.

Buddha continued telling Sergeant Jones his story. Jones diligently took notes, kept his mouth shut, and listened to the young man.

"We all—Craig, Justin, Lorrie, and I—got into Justin's car," Buddha continued, "and headed toward the I Love Yogurt Shop on Anderson Lane."

Jones did not bat an eye at Buddha's incorrect naming of the store. "What time was this?" he asked.

"Before the yogurt shop closed. When we got there . . . the door was locked, but we could see Eliza and three other girls inside. Eliza came to the door. There was one behind the counter and two in a booth. Eliza came to the door and let us in. I knew it was Eliza, because when [Craig] saw her, [he] started saying, 'There she comes, that bitch.'"

Buddha claimed that Eliza let them all inside the store. Vick supposedly locked the door behind them. Davis approached Eliza and demanded to speak to her in private.

"Don't do this here. I can get fired," Eliza allegedly appealed to Davis.

"No, we need to deal with this now!" he screamed at her as he pointed a finger into her face. He pushed Eliza to the floor and hovered over her.

"What happened to my money?" he demanded.

"I don't know," she cried.

"Fuck that shit," he yelled at her. The two younger girls kept quiet in the booth. Jennifer Harbison, however, stepped out from behind the serving counter and walked right up to Davis.

Bad move.

Davis whipped out his pistol and pointed it at Jennifer.

"Everybody, go to the back!" Davis ordered. "We are going to get this shit straight." The three girls did as they were told, as did Buddha, Vick, and Hoefling. As they corralled the girls in the back of the store, Eliza and Davis started to scrap. Suddenly a gunshot was fired. Buddha heard the sounds of the bullet ricocheting off the walls. He and Vick immediately turned around and headed for the front of the store. He saw Davis holding Eliza from behind.

"Go get something to tie them up with," Davis ordered Vick. He turned his attention to Eliza and said,

"This bitch is gonna tell me where my fucking money is." Amy, Sarah, and Jennifer began to cry. Davis turned around and smacked Sarah in the face.

"Shut these bitches up," Davis commanded Smith and Hoefling. Buddha froze. Vick, meanwhile, was reassuring the girls that everything would be cool just as soon as Davis got his money back.

Sergeant Jones broke up the remembrance by asking Buddha if Vick was brandishing his gun. No, he did not, recalled Smith, who continued to tell the story. He spoke of Hoefling telling everyone to be quiet and how Davis screamed at Eliza.

"This bitch is going to pay me back somehow."

"How?" Eliza wondered through tears.

"This bitch is going to pay me back or I'm gonna take it out of her ass. I want my money today. Now!"

Vick returned with something that resembled stage cord. He tied Jennifer's hands in front of her with the long, skinny cord. He tied Amy's hands together. Buddha tied up Sarah.

"She and I were the only calm ones," he recollected. Davis got fed up with Eliza's denials.

"I don't have any money." She begged him to leave her alone.

Davis had enough. "Well, fuck it then." He pointed the gun toward Eliza. "Strip," he commanded. He looked over at Vick and Hoefling and told them to strip the other three girls.

"What the fuck's your problem?" Buddha wanted to know.

"You'll get over it."

Buddha watched as Vick and Hoefling grabbed the girls and tore the clothes off their bodies. He stood silently as Davis ripped off Eliza's clothes. He did not move as Davis tore her panties off and shoved them into her mouth. Buddha joined in and shoved Sarah's panties into her mouth as well.

Buddha told Sergeant Jones that Davis tossed Eliza to the hard floor and began to rape her. Eliza screamed at Davis, calling him a "fuckhead" and "bastard" and threatening that "they're going to get you for this. You-all are all going to jail."

Davis just laughed as he continued to rape her. "I'm gonna get my money's worth."

When he finished with Eliza, he walked over to Jennifer. He proceeded to rape her as she lay on her side. When he finished, he motioned to Vick, who dropped his drawers quicker than a greased-up pig on a Slip 'n Slide. Vick jumped on top of Jennifer and began to rape her. His girlfriend, Lori, sidled over next to Jennifer and restrained her arms as her boyfriend continued to brutally rape her.

At this point, Amy bolted for the back door. Davis, who went back to rape Eliza, dismounted and yelled at Vick, "Shoot her. Stop her!"

"You shoot her," Vick yelled back. Both boys pulled out their guns and simultaneously shot Amy, who crumpled to the floor.

The other girls' screams could be heard through their gags. Davis began to freak out.

"Fuck it, fuck it, fuck it." He turned toward the three surviving girls. "I want you all on the floor, face first, now," he screamed at them. The girls did not comply, so Davis walked up behind them, took his foot, and pressed it on each one of their heads until their faces were mashed into the floor. He calmly walked up behind Jennifer, stuck his gun to the back of her head, and pulled the trigger.

*Bang.*

Then Sarah.

*Bang.*

He saved Eliza for last.

*Bang.*

Just like that, they were all dead.

Buddha stood in dumbfounded silence. Vick stared off into space. Hoefling leaned against a kitchen wall and slid down to the ground. Vick snapped out of it and walked over to Davis. He began to push the bodies of the dead girls together in a big pile.

"What are we going to do with the bodies?" he asked.

"I don't know," replied his girlfriend.

"Let's burn them and get rid of them," Davis asserted. "Go get that lighter fluid out of the car," he ordered.

"I ain't moving."

Instead, Hoefling got up, left the yogurt shop, walked through the parking lot, crossed the street, opened the car door, grabbed the yellow plastic lighter fluid bottle, and walked back into the store. She handed the container to Davis, who poured it over the pile of bodies. He handed the bottle to Vick, who also doused the girls.

Buddha left the building. He could not take it anymore. He ran toward the front door, through the parking lot, onto Rockwood Lane, up to Foster Lane, and then to the Metro bus stop, where he caught the number 3 Burnet Road bus. He had no destination in mind. He just wanted to get rid of the images that he witnessed.

Buddha did not see Davis, Vick, or Hoefling again for almost ten days, until the couple stopped by to score some Ecstasy. The buy went down and nothing was said about the night at the yogurt shop. Everything seemed back to normal.

Shawn "Buddha" Smith completed his disturbing recounting of the yogurt shop murders. Sergeant Jones asked that he commit his statement to paper. It would be the first of such written statements in the case.

After Smith wrote and signed his statement, Jones asked if he could conduct a polygraph examination on him. Smith agreed, but asked during the preinterview,

"What if my statement is a lie?" Nothing was said and the polygraph was administered.

The results came back negative.

Smith's story was bullshit.

When asked why he lied, Smith stated that after his conversation with Sergeant Polanco, he believed he was at the scene of the crime. He claimed that Polanco told him they had videotape of him at the yogurt shop. Smith also claimed that he and some buddies sat around one night at a party and discussed how they would have committed the crime. He blamed these factors for why he falsely confessed.

Back to square one for Sergeant Jones.

# CHAPTER 17

*Thursday, February 6, 1992*
*Interstate 35 and Seventh Street*
*Downtown Austin, Texas*

WHO KILLED THESE GIRLS?

The smiling faces of Amy Ayers, Jennifer Harbison, Sarah Harbison, and Eliza Thomas stared back at the passing motorists of Austin's main thoroughfare that connects the state capital to San Antonio going south and to Dallas going north. The billboard, measuring twelve by twenty-four feet, donated courtesy of the Patrick Media Group, asked "Who Killed These Girls?" and listed the police task force telephone number. It also listed the amount of the reward money available to anyone who could provide tips in connection to the murders. It was one of twelve billboards the company donated for free.

The parents of the girls were moved by the gesture. Through tears, Barbara Suraci insisted that the "murderers just have to come forward. They can't look at this and not feel so much guilt and shame. They have to come forward."

Meanwhile, two months after the murders, Lieutenant Andy Waters, police spokesman, offered, "I think it will be solved. We don't feel like this type of information can be covered up forever."

# CHAPTER 18

*Saturday, March 14, 1992*
*3:45 P.M.*

Shawn "Buddha" Smith gave the first written statement in the yogurt shop murders case. He also gave everyone a major headache. It would not be the last.

Detective Mike Huckabay sat down with another criminal to discuss the yogurt shop case. Alex Briones was recently arrested for the murder of an elderly woman in Windcrest, north of San Antonio. He bound the woman, raped and sodomized her, shot her in the head, and lit her body on fire. Briones decided it was time to come clean about another murder.

Or rather, murders.

Briones's written statement started off with, "I want to tell Sergeant Huckabay . . . about my involvement in the deaths of the four girls who were killed on December the 6th, 1991, at the I Can't Believe It's Yogurt shop on West Anderson Lane."

Briones claimed that he and an unnamed buddy "borrowed" a truck earlier that day and drove over to the Hillside Center to plan a burglary. Briones added he burglarized a nearby apartment a few weeks earlier, so he felt comfortable in the neighborhood. After they cased the shopping center, Briones went home while his buddy returned the stolen truck.

Later that same evening, Briones and his friend hopped the Metro bus to Anderson Lane. The two men got off and began looking at various stores. They stopped in front of the yogurt shop, peered through the front window, and noticed that there were no customers inside. Briones spotted one girl, Eliza, cleaning tables in the front dining area. He spotted another girl, Jennifer, behind the counter. He motioned to his friend and the two men slithered inside.

"I noticed that the keys to the door were in the lock on the inside of the door," Briones recalled. He asked Eliza if he could use their rest room. She smiled and told him yes. Briones headed toward the back of the store, behind the serving counter, and into the men's rest room.

"I went inside the rest room and I smoked some crack." He stayed there for ninety seconds or so, while his buddy hung out in the front of the store. He returned and stood beside his pal.

Without warning, Briones grabbed Eliza by the arm, pulled out a gun, and stuck it to the back of her head.

"If you cooperate, I ain't gonna hurtcha," he whispered to her. He forced her back to the counter, where Jennifer stood. He pointed the gun at her and told both girls to get down on the floor behind the counter. His buddy dragged the girls over to the cash register. Briones grabbed Eliza and pulled her up on her feet. He pointed his gun at her and demanded she open the register. She took out the register key and did as she was told.

Briones could not remember if he took anything from the register. He did remember herding the two girls to the back of the store. He could not believe his eyes. His friend had two additional girls on the floor, one on her back and one on her stomach. They were younger than the two girls in the front.

Briones's buddy was stripping the clothes off the two girls. He tied their feet together and their hands behind their backs. He inserted gags into their mouths. He grabbed the girl who was on her stomach and raped her. The other girl's sobs were muffled by the gag.

While his buddy violated the girl, Briones tied up Eliza and Jennifer. Both girls' cries for help were upsetting him. He asked them to "be quiet" but they would not listen. After he constrained both girls, he began to disrobe them.

"One of the girls that was with me was real young and pretty," he recalled to Huckabay. "She had blondish colored hair and a real good body. I don't know what I did with the other girl, but I raped the young one." He forced her to lie facedown while he ravaged her from behind, her hands tied behind her back.

Briones claimed to not quite remember everything else so vividly. He blamed it on alcohol, crack, and cocaine. He did, however, remember hearing gunshots ring out.

"All of a sudden, I started hearing shots. They were real loud. My ears started ringing." In his drug-fueled haze, he claimed that he looked down at the girl.

"I remember shooting the girl that I had raped, in the back of the head," he solemnly admitted, "and she was screaming."

After he shot the girl, he grabbed some paper napkins, lit them on fire, and placed them on top of some cardboard boxes near two metal storage shelves.

"I wanted to burn the place because I couldn't recall what all we had touched." As smoke filled the store, Briones scurried out the front door. He ran to the end of the building, stopped, and lit a cigarette. He then pulled out his crack pipe and smoked crack. He pulled out his vial of cocaine, dabbed it with his finger, and glazed his lips. He had no idea which way his buddy went. Briones headed over to a black neighborhood and scored more coke.

A few days later, he tossed his gun, a black .22-caliber automatic, off the Congress Avenue bridge into Town Lake. He also mentioned that his buddy's gun looked like a .38 automatic, but he was not sure.

At the conclusion of Briones's statement, Huckabay showed him several photographs of Hispanic males who matched the description of his buddy. After sorting through most of the photos, Briones picked out the picture of Abel Arredondo.

Huckabay released Briones back into custody. When the man left the room, the detective slowly shook his head. Once again, they had been fed more bullshit.

Abel Arredondo, Briones's "buddy," was sent to prison in the summer of 1991 for attempted burglary. While in prison, he was diagnosed with AIDS. He was eventually paroled, but not until January 1992. He was almost dead upon his release.

Disgusted, Huckabay marched out of the room, where he encountered Sergeant Polanco.

# CHAPTER 19

*Monday, March 23, 1992*
*Austin Police Department*
*Austin, Texas*

Several members of the yogurt shop task force were concerned about the Alex Briones confession. They were also concerned about the Shawn "Buddha" Smith false confession. There was one common denominator in each questionable situation: Hector Polanco.

Polanco was removed from the task force completely. Many on the force believed he may have engaged in questionable tactics that led to the various false confessions. Austin chief of police Jim Everett stated that Polanco had been reassigned from homicide altogether to the Field Services Bureau and Patrol Department.

According to the University of Texas student newspaper, the *Daily Texan*, Victor Polanco, Hector's father, leveled charges of racism. He believed his son was removed from the task force because the higher-ups did not want a Mexican-American to head such a high-profile case.

"He's not a 'yes boy,'" Victor Polanco said of his son. "That's why they fired him." Polanco's father also spoke of an earlier incident when his son supported a fellow Hispanic officer, Rodrigo Herrera, in a contentious situation with the police department. Someone in the police force apparently accused Herrera of writing a memo that criticized his supervisor. Herrera hired a lawyer to disprove those claims and Polanco stood behind him. Victor Polanco believed that that situation, combined with his son's skin color, led to his removal from the yogurt shop murders task force.

The task force needed every top-quality individual it could get to help crack the continuing investigation. Polanco's track record up to that time definitely placed him in that category. He joined the Austin police force in March 1976. He worked his way through the ranks for several years before he landed a coveted investigator position in the homicide division. He held that position for 3½ years before being promoted to senior sergeant.

Polanco was considered one of the best investigators on the police force. He was also a highly decorated officer. He received well over forty commendations—many because of his ability to assist in homicides in which Hispanics were involved as suspects, victims, and/or witnesses. His ability to speak fluent Spanish made him a go-to guy in numerous cases.

According to court documents, Polanco was also a strong supporter of minority causes within the police department. Polanco was not shy about promoting his Mexican heritage. In fact, he practically wore it as a badge of honor. Needless to say, he considered it a personal affront when his boss, Lieutenant David Parkinson, called murders of minorities "misdemeanor murders." Polanco considered such derisive comments par for the course with the Austin Police Department and their substandard treatment of Hispanics and other minorities. He often argued about the disparity in pay between minority police officers and white police officers; lower funding for research for minorities; and less time provided for proper investigations by minorities.

Despite Polanco's vociferous style, he still was named supervisor of the yogurt murders investigation. After Briones's false confession, however, other members of the task force, especially Detective Mike Huckabay and Sergeant John Jones, wanted him off.

The district attorney's office began its own investigation into Polanco. They did not find anything that proved he coerced a confession out of Briones. The DA's office took no action against Polanco.

But that was not the end of the turmoil.

The Austin Police Department Internal Affairs (IA) unit decided to look into the allegations against Polanco. Internal Affairs extended its search of the sergeant even further back. The main focus shone on the case of a February 1991 murder of Travis County sheriff's deputy William Redman. Allegedly, a suspect by the name of John Salazar was brought in for questioning by Sergeant Brent McDonald. Polanco was not working for Redman, but he did assist in eliciting a confession from Salazar. McDonald sat down alone with Salazar, who started to confess to the murder of the sheriff. He abruptly stopped talking, however, leaving McDonald high and dry. Polanco decided to take a crack at it. He entered the room with Salazar. Three hours later, Polanco emerged from the interview with a signed confession from Salazar.

There was one problem with this scenario. Unbeknownst to either McDonald or Polanco, the real killers had already confessed to the murder of Sheriff Redman. Furthermore, it was later determined that Salazar was in the custody of the Austin Police Department at the same time as the Redman murder. In other words, he could not have been physically present to kill the sheriff.

As a result, the police department determined that Salazar had lied. His confession was false. No charges were filed against him. Polanco, however, was still inexplicably rewarded with the department's Basics Award for his help in the Redman case.

IA took the matter very seriously. On April 15, 1992, they charged Polanco with aggravated perjury, failure to supplement police reports, and for "bringing discredit upon the police force." The Austin Police Department and the Disciplinary Review Board supported the charges. They offered Polanco a thirty-day suspension, which he refused. Subsequently they suspended him indefinitely.

According to Mike Huckabay, Polanco nearly crippled the yogurt shop investigation.

"Hector is a good, good investigator," stated Huckabay, "but Hector is very unethical and very unprofessional in some of the things that he does.

"He crippled the case more than he helped it, because Hector would create tips through informants that didn't exist and have us go sit on this house and sit on that house and run this down and run that down so he could generate overtime for himself.

"Hector lied about stuff. In my opinion, he sabotaged the investigation."

# CHAPTER 20

*Thursday, May 14, 1992*
*Lanier High School Future Farmers of America*
*Awards Banquet*
*Austin, Texas*

Nearly 250 students, teachers, parents, and friends gathered together for the twenty-ninth annual FFA Awards Banquet. The occasion, of course, was colored with tears of sadness and longing for their four fellow FFA members. Large framed photographs of the four girls decorated the podium set up before the audience.

The parents of all four girls attended the banquet as well. Skip Suraci commented that the kids in attendance that evening were the "cream of the crop, the best of the best." These included students such as Sandra Hadja, the school's official "Country Bumpkin," who was good friends with Jennifer and also the chapter vice president when Jennifer died. Hadja reluctantly took over her friend's position in the chapter after her death. "We were like sisters," she recalled. "I still remember what she said and how she makes me laugh." Hadja wistfully stated, "I tried to accomplish the goals she set."

Several other FFA members were also inspired by the girls. Five students received awards that evening for carrying on the work that the girls began. One of those was Eliza Thomas's sister, Sonora, who won Grand Champion honors with her sister's pig, Stoney, at the Austin/Travis County Junior Livestock Show earlier in the year. Another student, Melissa Gallimore, also received recognition for her efforts with Amy Ayers's hog, which took fourth place at the livestock show.

Hadja introduced Kristal Blaha, a fellow FFA member and Lanier High School student. Blaha carried a few items up to the podium. As she stepped to the lectern, she caught the eye of Barbara Suraci and smiled.

"You all have given us some of the most beautiful people we have known," Blaha confidently stated as she continued to look at the girls' parents. "We thank you very much." Blaha asked the parents to come up to the podium. She held four crosses in her hands. She silently walked up to the parents and handed out the crosses. The name of each daughter was engraved on each individual cross. Another student handed out flowers to the other family members of the girls.

Blaha walked back to the microphone and said, "We wanted something the mothers could keep with them at all times."

The families were visibly moved by the gesture. Barbara Suraci thanked Blaha and the FFA gathering. "You have thought of us so often. We love you all so very much and appreciate these kids, your leadership. The world will be a better place for all you have done."

As the families returned to their seats, the entire audience got up and gave them a standing ovation.

The following day, the remembrances continued. Lanier High School dedicated two memorials to the girls. The first was a garden of four oak trees planted on the school grounds. The second was a large marble plaque with pictures of all four girls. The presentation of the plaque took place in the campus assembly room in front of 350 students. The inscription on the plaque said, "Their light still shines even though they are not here physically, but are still here Mentally and Spiritually." The plaque would be hung in the main foyer of the Lanier High School Agricultural Building behind the main campus.

Several students shared memories about their friends. Michelle Froh reminisced about Eliza's silly laugh and how she would sing country songs to her pig.

"I want to keep alive our memories," she calmly told the audience. "And someday we'll talk about them together again."

Sonora Thomas, Eliza's younger sister, also spoke of memories. She related the story of how she and her big sister, who had separate bedrooms, communicated via a code that they rapped through the walls with their hands.

"Sometimes I knock on the wall and start crying and remembering everything." As she spoke, the gathered crowd began to cry along with her. "Now, I'm an only child and it's very lonely without her."

In addition to the Lanier students, Mayor Bruce Todd also appeared. He wanted to let everyone know that someone would be caught. He spoke briefly before the rapt crowd.

"The entire community has grieved over this. More so than any single event in the past three decades." At the conclusion of his speech, he expressed a sentiment that many were beginning to share. "It's frustrating that we've not solved this case yet."

*Wednesday, June 3, 1992*

To help solve the case, an additional $75,000 was added to the reward money. Merriman Morton, chairman and CEO of Texas Commerce Bank, announced the good news to the press.

"The money was raised by many business people in the community whose names may not come as a surprise to some, but who do want to remain anonymous."

The additional $75,000 increased the total reward amount to $100,000. To emphasize how much money he was talking about, representatives from the bank rolled out a stack of one hundred thousand $1 bills.

"This is the largest reward I've ever heard of," opined acting police chief George Phifer, "certainly in the history of the Austin Police Department." Phifer believed increasing the reward money would inspire someone to come forward finally and give out critical information that would lead to the arrest of the killer or killers. "The community [and] the families need the peace that would come with the solution of this crime."

*Friday, June 5, 1992*
*State Capitol Building*
*Downtown Austin, Texas*

Nearly six months to the day after the murders, Governor Ann Richards, who once received a free serving of yogurt from Jennifer Harbison, was ready to give something back. The governor declared June 5, 1992, "We Will Not Forget Day," in honor of the girls.

Twelve hundred citizens of Austin descended upon the Congress Avenue Bridge, which overlooked placid Town Lake. Many wore white ribbons on their lapels and T-shirts with the WE WILL NOT FORGET slogan. The throng gathered to show their support by marching from the bridge, straight down Congress Avenue, up to the steps of the Capitol. The front of the group held up a long white banner that read, WE WILL NOT FORGET.

Again the tears flowed. Hugs were abundant. Austinites once again showed how much they cared.

"It makes me feel good to see all these people come out to show support, love, and concern," said Pam Ayers. "It's a good feeling to know the community cares and hasn't forgotten."

Travis County district attorney Ronald "Ronnie" Earle spoke to the crowd assembled at the Capitol. He encouraged full community participation in the fight against crime. He also informed the audience that they "needed to push legislators to pass bills that will make sure criminals like [Kenneth] McDuff don't get parole." Earle was referring to Kenneth Allen McDuff, a death row inmate who was paroled from death row due to prison overcrowding. He was also the man who kidnapped Colleen Reed from the car wash on Fifth Street in Austin three weeks after the yogurt shop murders. He also murdered at least four other young women.

Maria Thomas, Eliza's mother, also addressed the crowd. She covered a wide range of topics, from giving thanks to the supporters to questions about the need for a "life without parole" sentence in Texas to the vagaries of the death penalty. The statement with the most impact, however, came when she asked the crowd to put themselves in her shoes.

"Think of this," she told the crowd. "Think of a mother at a cemetery trying to sing 'Happy Birthday' to her child."

There was not a dry eye in the house.

As the rally ended and the supporters went back to their own lives, four white doves were released above their heads, high into the heavens.

*Saturday, June 6, 1992*
*Toney Burger Center—Jones Road*
*Austin, Texas*

The following morning the Suracis and the Thomases made their way over to the Toney Burger Center in South

Austin. It was graduation day for the seniors of Lanier High School. Jennifer and Eliza would have been there wearing their caps and gowns.

When the families arrived for the ceremony, they were greeted with three empty chairs. Someone had adorned them with graduation gowns, white ribbons, and a single white rose. Two of the chairs were for Jennifer and Eliza. The third chair was for Corey Armstrong, a leukemia sufferer, who died two years before.

The ceremony straddled a difficult line between celebration and mourning. While the seniors were excited about their accomplishments and looking forward to their futures, they could not help but feel the pain of loss.

"Every time I think of graduation, I don't think of it without thinking of Jennifer and Eliza," proclaimed senior Amy Hettenhausen. "I feel everything I enjoy, I enjoy for them too."

Senior Class president William Boyd gave the invocation. As he asked for guidance and support for his fellow classmates, he also recalled the missing seniors. "They will always remain with us, spiritually, in our hearts and in our memories." Boyd looked up at the more than two hundred graduates in front of him.

"We will not forget."

James Thomas, Eliza's father, definitely did not want to forget. "I mostly came because I was afraid I'd be kicking myself in ten years if I didn't."

After the graduates received their diplomas, a Lanier school official quietly walked up to one of the empty chairs, grabbed a white rose, walked up to Thomas, and handed it to him. Thomas was unable to stifle his emotions. "Damn it, she should have been here."

Barbara Suraci had a different take on the event.

"Oh God, that was horrible," she recalled. "That was horrible. It was horrible. It was so sweet, but it was really, really awful. What they did was wonderful. But for us to go through that, it was really awful."

*June 6, 1992*
*Anderson Lane and Rockwood Lane*
*Austin, Texas*
*10:00 P.M.*

Later that night, six months after the girls were murdered, a group of three hundred people gathered to remember. Several graduates decided to spend their evening at the vigil to honor the memories of their friends. Lanier graduate John Schultz stated, "It wouldn't really be graduation without doing something with your friends." He glanced toward the empty yogurt shop and said, "They were friends."

Vigil organizer Neil Stegall put together the event to keep the public focused on the tragedy and to address the growing issue of crime in Austin. "Remember, this happened in your community, by someone who called themselves your neighbors."

Stegall reiterated the mantra of this case.

"We can't afford to forget this."

# CHAPTER 21

*August 6, 1992*
*Austin Police Department*
*Austin, Texas*

Eight months after the murders, a ray of light broke through. The Austin Police Department announced they had reason to question three men in connection with the yogurt shop murders. The men, Alberto Cortez, twenty-two, Ricardo Hernandez, twenty-six, and Porfirio Villa Saavedra, twenty-three, were not your average men off the street. All three had been indicted by a Travis County grand jury on March 23, 1992, for the abduction and sexual assault of a young woman in November 1991.

The apparent ringleader, Saavedra, a stocky five feet four, used several aliases, including "Carlos Martinez" and "Carlos Saavedra." He was also known euphemistically as "The Terminator." Cortez was also five feet four. Hernandez was the tall one of the group at a whopping five feet six. He was also known as "Ricardo Sanchez," "Ricardo Hernandez Albarran," and "El Brujo," or "The

Witch," due to his hooked nose. He was also called "El Dienton" because of his big teeth.

Cortez and Saavedra had previous encounters with the law. In September 1990, Cortez was sent to prison on a five-year sentence for burglary and theft but was released in little over a year. Saavedra had recently been deported from Houston, Texas, to Mexico in September 1991 after being released from prison.

Despite having been relocated to Mexico, Saavedra was arrested on November 21, 1991, in Belton, Texas, home of mass murderer George Hennard, for unlawfully carrying a weapon. His parole should have been revoked; however, he showed officers a fake Florida identification card. When the officers looked up his name, there was nothing to be found. He then failed to appear in court on the weapon charge.

Austin police sergeant Joy Mooney worked the kidnapping case. According to Mooney, a young woman was standing outside the Cavity Club, located on Red River Street, near Sixth Street, Austin's internationally known locale for live music entertainment. The Cavity Club veered just off the beaten path of Sixth Street, and with good reason. Within its walls pulsated the sounds of industrial music, bruising death metal riffs, or anything out of the mainstream realm of cover bands or blues music for which Austin is known. The Cavity Club became infamous in Austin just a few months later when naked, bloody punk rocker GG Allin was arrested for starting a riot in concert after hitting audience members in the face with his feces.

The March 23 indictment against the three men claimed that Saavedra, Cortez, and Hernandez spotted a young woman leaving the Cavity Club on November 17, 1991. It was raining that night. The three men drove along Red River Street beside the club. One of the men rolled down his window and asked the woman if she wanted a ride. Since it was raining, she accepted, but only if they would take her to her car, which was parked several blocks away. The men agreed. The woman hopped in.

She never made it to her car.

Instead, the men drove to the Galewood Garden Apartments, located on Galewood Drive in North Austin. The driver got out, went inside one of the apartments, and returned with a handgun. The men pulled the woman out of the car and switched over into a white four-door Ford. They took off and headed south on Interstate 35 toward San Antonio.

The men took turns raping the young woman while in the car. One man pointed the gun at her while another man violated and abused her. They would then switch positions. This torment took place for over an hour, about the time it took to drive from Austin to San Antonio. When they arrived in the Alamo City, the men dumped the woman out of the car onto the side of the highway. She was left bedraggled and discombobulated, but she was determined to remember their faces.

Four months after the abduction and rape, a composite sketch of one of the Hispanic suspects was created and distributed. One week later, indictments were made against Saavedra, Cortez, and Hernandez.

It just so happened that the sketch of one of the men closely resembled the description of a man who was seen outside I Can't Believe It's Yogurt on December 6, 1991. For the next several months, authorities attempted to locate the three kidnappers/rapists. They were unable to find them. Some authorities believed they may have crossed the border into Mexico.

Sergeant John Jones held a press conference to discuss the young men and their potential involvement in the yogurt shop case. He laid out four reasons why authorities sought out the men in connection with the case:

- The similarity of Alberto Cortez and the sketch of the man seen outside the yogurt shop on December 6, 1991.
- The similarity of a vehicle used by the three men in the abduction/rape and one seen at the yogurt shop.
- FBI agent Ed Richards's profile claimed that the killer or killers would be familiar with the Anderson Lane area. The three men had family and friends that lived in that exact area.
- The three men blazed out of town immediately after December 6, 1991, and had not returned.

To help locate the three men, the television crew from *America's Most Wanted* agreed to offer assistance. Sergeant Jones was ecstatic. He knew how *America's Most Wanted* had recently played an integral part in the capture of serial killer Kenneth McDuff. He hoped they could produce a similar result with these three men.

The *America's Most Wanted* crew researched both the yogurt shop murders and the Cavity Club abduction. That Friday, a five-minute segment about the three men aired to a nationwide audience. The APD received more than sixty phone calls from people who claimed to have information about the fugitives. It was unknown how many calls were received by the *America's Most Wanted* staff.

The information came as good news to the parents of the girls. They were hit hard with the knowledge that the windows of the yogurt shop were bricked up earlier that day. Charles Morrison owned the property where the yogurt shop stood. He stated that the yogurt shop and the clothing store next to it were to be conjoined to form a photocopying business. The new store would not be accessed through the old yogurt shop doors.

The investigators were hurt by the move as well.

"There used to be flowers there," Sergeant Jones

stated ruefully. "Now they're gone. It might be out of those people's memories, but not ours."

After eight months, the investigation had begun to take its toll on Jones. His health took a downward spiral, as did his home life.

The task force had already received more than two thousand tips. There were already over 750 suspects. Almost half of those had been ruled out.

Jones was determined to not seal this case shut like the doors of the yogurt shop.

"December sixth is every day for us."

# CHAPTER 22

*Wednesday, October 21, 1992*
*Mexico City, Mexico*

Mexican police officials escorted the man known as "The Terminator" up to the swarm of microphones. Porfirio Saavedra stood behind several police officers and Mexican assistant attorney general Jose Elias Romero Apis, who spoke of how Saavedra was responsible for the yogurt shop murders.

"He forced the young girls to submit," Apis informed the press. "Then he raped them, tied them up, and shot them."

The police officers forced Saavedra toward the microphones.

"Did you kill those girls in Austin?" asked one reporter.

"Yes," replied the sullen captive.

"Why?"

Saavedra, looking down at his feet, shook his head.

More information was given out regarding the two men. Saavedra was hiding out in the resort town of

Puerto Vallarta when police descended upon him. Alberto Cortez was arrested in his home in Nezahualcoyotl, a poor suburb outside of Mexico City. Ricardo Hernandez, the third suspect, had not been located.

It was uncovered that Saavedra led a sixty-member motorcycle gang in Nezahualcoyotl called the "*Mierdas* Punks*," or the "Shit Punks." Cortez was, allegedly, also a member of the biker gang. Saavedra was believed to have worked as a deliveryman for a company that delivered products to I Can't Believe It's Yogurt.

Mexican officials had long suspected the gang of being involved in organized crime and drug trafficking. The capture of these two men was considered a major coup for the Mexican police.

The yogurt shop murders confession was a bonus.

The police reported that Saavedra told them that he had planned to rob the yogurt shop. He assumed it would be empty when he broke in. Instead, he was surprised to find four young girls inside. He raped them and desecrated their bodies. He claimed that Cortez helped him out.

Cortez did not confess.


"They caught them! They caught them!" Austin resident Erik Eichorn yelled to his mother, Kat. Mother and son cried together. Kat and Erik headed over to Anderson Lane after they heard the news. They wanted to pay their respects to the girls. The Eichorns lit four white candles and rested them on the store's window ledge.

Anderson High School student Brandy Arlitt also visited the yogurt shop after she heard the news. "It doesn't matter if you knew them or not," said the youngster, who did know all four girls. "Everyone in Austin knows them now." Arlitt presciently stated that "it's not the fact that it was Sarah, Amy, Jennifer, and

Eliza. It was four young girls. It could have been anybody." She then voiced a sentiment shared by everyone at the yogurt shop.

"I think mothers, sisters, brothers, family members, friends—everyone is going to sleep better tonight."

Some people, however, expressed skepticism about the arrests. Lanier High School principal Paul Turner stated, "I would rather there be some kind of closure to it than for us to be left hanging. I don't know whether this will bring closure or not."

The victims' families had their own reactions. James and Maria Thomas elected not to speak to the press until they heard directly from the Austin Police Department. Barbara Suraci felt sick at the news. "I've been sick all day. You want to feel good about it, but it brings all the reality back."

Pam Ayers, like Paul Turner, did not want to get her hopes up. "It would be nice if it is him (Saavedra)," she explained with a sigh, "so we could let go of the drudgery of waking up and wondering if this will be the day we'll find out who killed our girls. Until Sergeant Jones tells me it's real, I won't let the numbness settle back in."

Amy's father, Bob Ayers, wanted answers.

"I want to know why," he questioned. "You're talking about a lot of innocence here with four young girls. I can't believe someone would do this to them.

"The end may be near," Bob Ayers reasoned, "but it'll never be over."

He could not have hit the nail on the head with any more precision.

# CHAPTER 23

*Saturday, October 24, 1992*
*Mexico City, Mexico*

Porfirio Saavedra appeared before Federal Magistrate Francisco Nieto Gonzalez to answer rape and murder charges in regard to the yogurt shop case.

"I don't know how to begin," whispered a sullen Saavedra, "except to say that in regard to the murders, none of it is true. I don't know who killed the girls."

Saavedra insisted that Mexican federal agents had tortured him into making the confession. He claimed authorities nearly killed him during interrogation by placing a plastic bag over his head and almost suffocating him. In addition, the agents allegedly threatened to terminate his entire family if he refused to confess.

Saavedra cried as he pleaded with Gonzalez.

"I am innocent. I did not commit the murders. I'd rather be killed for telling the truth rather than be thrown in jail for something I didn't do," he proclaimed after more than an hour of testimony. "Please, Your Honor. I beg you for justice. I believe that God will help me. Only He and I know the truth."

The Austin Police Department, which had remained quiet on the subject of Saavedra up to this point, admitted that two members of the yogurt shop task force, Mike Huckabay and Hector Reveles, were present during the interrogation, as was Alejandro Diaz de Leon, the legal attaché for the attorney general's office.

De Leon admitted that claims of torture are commonplace amongst defendants in Mexico. In this case, however, "there was no torture." Huckabay and Reveles also claimed not to have witnessed any torturing of Saavedra by Mexican officials. Austin interim police chief George Phifer stated, "Obviously, nothing like this was reported to me. In fact, an indication was made to me that at no time that they were present did any duress occur."

Alberto Cortez eventually also gave a statement. He claimed that he, Ricardo Hernandez, and Saavedra *were* outside I Can't Believe It's Yogurt on December 6, 1991. He also claimed that the two men sat in the car while Saavedra killed the four girls alone. Cortez claimed that Saavedra came out of the shop twice to retrieve something from the car. The second time he came out, Cortez alleged, Saavedra pulled out his .38-caliber pistol, pointed it at the two men, and told them to stay put.

"I don't know what was going on inside there, because I was sitting in the car," Cortez pleaded. "I wasn't looking. I was just waiting. Next thing I know, he comes out of the shop again and he's covered in blood." Then Cortez saw flames come out of the building. He claimed they drove off and headed for Mexico.

While both Saavedra and Cortez denied direct involvement in the yogurt shop murders, both men did admit to committing the Cavity Club abduction and rape. The men admitted kidnapping, raping, and kicking the victim to the curb in San Antonio. They were nice enough, however, to give the woman $10 for bus fare.

The plight of Porfirio Saavedra was presented during his hearing. He was born in Mexico City in 1968, the same year the Summer Olympics were held in that city. He was the second of six sons, and eight children overall. His father bailed out on his mother, Erminia Saavedra Guerrero, shortly after the family moved to Nezahualcoyotl, when Porfirio was two years old.

Stories of alleged physical and sexual abuse as a child at the hands of his older brother, Mario, dominated the proceedings. Porfirio claimed that the abuse went on for several years. At the age of thirteen, Porfirio had enough of the abuse. He ran away from home. He participated in numerous criminal activities such as stealing cars, burglary, drug dealing, gun smuggling—you name it. His ventures led him back and forth between the United States and Mexico. In the United States, he would stay with his brother Marcelo Villa Saavedra.

In 1991, after he was released from prison, Porfirio moved back to Mexico with his mother. She believed he was a reformed man. His sweet nature only lasted a few months before he got into a fight with his brother Mario. No one knows what the fight was about, but Porfirio stabbed his brother, who nearly bled to death. He immediately returned to Texas, where he found himself outside the Cavity Club and possibly I Can't Believe It's Yogurt.

His nearly blind mother lamented the state of her son.

"It hurts me to think he could have been involved in the killings. But when I think back about what he did to his brother, I cannot help but wonder."

Marcelo Villa Saavedra, Porfirio's brother who lived

with him between 1985 and 1987, did not wonder. He defended his younger brother.

"My brother Mario would hit Porfirio for no reason," Villa exclaimed. "One day, he said he didn't want anyone to hit him anymore." Apparently, the rage inside Porfirio was too strong to suppress. "That's when he started the violence to(ward) the people. He had a lot of hate inside."

At first, Villa believed that Porfirio *was* involved in the yogurt shop murders. He had seen the *48 Hours* episode that aired back in March and saw the sketch of the man who was supposedly seen outside the yogurt shop. He called his brother in Mexico, told him what he saw, and said, "Why did you do it?"

"I didn't do it," Porfirio replied.

"Why did you leave town?" his brother wanted to know.

"Because everybody thinks I did it."

"Why don't you talk to the police?"

"That'd be like turning myself in," his younger brother responded.

Over time, however, Marcelo came to believe that his brother did not commit the murders. He also believed Porfirio's arrest was nothing more than a political ploy. He believed that Mexico was merely trying to improve relations with its more powerful neighbor to the north.

"These are the girls the United States has made such a big deal about. Mexico wants it to be true."

# CHAPTER 24

*Tuesday, October 27, 1992*
*Mexico City, Mexico*

Porfirio Saavedra and Alberto Cortez stood before Federal Magistrate Francisco Nieto Gonzalez in the tiny courthouse. Gonzalez charged the two men with drug trafficking, kidnapping, and rape in the Cavity Club case. Since Mexico did not allow its citizens to be extradited to the United States, the men would face criminal charges in a Mexican courtroom. The penalties were potentially substantial: the drug charges could net them anywhere from ten to twenty-five years, while the kidnapping and rape charges would carry a sentence of twelve to twenty-one years.

More important for APD officials, it would keep the men in custody, while they determined whether their confessions were legitimate or not.

Mexico's attorney general spokesman George Natanson said, "These guys are in the slammer and they cannot get out on bail." By placing them on trial, Natanson informed the press, Judge Gonzalez assured all interested parties involved that Saavedra and Cortez were not going anywhere for at least one year.

The yogurt shop task force made sure they were ready for anything. They already had representatives down in Mexico City from the FBI, the ATF, the AFD, and the Travis County District Attorney's Office. They were ready to pick Saavedra's and Cortez's brains for the "tremendous amount of information" concerning the murder of four innocent girls.

*Tuesday, November 17, 1992*
*Mexico City, Mexico*

Three weeks after the announcement of charges against Saavedra and Cortez, police met with Mexican prosecutors to garner more details of their possible involvement in the murders. No information was given about the meeting. The Mexican prosecutors did state that they needed more evidence to bring charges against the two gang members.

Word on the Texas side of the border was not any more forthcoming. Austin police lieutenant David Parkinson claimed to have struck an agreement with the Mexican attorney general not to discuss the case through the press.

One week later, confusion set in. George Natanson, spokesman for the Mexican Attorney General's Office, reported that Saavedra and Cortez "are now officially suspects."

Sergeant John Jones, however, had a different story. "I don't know what they're talking about. Nothing has changed as far as their status."

When asked why there seemed to be differing opinions as to Saavedra and Cortez's suspect status, Natanson responded, "That's what Austin police told us." The distinction was important for Mexico because if the men were declared suspects, it would allow the Mexican public ministry the opportunity to conduct an official investigation into the murders. They were prevented from doing so, since the murders did not occur in Mexico.

The international goodwill seemed to be fading. Sergeant Jones reiterated, "It's our investigation and we're still investigating to our standards of justice."

# CHAPTER 25

Sergeant Jones may have had another reason to be less than forthcoming about the alleged torture of Porfirio Saavedra and Alberto Cortez. Just a few weeks earlier, on October 30, a new bombshell detonated, which involved former task force supervisor Sergeant Hector Polanco.

ADA Robert Smith informed state district judge Bob Jones of a serious problem with one of his cases. Smith discovered that another man confessed to a murder other than the defendant, Alva Eziel Curry, who was found guilty of capital murder two weeks earlier. A jury decided that Curry shot and killed a convenience store clerk named David Vela.

Smith found out about the confession from Bruce Bowser the night before Curry was to be sentenced. The discovery was relevant because Texas law, as well as federal law, states that all information that is or could be beneficial to a defendant must be turned over before or during the trial phase. Smith had not been told by anyone in the APD that there was another confession.

The kicker for Sergeant John Jones was, once again, that a questionable confession involved Hector Polanco. Bowser, twenty-two, was interrogated by six Austin police officers, including Polanco, over a six-hour period that stretched over two days. Bowser claimed that Polanco threatened him. Polanco also allegedly threatened Bowser's family members by saying that one of Bowser's previous robbery victims would kill his mother and grandmother if he did not confess. Bowser stated that he relented to the pressure and decided to "tell them what they wanted to hear." He gave a statement that implicated himself in Vela's murder.

Bowser refused, however, to put the confession in writing.

He told police everything he said was a lie.

After the interrogation ended, another police officer approached Bowser.

"Why did you confess?" the officer wanted to know.

"I was scared," Bowser quickly replied. He described the alleged threats from Polanco. "I think they just wanted me to confess to it because they didn't have any evidence at all, but he wanted me to have something to do with it."

The Austin Police Association, a labor organization that represents Austin police officers, agreed to look into the matter and determine why no police officers informed the district attorney's office about the confession. District Attorney Ronnie Earle said he would look into the matter. He also stated that Curry's status would not change.

*Tuesday, November 10, 1992*

Earle was joined by the new police chief Elizabeth Watson, who had been appointed in August and had become the first woman in the city's history to obtain the position, and Mayor Bruce Todd for a Monday-morning press conference. (According to Barbara Suraci, Watson had not expressed much concern for her daughters' case, as she told the mother that the "crime didn't happen on her watch.") Earle had an announcement to make in regard to the practices and procedures of the Austin Police Department.

"There are a number of serious cases in which past convictions and pending prosecutions may be jeopardized because of possible police misconduct," Earle told the media. "Specifically, the police misconduct involves using improper methods to obtain confessions and statements, obtaining false and incorrect statements and confessions, and concealing evidence possibly favorable to the accused in violation of state and federal law."

Mayor Todd chimed in with "there are some very difficult problems that need immediate attention. We need to make sure it doesn't occur again."

Earle wanted to make it clear that "unfortunately, this behavior is not the result of the work of just one person. . . . It appears to arise from attitudes among some criminal investigators of 'anything goes,' and 'the end justifies the means.'"

This public criticism of Austin police tactics by the district attorney was quite shocking. Earle had never chastised the police department in public. District attorneys and police officers often work in concert. It is the tendency for both sides to support one another. Apparently, the egregiousness of the officers' actions was far too great to ignore.

Earle lamented the current state of police methods. "This is especially sad for those of us who have for years admired the way that APD has reflected the standards of its community."

The Austin Police Association quickly jumped to the defense of the police officers. Sam Cox, senior sergeant, head of the organization, protested that officers were overworked. "Maybe there was not enough time to do as thorough an investigation as they should."

Earle understood the pressures placed on law enforcement, but "that sometimes leads people to want to cut corners and fudge on the rules."

A task force comprising police officials and prosecutors was created to look into at least ninety homicide cases for questions of potential police misconduct. "Ninety cases is a very conservative estimate," stated first ADA Steve McCleery, who alluded that the task force might also add cases of manslaughter, attempted murder, robbery, and more. "Our interest is to reexamine these cases and make sure they are what they are supposed to be. Our interest is not to conduct an investigation of the police department."

Several of the cases that would be reexamined involved defendants questioned by Sergeant Hector Polanco. Attorneys for several defendants had already made noise about taking their cases back in front of a judge.

Earle closed out the press conference with a telling quote: "Police misconduct directly jeopardizes public safety because [the] cases are unprosecutable and criminals go free."

# CHAPTER 26

*Sunday, December 6, 1992*
*First Anniversary of the Murders*
*Austin, Texas*

Opening the December 6, 1992, *Austin American-Statesman* to page A24 led to many tears. Inside were letters from the parents of Sarah, Jennifer, Eliza, and Amy on the one-year anniversary of their untimely deaths. Skip Suraci, stepfather to Jennifer and Sarah Harbison, recalled the horror of being notified of his daughters' deaths at 3:15 in the morning. He described the unbelievable feeling that immediately came over him upon hearing the news.

The need to contact any and all family members immediately.

The numbness that quickly settled over him.

Having to call the girls' biological father, Mike Harbison, and break the news to him.

"Michael?"

"Uh?" he mumbled through his haze of sleep.

"Is Debbie there?" Debbie Harbison, Mike's wife. Skip Suraci wanted to be sure that Mike was not alone when he told him.

"Uh," Mike mumbled again.

Suraci blurted it out: "Mike, Jennifer and Sarah were killed in a fire. Mike, did you understand what I said?"

"Yes," came the lone reply. He hung up the phone.

Seconds later, the phone rang at the Suraci household. It was Debbie Harbison.

"What did you say to Michael?" she asked. "He's babbling incoherently."

Skip Suraci could only think, *Please don't ask me to say it again. I don't believe it myself.*

Suraci wrote about the support they received from friends and family. "We may never have their killers; but, one and all, we do have each other."

Bob and Pam Ayers reminisced about their youngest child, Amy.

"The murder of our little girl, Amy, has altered our lives forever and actually causes our hearts to ache," their article started off. "Each sunrise begins with thoughts of Amy as does each waking hour of every day. 'We Will Not Forget' is not only a slogan for the public, but a reality we must face."

The parents spoke of the things they missed about their daughter—the laughter and the smiles. "We have learned not to take anything, especially life, for granted. Our wish and dream is that no parent would ever have to experience the pain that the murder of a child brings, but, unfortunately, we know that others will have to bear the same grief."

The Ayers also thanked their friends and family, as well as the entire community, for their continuous support. They closed with these thoughts: "Please don't take life for granted. Cherish each moment you have as it might be the last. Love your children, hug them, appreciate them to the very fullest and please always remember to tell them you love them."

Norma Thomas, Eliza's mother, addressed her letter to her daughter. It started off:

*My sweet daughter Eliza,*

*I would like to tell you about this year. It has been the worst year of my life. Because I was blessed with you and Sonora, the world was an okay place to live in. How could a Mom be as lucky as I? I had Eliza and Sonora for my daughters.*

*But E.T., you are no longer of this world. I make believe you will come back. That everything which has gone on for the last year is just a hoax. I sure wish they all (the media) could find another story and another sad mommy.*

Maria Thomas's despair was clearly evident when she wrote, "All my hopes and dreams are gone. And, my sweet, beautiful daughter, what about all your hopes and dreams?" She lamented the fact that she did not get to help Eliza prepare for the prom, graduation day, or her first day of college. Or her wedding day or the birth of her grandchildren.

"Eliza, the pain of losing you has been so intense. But I would go through it a million times if I knew that was the only way I'd been able to have you for my kid."

She also thanked the members of the community for their caring and support. "I am so very sorry you did not have the pleasure of meeting Eliza. She was, is, a daughter, sister, relative, neighbor, friend you would have had the pleasure of getting to meet and know."

James Thomas and Norma Fowler, Eliza's father and stepmother, thanked everyone in the community as well and asked that people contribute to several local grief-support services such as Parents of Murdered Children, Compassionate Friends, and For The Love of Christi. They also expressed their gratitude for the Austin Police Department and the task force. The couple wrote that they "have been extraordinarily kind to us. Their professionalism and dedication are impressive. They are truly Austin's finest."

The members of the task force had to deal with a certain grief of their own: the one-year anniversary of not having caught the killer or killers. Detective Mike Huckabay came home every day to the same question from his youngest son: "Daddy, did you solve the yogurt case?"

Sergeant John Jones was stressed about several factors that surrounded the case: "Black Thursday," which is what he called the Mexican confessions that turned out to be false, the Polanco problems, and the December 6 anniversary. He chose to sleep most of the day.

Assistant Police Chief George Phifer, a forty-year veteran, described the pressure as the most intense of any case in Austin's history. Not even the Charles Whitman UT Tower massacre held a candle to the yogurt shop case.

"We didn't use near the resources [on the Whitman case] because he was killed at the scene," the veteran recalled. "There was a tremendous amount of paperwork afterward, but we closed up the books after a month."

Phifer described the pressure on the detectives, however, as minimal compared to others. "It's tough, but no matter how tough it is, it's nothing compared to what the families are going through. We owe it to them to solve the case."

Detective Huckabay summed up the dichotomous

feelings of most officers when he said, "I wish I could just get my hands on these creeps. Look what they've put everyone through. But, if someone came forward, I'd almost want to hug them for ending all this."

# CHAPTER 27

*Wednesday, January 27, 1993*
*Austin, Texas*

The lawsuits began.

The week kicked off with the arbitration hearing of Sergeant Hector Polanco. The former yogurt task force supervisor initiated proceedings against the Austin Police Department after he was indefinitely suspended for the William Redman case. Polanco levied charges of racism against his employer. He emphasized the fact that he, a Hispanic, had been suspended, while Sergeant Brent McDonald, a Caucasian, only received a reprimand. Polanco desired to regain his position back in the police department.

On Wednesday, the parents of the murdered girls filed a lawsuit against Brice Foods, owners of I Can't Believe It's Yogurt, under the Texas Wrongful Death Statute and the Texas Survival Statute. Also named in the lawsuit were Rockwood Plaza Associates Ltd. and Charles Morrison, of Morrison Properties, owners of the Hillside Center.

The suit, filed by Jeff Rusk, of Shields & Rusk, PC, stated that "the owners of the yogurt shop knew of the security problems . . . but they did nothing to protect these children."

Rusk contended that there had been a rash of crimes in the West Anderson Lane area prior to the murders. The suit stated that the listed parties were negligent in not providing security, keeping the store open until late in the night when most other stores in the strip center were closed, and in staffing the shop with teenage girls late at night.

Representatives from Brice Foods were reluctant to speak about the lawsuit. A few weeks earlier, one official from the company told an Austin television station that "the yogurt store employees were briefed about security one week before the killings."

All calls made to the corporate headquarters in Dallas in regard to the lawsuit were forwarded to an Austin attorney named Carl Pierce. Pierce acknowledged the tragedy, yet he refused to comment on specifics of the suit.

"I will say that any allegation of wrongdoing will be denied," claimed Pierce.

The families insisted that they were not after money. They were angry that Brice Foods had done nothing to improve security in the area in the more than one year since the murders.

"While no money will fully compensate for the loss of their children, perhaps it will serve to deter these defendants," the lawsuit stated, "and set an example to others who place a higher value on their image and financial considerations than the health and well-being of their employees and their customers."

The amount of damages sought by the families was not specified.

Some people in Austin were not so sure of the purity

of the parents' motives. Ted Willmore, a senior music major at the University of Texas, questioned the parents in an editorial in the *Daily Texan*, the campus student newspaper.

"It seems that out of frustration the parents have struck out for retribution." Willmore was not kind to Rusk. "Jeff Rusk is the local lawyer who smelled a sure-fire multimillion dollar settlement and went in for the kill."

Willmore appeared to feel sorry for the companies; he wrote, "The defendants are not likely to go to court—they would be perceived as evil corporate monsters, insensitive to the human suffering involved.

"Settlement is virtually guaranteed, allowing Rusk to reap millions."

Willmore also questioned the judgment of the parents. "The parents claim that it was dangerous to have only two female teens working at night in the shop. If they actually believed this, it seems that they should have insisted that their children quit the job."

The editorial insinuated that businesses should not be liable for the actions of criminals. "Draining the coffers of the defendants," Willmore posited, "is not the way to promote social change in this case." He stressed that change could only take place through activism, such as the example of Candy Lightner, founder of Mothers Against Drunk Drivers (MADD). In 1980, Lightner's thirteen-year-old daughter, Cari, was murdered by a drunk driver, fifty-two-year-old Clarence Busch, in Fair Oaks, California. MADD, of course, has gone on to promote awareness of drunk driving and has potentially saved thousands of lives.

"It is a pity," wrote Willmore, "that the girls died. But their parents should drop this suit in favor of effective social action.

"The only outcomes of this suit will be a large cash settlement for the parents—not to mention their attorney—and a slight but barely perceptible loss of public sympathy."

# CHAPTER 28

*Monday, March 15, 1993*
*Yogurt Shop Task Force*
*Austin, Texas*

Reality began to set in for Sergeant John Jones, Detective Mike Huckabay, and the rest of the yogurt shop task force. After one year and three months and more than five thousand tips, they received word that the task force would have to be reduced. A cost/benefit analysis indicated that the task force was a losing proposition. They had until June to solve the case before cutbacks were made.

To help make a last-ditch effort, six more police officers were added to the team. The total number of officers involved rose to eighteen.

They had less than three months to get the work done.

The goal was to plow through as many of the remaining two-thousand-plus tips as possible.

Austin police lieutenant David Parkinson spoke about the imminent shutdown of the task force. "The only way you can face this is by thinking that someday, somewhere, you'll find information that leads to solving it."

Optimism still remained.

"Who knows, with five thousand tips, we may be down to five hundred seventy-three and solve it. All we can do is try."

*Sunday, March 28, 1993*
*West Anderson Lane*
*Austin, Texas*

A fair-size group of mourners gathered outside, across the paved street, from the I Can't Believe It's Yogurt building. Sprinkled amongst the crowd were family members of the four girls. They had gathered yet again to honor their daughters, Amy, Sarah, Jennifer, and Eliza.

Yogurt shop patron Neil Stegall wanted to dedicate something special for the two girls he knew as the friendly employees behind the counter—a pink granite "remembrance stone," measuring twenty by twenty-eight inches. On the face of the stone was a gold-colored plaque with a maroon inlay with the inscription IN LOVING MEMORY—AMY AYERS—SARAH HARBISON—JENNIFER HARBISON—ELIZA THOMAS—FOREVER IN OUR HEARTS. The stone was set in a white rock garden inside a white small wooden fence. An oak tree stood watch.

*Wednesday, May 26, 1993*
*Yogurt Shop Task Force*
*Austin, Texas*

Two months after the memorial ceremony, a rather unceremonious occasion took place; the official reduction of the yogurt shop murders task force. The additional officers that were brought in were unable to crack the case. Cuts had to be made. The task force was reduced in size from eighteen people to five. Sergeant Jones remained as case agent.

"We are currently working on what we consider to be ten to fifteen solid . . . leads concerning the case," Jones informed local reporters. He stated that more than fifteen hundred tips were to be looked into. He also mentioned the Hispanic suspects. "The investigation is still open despite the perception that the guys in Mexico did it and that's that," he replied. "Well, no, the jury is still out on that. And until it is proven to our satisfaction, the investigation continues."

Lieutenant David Parkinson informed the media that "it is still a priority to solve this case."

The families spoke with the task force about the reduction. They were concerned, but understanding. Skip Suraci relayed that the families "were all pretty upset," but pleased that the police department assured them that "we are still a priority case, not just for the one investigator . . . but for the whole force."

The revised staff included Jones, Huckabay, one full-time investigative assistant, and two part-time investigators.

# CHAPTER 29

The support for the girls continued to resonate throughout the Austin community—sometimes in a very traditional manner, sometimes in a uniquely Austin manner, sometimes in a wholly bizarre manner.

The traditional recognition took place at the St. Louis Catholic Church, where three of the girls attended church (Amy Ayers was not Catholic) and where Sarah and Jennifer graduated from junior high school. A memorial plaque in honor of the four girls was introduced. The plaque dedicated all of the youth rooms in the church on behalf of the girls. In addition, officials from the church planted a strong oak tree behind the school office building.

The uniquely Austin-style remembrance actually came a year earlier from a group of musicians led by two Joes: Joe Ely and Joe "King" Carrasco. Ely, the eclectic country-rocker, and Carrasco, the "Tex-Mex Party King," joined forces to pen a song entitled "We Will Not Forget." In a "We Are the World"–type setup, the recording included several musicians and local media personalities. The musicians gave the rights of the song to the families to do with what they wished. Proceeds of the song benefited Child, Inc.

The bizarre remembrance of the case came from a local punk band known as the Fuckemos. The band, formerly known as Warthog 2001, changed its name to the Fuckemos after its lead singer, Russell Porter, was unceremoniously tossed out of Emo's, the long-standing punk rock venue and hipster hangout.

With such song titles as "Pedophile," "2 Punk 2 Fuck," and "The Screams of the Wild Women," the Fuckemos were not known for their restraint.

Obviously.

Porter was also intrigued by conspiracy theories. The yogurt shop case held an unusual fascination for him. The band recorded a song about the case entitled "YM."

"The song's not that deep, but it hits close to home." Porter commented that several people in the club scene were being unfairly brought in for questioning. The band wanted to poke fun at the Austin Police Department for going down the "scary-looking-kid route." Lyrically, the song talks about the wide range of potential suspects and how the cops seemed to have no clue.

The chorus of the song goes: "I know who killed the girls. But I'm not telling you."

# CHAPTER 30

*November 1993*
*Mexico City, Mexico*

The task force was also rather low-key. Since the reduction in staff, not much progress had been made. While the current team continued to plow through tips, they did not completely write off Porfirio Saavedra and Alberto Cortez. Even though the bikers confessed to the murders one year earlier, then recanted, Austin police were still considering them as possible suspects.

Lieutenant David Parkinson and two other Austin police detectives returned to Mexico, this time hopefully armed with evidence to implicate the two men.

"They want to prove what the suspects confessed to," stated Jaime Gonzalez, attaché to the Mexican attorney general. He stated that the Austin police were not prepared the previous year when they visited Mexico; that they did not bring any proof. "Now they want to make sure that they have a good case."

Police were not so sure that the trip would amount to anything.

"We don't have more or less evidence than we had a year ago," an unnamed inside source told the *Austin American-Statesman*. "At some point we may eliminate them, but I don't think we're at the point of saying, 'Let's move on,' with these guys."

The uncertainty of the status of their daughters' cases began to creep into the parents' words. "I hope they figure something out," stated Maria Thomas. "A lot of people think it's them, but we don't know for sure."

Barbara Suraci feared learning more about how exactly her daughters were killed. "I have not dealt with how my children died yet. I'm not ready to think about what they were thinking and how scared they were."

# CHAPTER 31

*Monday, December 6, 1993*
*Second Anniversary of the Murders*
*West Anderson Lane*

For the second year in a row, a group of people gathered outside the former location of I Can't Believe It's Yogurt to remember the four girls. The crowd was not quite as large as the previous year; however, the impact of their loss was evident.

Pam Ayers, Amy's mother, spoke of how those not related to the girls were able to move forward. "For a lot of people, they're aware it happened, but their lives can still go on." She harbored no resentment toward people who had "moved on."

"I know they think about it, but it's not the daily agony we all have to deal with."

Earlier that Monday morning, Barbara and Skip Suraci attended mass for the four girls at St. Albert the Great Catholic Church, where Sarah had attended during her preparation for confirmation.

"She was murdered before she could be confirmed," informed Barbara Suraci.

The gathering, however, was not to continue to mourn the girls' deaths, but to celebrate the bright light that was their lives. Friends reminisced about the fun times they had with the girls.

"I would much rather spend my time talking about Jennifer and Sarah than talking about how they died," Barbara Suraci stated. The brave, elegant woman smiled and gave strong hugs to friends and supporters as she entered the chapel.

Later, at the candlelight vigil held at the Hillside Center, two of the mothers spoke out about the investigation. Pam Ayers feared that someone else may be killed. "Whoever did it is still out there, and it could happen again. And somebody else is going to have to go through what we're going through."

Barbara Suraci announced that the coffers of the reward money had been stuffed with an additional $25,000, bringing the total to $125,000. "We want to encourage people to give us a Christmas present."

The two mothers spoke of how their lives had changed forever. "We'll never be the same," a wistful Pam Ayers stated. "Whoever did this is still out there probably still enjoying themselves. They're able to live with what they've done, and they have ruined my family."

"We're not the same people we were," added Barbara Suraci. "We were very busy people. We had teenagers. They were involved in everything in their schools. Our whole life revolved around them.

"Our whole life is now revolving around their memory."

The parents, however, were not there for a pity party. They continued to stress the need for someone to step forward and provide some pertinent information.

"I have said from the beginning that I thought this

would be a two-year process," Barbara Suraci said. "I don't think it will be [today], but I do think it will be soon."

Pam Ayers was not quite as optimistic. "I used to think they are going to solve it. Now, I don't think so. We're getting too far down the road." She feared the only way it would come to an end would be for another person to be killed.

Barbara Suraci was determined to keep a positive face on the tragic anniversary. "There are moments of these two years that have been filled with pain and anxiety that have lasted a lifetime. The moments are eternity and the years are just a blink.

"I believe that we can, as individuals, make a difference. We can help each other, support each other." Her goal was to help other children who had suffered at the hands of violence, and those who may dole it out. "We can take care of all the children so that no one's child falls through the cracks and ends up on the streets with a gun and a broken heart." She emphasized that it was the kids who "have not been loved enough or cared [for] enough" who usually committed violent crimes.

"With that in mind, I will continue to have this little crusade to save all the kids." Barbara Suraci spoke with no bitterness in her heart. "I know that sounds optimistic and probably silly to a lot of people, but I think it's important that I remain optimistic.

"Because as long as there is hope, we will survive."

# CHAPTER 32

*Monday, January 10, 1994*
*Austin, Texas*

One year after the parents of the slain victims filed a lawsuit against I Can't Believe It's Yogurt Ltd., Brice Foods Inc., and Charles Morrison, of Morrison Properties, the defendants in question offered to settle. The case was set to be heard before a judge on February 28. Instead, the defendants made an offer of $12 million, which the parents accepted.

Jeff Rusk, attorney for the families, said that one main reason the families settled was because I Can't Believe It's Yogurt instituted changes and upgrades in security after the suit was filed. Records indicated that in 1991, the West Anderson Lane yogurt shop's budget was $271,000. The total budget for security for that store had been only $50.

"There will be some people who are still alive because of these changes," stated Barbara Suraci. Not only were better safety measures being implemented in all ICBY stores, but also in other restaurants in Austin.

Burger King Central Texas district manager Lewis Jernigan snapped to when he heard about the lawsuit settlement. "Something like that will get your attention in a hurry."

Others were encouraged to reassess their safety precautions right after the murders. Doug Thomas, president of Schlotzsky's, a submarine sandwich chain that originated in Austin in 1971 and has kept its home office there, said, "We went and reassessed all our security measures and we did add some things. But there's a limit to what you can do."

A similar sentiment rang throughout the food-service industry in the state. Texas Restaurant Association representative Julie Sherrier stated her opinion very clearly: "Restaurants are public places. As an industry, we can't be responsible for every Joe Schmo with a gun."

I Can't Believe It's Yogurt CEO Bill Brice mentioned his company's nearly spotless safety record for fifteen years before the massacre: "We have gone through a painstaking process of deciding what to do in an increasingly crime-ridden society to keep people safe."

But much like *Daily Texan* writer Ted Willmore, Brice wondered how far restaurants needed to go to provide security. "We can't put up barbed wire and armed guards and search people going into our stores."

The parents of the girls were determined to insure that their daughters' deaths were not in vain. According to Rusk, they planned to use a large portion of the settlement money to create an organization, SAJE: We Will Not Forget, to help educate parents, businesses, and teenage employees about workplace safety. The name SAJE was derived by using the initials of each of the girls' first names.

In January 1994, Skip Suraci, Jennifer and Sarah Harbison's stepfather, decided a career change was in order. Motivated by the deaths of his stepdaughters,

Suraci made the choice to attend law school. He was accepted to Tulsa University in Oklahoma, about seven hours north of Austin.

"What brought me here was this terrible event that thrust me into this world of law enforcement and criminal investigation," Skip Suraci told the University of Tulsa *Collegian*. "Unfortunately, in today's society, the prevalence of violent crime makes each person a potential victim. I needed to know more than just a passing overview of the law to be a figure at all in the investigation."

Skip Suraci was so consumed with his daughters' case that he could not properly focus on his job as a project manager for Dell Computer. He needed to become a part of the investigation. He believed law school was the best avenue.

"At my age, it was a rather gutsy move to leave home and arrive at some foreign location three weeks before classes. It was a leap of faith."

It was not a decision he made lightly.

"I had to do some deep soul-searching as to what was next for me," he stated. "I came to realize that my children are gone, but, good or bad, I'm not. It would have been easier if we all had gone together. But we were left behind."

Suraci spoke of his plans for after graduating. "First, I want to move back to Austin and see what my wife wants to do." He continued to speak of some lofty goals. "I might also practice law, both as a prosecutor and a defender, helping underrepresented people." He knew that some people would be surprised by that admission "because I naturally have more of a prosecutorial bent from what happened to me. However, to be a good prosecutor, you have to know the other side too."

Skip Suraci summoned the memories of Sarah and Jennifer when he talked of his reason for studying law:

to be a part of the investigation of the deaths of his two lovely daughters.

"I'm still searching for answers. I want to be able to open the doors."

# CHAPTER 33

*Monday, June 27, 1994*
*Yogurt Shop Task Force*
*Austin, Texas*

The four girls were not the only people who suffered from what occurred on December 6, 1991. Sergeant John Jones, after 2½ years of leading the investigation on the case, had enough. He ate, drank, and slept the case. It consumed him every waking hour. It devoured him during rare moments of sleep.

It also took its toll on him physically and emotionally. The yogurt shop case almost destroyed him and his family. Jones was tired and he needed off the case. He was burned-out.

Jones did not want it, but he received a reassignment. He was relocated to the Assault Unit.

"The case came before everything else. My own psyche was a victim of that," Jones admitted with a sigh. "My home life took a backseat a couple of times, which is a definite no-no.

"It almost ended my family. It came close, too damned close."

Jones suffered from severe bouts of depression over the case. His temper flared. He was diagnosed with post-traumatic stress disorder. He sought secular help from a psychologist. He sought higher help from his church. He described himself as "haunted."

"It sent me to a psychologist, and I'm still going . . . to keep my head above water. In between battling the administration and trying to do justice in this case, it was draining me down to zero.

"If there's anything that's been positive that's come out of this case, it's been my renewed faith in a Supreme Being, someone to watch over me."

Detective Mike Huckabay took over the case. He, too, had suffered mental anguish over the investigation. "I've burned more sick leave in the last two-and-a-half years than I have in the last twenty or twenty-five years," Huckabay emphasized. He informed Jones that he was deeply depressed. Jones suggested a visit to his psychologist. Huckabay said it was "probably the best move I ever made, because she made me realize all this is normal."

Neither man was pleased with Jones's reassignment. Jones felt that the task force would always get bogged down with "petty politics" among the departmental divisions—usually surrounding a lack of personnel. Police officials disagreed.

"I never heard one concern about a personnel shortage or any lack of human resources on that case," claimed Deputy Chief Bruce Mills.

Alas, when Jones was told he was not only off the yogurt shop case, but out of homicide altogether, he claimed, "The bottom dropped out of me." He summed up his mental state best with a song lyric from the 1970s television variety show *Hee Haw*: "Deep, dark depression, excessive misery."

Jones continued to discuss the logistics of the task force and how it fell apart at the seams. "The mechanics is where this thing fell apart. What I got was a call on my day off saying, 'Come in. You're being transferred in a week.'

"That was a slap in the face. It hurt."

"I personally don't like the way it was handled with John," asserted Huckabay.

The parents of the four girls were not happy, to say the least. They had grown quite fond of Sergeant Jones and believed that no one knew more about the case than did the respected detective.

"We feel abandoned," complained Barbara Suraci. "We're being processed out just like John Jones was." She continued: "The man dedicated his life to what happened to our children, and we can't help but love him for that."

Norma Fowler, Eliza Thomas's stepmother, was also sorry to see Jones go. "I think that we have just been unbelievably, uniquely lucky in how positive our interactions with the police have been, and I think a lot of that is due to John."

Despite the frustration of the transfer, Jones understood the necessity of a fresh pair of eyes on the case. His rekindled affair with a Supreme Being also may have led to a more rational outlook. "Two years ago, the line would have been, 'This son of a bitch is going to be solved soon.' Now, it's going to be solved when it's ready to be solved. It's up to the man upstairs." Jones continued: "It might be tomorrow, it might be a year from now, and it might be twenty years from now. It might be those guys in Mexico. It could be somebody we've already talked to. It could be McDuff."

Jones spoke of the shirt he wore on December 6, 1991. He hid the shirt and vowed never to bring it out again until the girls' murders were solved. "I told the families that the next time they see me wearing that shirt, they'll know it's over."

Sergeant John Jones's shirt would remain in the closet for a long time.

# CHAPTER 34

*Tuesday, December 6, 1994*
*Third Anniversary of the Murders*
*Santa Marta Prison—Outside of Mexico City, Mexico*

Three years later, and still no definitive answers. The Hispanic suspects Porfirio Saavedra and Alberto Cortez were still in jail in Mexico, but not for the yogurt shop murders. They received fifteen-year sentences for rape and cocaine possession in the Cavity Club abduction. They were imprisoned in Santa Marta, a medium-security prison outside of Mexico City, where they received visits from their wives and children.

Austin police did not seem to place any more attention on the two men. "We're kind of stalemated on the guys in Mexico," said Lieutenant David Parkinson.

Barbara Suraci, however, was much more definitive in her belief of how Austin police were handling this aspect of the case. "The investigation has ground to a halt," she said. "Unfortunately, the Austin police don't have the clout [or] the expertise to pursue these men in Mexico because of all the international laws."

Saavedra gave more details about why he confessed to the yogurt shop murders: "The Mexican police said they would beat my wife and rape her." According to police authorities, confessions extracted via beatings are not uncommon in Mexican prisons. Saavedra feared for his wife. "I refused to confess until they said they would rape my wife."

Saavedra and Cortez had not even been interviewed by any of the Austin police detectives in more than two years. Saavedra claimed to have taken a lie detector test with Lieutenant Parkinson, which he supposedly passed with flying colors. He also claimed that Parkinson told him, "I don't think you did it, but I think you know who did."

Alberto Cortez added, "They have the wrong people. We did bad things, but we didn't kill anyone."

Apparently, Mexican government officials did not even remember the yogurt shop murders or the two suspects. This discouraged Barbara Suraci.

"The chances are that this is a forgotten case," the crusading mother stated. "Not in the hearts and minds of the people, but we're talking about a system, and systems don't have hearts and minds."

She, like the other parents, were left once again to face Christmas without their loving daughters.

# CHAPTER 35

*1994–1996*

Over the next three years, things remained relatively quiet with the case. According to Mike Huckabay, in 1994, Doug Dukes took over as lead investigator and Sergeant Butch Biehle took on the role of supervisor. No major developments surfaced in the case during that year.

In October 1994, Barbara Suraci moved out of her home on Tamarack Trail into the Scofield Farms neighborhood in North Austin to be closer to her daughters.

In 1995, the Ayers moved out of their cozy little home on Ohlen Road in North Austin to a quarter-horse ranch in the Texas Hill Country. It would have been the perfect setting for their daughter to raise pigs and ride cutting horses, which are used to separate cows on the open range. Robert Ayers became a full-time rancher, while Pam Ayers worked in the cafeteria at Dripping Springs Middle School.

In March 1996, Yogen Fruz Worldwide purchased I Can't Believe It's Yogurt Ltd., and Brice Foods CEO

Bill Brice netted a cool multimillion-dollar payday for the transaction.

In June 1996, a case that had already been populated with all sorts of bizarre characters took another unusual twist. Erik Moebius, a former Texas assistant attorney general, became immersed in a legal imbroglio that managed to drag in a vast conspiracy theory involving the yogurt shop murders.

Moebius was convinced that the yogurt shop murders were the result of corrupt insurance frauds perpetrated by several high-ranking officials and bigwig attorneys in Texas. Some of the names bandied about were Roy Minton, one of the lawyers who settled the $12 million lawsuit against Brice Foods, San Antonio attorney Jerry Gibson, who helped on the Brice Foods settlement, Attorney General Dan Morales, state district judge Paul Davis, and possibly several police officers.

Moebius theorized that the yogurt shop case was a "no liability" case and should not have been settled. Moebius believed that the $12 million did not come from insurance money, but rather, from laundered money. He postulated that the money might have been laundered through insurance companies and "murdered out," or paid out through a settlement death claim.

Moebius believed it was all a part of a pattern throughout the United States known as "reserve fraud." He claimed that reserve fraud involved "severe injury cases, including murder and arson, in which people were being intentionally injured, murdered, or burned on preselected premises with the intent of creating personal injury claims." He also wrote that "claimants were also 'separated' from their claims by attorney fraud or court action."

Moebius called the money-laundering scheme a "site-specific murder" that involved "gross premeditation and planning." He believed that the yogurt shop murders were preplanned and staged. Part of that planning involved hiring a killer to do the deed.

Moebius has even implicated a specific individual in the murders: Bill Moerschell, a thirty-four-year-old unemployed gambler. Moebius claimed that Moerschell was hired as a hit man six months before the murders, and that he was embedded in a condominium directly behind the Hillside Center and the yogurt shop. Moebius also claimed that Moerschell visited the yogurt shop every day for six months straight and that he befriended Eliza Thomas and Jennifer Harbison. He alleged that Moerschell's name even appeared in Jennifer's diary. And that both girls visited him at his condo and took care of his dogs.

Moebius claimed that Moerschell moved out of the condo the day after the murders and into his girlfriend's place. He also stated that the hit man received a cash infusion of $40,000 one week after the murders.

Moebius has also implied that the parents of the girls may have been involved in the murders. He stated that the Suracis made it possible for all four girls to be together at the same time. He also stated that Moerschell was a gambling associate of Skip and Barbara Suraci's. Moebius also claimed that Moerschell received a postcard in 1992 from Skip Suraci thanking him for "everything."

Moebius, however, tended to misstate several of the most basic facts. He called Eliza Thomas, Eliza May. He has given out the wrong ages of the girls. He claimed that the four girls were at a movie. He also listed several incorrect elements of the crime scene, such as his claim that all four girls were hanged and mutilated.

One year earlier, Moebius was disbarred from the state of Texas for nine counts of misconduct, including failure to communicate properly with his clients, lying about judges, violating court procedures, and "mental incompetence." Other sources indicated that he was disbarred due to accusations of child molestation.

John J. "Mike" McKetta, who prosecuted Moebius at the disbarment hearing, said, "Bless his heart, I'm convinced he believes everything he says. But I've never been able to follow what he's saying for more than a few consecutive minutes." McKetta added, "He never met a coincidence that wasn't conspiratorial."

Needless to say, Moebius's theories were met with disgust and disdain by many people.

In late November 1996, SAJE officially published a sixty-five-page safety manual entitled *How to Survive and Thrive at Work: A Guide for Teenagers (and Parents, Employers, and Other Concerned Adults)*. They also produced a twelve-minute companion video. The goal for the manual and video was to promote workplace safety.

Barbara Suraci stated, "We want to celebrate the lives of our children by saving other children's lives. We can't stop the violence, but we can make a difference."

Pam Ayers talked about when parents "send our children off to work and we assume the employers have done everything they have to do to keep it a safe place." She warned, "Don't assume anything. Look at what kind of workplace your children are going to."

The foreword to the manual cites statistics from the United States Department of Labor that indicate every year over seventy teenagers die at work, more than two hundred thousand are injured on the job, and nearly sixty-four thousand require emergency room medical treatment.

"If only we had known the right questions to ask," wrote the parents in the foreword, "we could have better evaluated the shop's security and the girls' risks in working there. Perhaps they would still be with us."

The manual provided numerous helpful tips for teenagers on how to deal with potential threats or dangerous situations on the job. There was even a chapter entitled "How to Survive a Robbery."

The families printed up one thousand booklets initially. SAJE's goal was to distribute the book to as many employers, parents, and kids as possible. "Knowledge is power," stated Pam Ayers, "and that's what we want to give them."

# CHAPTER 36

*Friday, December 6, 1996*
*Fifth Anniversary of the Murders*

Five years after the murders, the yogurt shop task force had dwindled down to two people. It was no longer a priority, and this frustrated several officers on the force. The APD homicide division had an impeccable clearance rate of 86 percent. Most United States cities with a population of 250,000 or more averaged only a 50 percent homicide clearance rate.

"To my knowledge, this case has received more attention and resources from the department than any other," stated Lieutenant David Parkinson.

Police officials were joined by the parents in their frustration. The parents, however, also directed some of their frustration toward Austin's finest. The lack of information given to the parents was cited. The switching of the case over to another investigative team was causing additional frustration.

One method to attempt to overcome the frustration was introduced by Crime Stoppers: a video with a speculative reenactment of the murders was introduced to a unique audience—Texas State prisoners.

Nancy Petkovsek, coordinator of the Texas Department of Criminal Justice Crime Stoppers program, stated that "approximately one hundred thirty thousand inmates will see this video. Even though they are in prison, criminals know more about what's going on outside than we do."

There were several incentives for a prisoner to inform on someone if they knew who killed the girls— 125,000 reasons.

After five years, everyone involved with the yogurt shop murders was desperate to solve the crime. Most were willing to try just about anything.

Just for one small glimmer of hope.

# PART II
# THE BOYS

# CHAPTER 37

*Friday, August 6, 1999*
*Austin Police Department Cold Case Unit*
*Clayton Lane—Twin Towers*
*Austin, Texas*

The Cold Case Unit headquarters was located in the gold Twin Towers, off Interstate 35 north, less than five miles away from the West Anderson yogurt shop location. The placid outward appearance of the buildings—well-manicured lawns covered with groomed shrubs, large oak trees that provided vast quantities of shade, and a relaxing eight-sided water fountain—belied the horrors that hid inside the second-floor location.

To reach the Cold Case Unit offices, Detective Paul Johnson would park his car in the parking lot, walk past the spraying fountain into the West building on the left-hand side, walk past a few small businesses on the first floor, head to the elevators, get off on the second floor, and take a quick left down the hallway. The view was uninspiring—a parking lot.

Detective Johnson strode confidently into his office.

The seasoned twenty-one-year veteran officer had solved several high-profile cases throughout his career. Probably the most notorious case Johnson worked on became known nationwide as the "Condom Rape Case." Johnson arrested Joel Rene Valdez for the rape of a young woman. Valdez claimed that he had engaged in consensual sex with the victim because she requested he wear a condom. Johnson's police work led to a forty-year sentence for the rapist.

Another well-known case that the forty-five-year-old Johnson worked was the 1997 abduction and murder of two young men, Brandon Shaw and Juan Cotera, whose bodies were discovered inside the trunk of a car in Town Lake. Johnson helped nail Ahmad McAdoo and Derrick Williams with the murders.

Johnson and fellow detective J. W. Thompson had been working on the yogurt shop case since 1996. Johnson was responsible for organizing the voluminous files of paperwork that had accumulated over the years. Thompson's duties included following up on any new tips that surfaced.

Due to the smaller number of homicides—only ten were committed during the first seven months—the APD determined it was time to reevaluate a few cold cases. There were more than one hundred unsolved homicides in Austin since 1967.

The yogurt shop murders were one of those cases.

Johnson felt confident because six new law enforcement officers were assigned to assist in trying to solve the case. They were Detectives Ronald Lara, Robert Merrill, John Hardesty, and Manuel Fuentes; Texas Ranger Sal Abreo; and ATF agent Chuck Meyer. The additional manpower could only help to lighten Johnson's overwhelming load. When he was handed the case two years earlier, he received two filing cabinets and numerous boxes of material related to the case: tips, leads, all sorts of paperwork.

As Johnson and Thompson organized the case files, they pulled out their most intriguing tips. By the time the new task force was created, the two officers had set aside the top sixty leads. These were the people on whom the new yogurt shop murders task force would focus their attention.

The first name, literally pulled out of a hat, belonged to Maurice Pierce. The same Maurice Pierce who was arrested at Northcross Mall on December 14, 1991, for carrying a gun, which he claimed was used in the murders. The same person who stole a Nissan Pathfinder off the Town North Nissan lot near the yogurt shop the night after the murders.

Also included in the Maurice Pierce tip file were the names of three of Pierce's buddies: Forrest Welborn, Robert Springsteen IV, and Michael Scott.

# CHAPTER 38

Maurice Pierce was born on September 3, 1975, in Houston, Texas, to William and Fonda Pierce. He was the only boy in a family of four children. Pierce came from a close-knit family that watched out for one another and shared a loving bond. He was especially close to his sister, Annette, with whom he spent much of his time.

Pierce's years at the Christian Academy elementary school were unremarkable. The young boy stayed out of trouble and was an average student. He went to class, did his schoolwork, and made decent grades.

According to William Pierce, he and Fonda divorced in 1983. Maurice's mother relocated to Austin. Despite the breakup, Pierce and his family still managed to stay close to one another. He and his father would visit his mother in Austin almost every other week. He maintained a loving relationship with his mother, father, and sisters. He also kept up his grades.

After elementary school, William and Maurice Pierce packed up their belongings and moved to Austin. William

Pierce wanted his son to be closer to his mother. The younger Pierce was excited about the move.

The excitement was short-lived.

One day, Maurice came home from Lamar Middle School very upset. When his father came home from work, Maurice informed him that a gang of black kids had tried to sell him drugs. They had also tried to pick a fight with him.

His father, incensed, wrote a letter to Governor Ann Richards. He wanted her to know that drugs were being sold in the schools and that young kids' minds were potentially ripe for corruption. He eventually received a letter from the governor, who told him to encourage his son to keep working hard.

William Pierce would have none of it. He immediately pulled Maurice out of school and away from the bad influences.

Soon thereafter, Maurice started taking drugs. According to probation records, Pierce started using "pot, coke, [and] acid" by the age of twelve. He claimed that he stopped taking drugs three years later, when he was fifteen. He claimed that he only drank on special occasions. And he only drank beer.

From twelve to twenty-four beers, that is.

Maurice eventually returned to school in 1989. He transferred to Dobie Middle School, where he met a girl named Kimberli. They were an instant item and it was not long before if you saw one, you saw both of them. William Pierce described them as "24/7."

Maurice just skated by academically at Dobie Middle School. At the time, he sported a very 1980s-era mullet haircut—"business in the front, party in the back." He enjoyed taking care of cars and was considered a bit of a neat freak.

He attended ninth grade at Robbins Academy, a learning facility for troubled kids and special-needs students, particularly special-education students, dropouts, and problem students.

Pierce was definitely experiencing his share of problems. He stole the Nissan Pathfinder on December 7, 1991. He later paid $350 for the damages to the vehicle. He was arrested on December 14, 1992, at Northcross Mall, for carrying a .22 revolver. He claimed that the gun was used in the yogurt shop murders; however, he was not involved in the crime. He was eventually written off the yogurt shop suspect list. In September 1992, he pleaded no contest to a misdemeanor drunk-driving charge. He was sentenced to two years' probation.

That same year, he received some good news. His girlfriend, Kimberli, gave birth to a baby girl. He was a father at the age of seventeen.

In 1993, he transferred to Anderson High School, but he only lasted three months. He dropped out in October 1993. He did not make the school yearbook.

After he dropped out of school, Pierce was arrested at least twice. Once, for public intoxication. The other time for acting as a lookout for a buddy who stole a car. Charges were dropped against him in both instances.

In 1995, Maurice, Kimberli, and their daughter moved to Lewisville, Texas, about twenty-five miles northwest of Dallas. Once they settled in, Pierce found employment at an industrial warehouse. He worked there for a few years and was considered a good employee. He fared so well that he was up for promotion as warehouse foreman. Pierce also lent his construction abilities to a Lewisville church, where he and his wife attended. He retiled the floors and tinted all of the windows in the church.

Pierce's former buddy Forrest Welborn was born on August 21, 1976, to Sharon and James Welborn. Forrest's parents divorced when he was in first grade at Blanton

Elementary School. He and his sister, India, stuck together until their father remarried. The newly formed family now included a half brother, a stepsister, and two stepbrothers.

Yvonne Greer, a Blanton Elementary classmate of Welborn's, recalled seeing Welborn riding by himself on the bus to school every day. She said he did not appear to have any friends.

Welborn's mother described her son as the reserved type.

"He is a very quiet person and he also pretty much keeps his emotions to himself."

Welborn's academic career was rather uneventful. He went to class, passed his courses, and stayed out of trouble. In seventh grade at Lamar Middle School, he played the upright bass in the school band.

Welborn started at McCallum High School in the fall of 1991, three months before the yogurt shop murders. He did not necessarily attend school like he once had. He began skipping classes and hanging out. He eventually flunked ninth grade and was forced to repeat it.

"Basically, after our freshman year," Yvonne Greer recalled, "we never saw him again."

Welborn made it through another semester as a freshman until he dropped out of McCallum in March 1993. A neighbor of his described him as "kind of wild" during that period. He did not, however, get into any serious trouble, except for a "driving with a suspended license" charge in late 1996.

The year before, Welborn impregnated his girlfriend. She gave birth to a boy. Welborn doted on his son.

"Forrest is a really good dad," said his sister, India Welborn. "He's wonderful. He's got a really good heart, and he'd do anything for anyone."

Welborn spent most of his time working on motorcycles. His passion for mechanics led him into a career in automotive repair. He moved to Lockhart, about twenty-five miles southeast of Austin, in 1997. He lived in an RV park just south of town. In the beginning of 1999, he worked for Lockhart Muffler. The muffler shop went out of business, so Welborn decided to put up his own shingle, Lockhart Automotive, that April.

Welborn had grown substantially since 1991. He stood well over six feet tall. He had long brown hair, flowing down the middle of his back, and a full-blown beard. He looked as if he stepped out of the musical *Jesus Christ Superstar*. He was quite noticeable in the tiny town of Lockhart.

Robert Springsteen IV was born on November 26, 1974, in Chicago, Illinois, to Michelle and Robert Springsteen. His parents, who married in 1973, divorced in 1976. He and his mother moved to West Virginia that same year.

Robert Springsteen III allegedly did not keep in contact with his son. According to Andrew "Brett" Thompson, Springsteen's stepfather, Springsteen III probably only saw his son three times in a span of twelve years. Robert Springsteen III, on the other hand, claimed to have visited his son at least one weekend every month when the boy was young. Eventually that dwindled down to two weeks out of the year.

As Springsteen grew older, he began to have serious problems at school and at home. Stonewall Jackson Junior High School former vice principal David Miller stated that Springsteen "wore out his welcome" there. Miller added that Springsteen was "not someone you wanted around a lot." Springsteen did not stick around Stonewall Jackson a lot. He was transferred to Cabell Alternative Education High School, an alternative school for students who were unsuccessful in their academic achievements due to either learning difficulties or too many behavioral problems.

Springsteen's favorite teacher at Cabell, Danny Decker, noticed that Springsteen did not fit in. "He was immature for his age, and he would do silly things to get attention." She cited the fact that his wardrobe was rather outlandish, from Nehru jackets to doo rags. "Robby would go to the far extreme."

Decker did, however, note Springsteen's creative side. "Robby was very artistic. At an alternative school, you don't have an opportunity to have an arts program, but he was very creative."

But more often than not, Springsteen would get into trouble. Decker recalled a fight he had with another student, who was picking on him.

"Robby grabbed a desk and lifted it over his head and was going to throw it." Decker yelled at Springsteen to put down the desk, to which he complied.

In addition to problems at school, Springsteen had several problems at home. He often fought with his stepfather. Decker claimed that the fights were some-times violent. "He just didn't listen to his stepfather," the teacher observed.

Springsteen also resented that his mother attempted to keep him in line. A fight between him and his mother led to the sixteen-year-old moving to Austin to live with his father in the summer of 1991. He moved in next door to his father in his own condominium on Dry Creek Drive, near Mopac and close to Anderson Lane, about three miles away from the yogurt shop. The two condominiums were owned by Robert Springsteen III's girlfriend, Karen Huntley.

Similar to Welborn, Springsteen attended McCallum High School, where he was enrolled as a sophomore. On December 4, 1991, he was reassigned to alternative-education classes, mainly because he had a propensity for skipping classes. Two weeks later, he dropped out of school.

By this time, Huntley had enough. She wanted him out of her condominium. Springsteen moved back to his mother and stepfather's home in West Virginia in late December 1991. He worked several odd jobs through the years, including selling newspaper subscriptions, working as a manager of a McDonald's in the Charleston Town Center, and being employed as a stock boy at Kroger.

One of Springsteen's jobs was working with his stepfather, Brett Thompson, as a second chef at the Charleston Civic Center (CCC). Thompson recalled the evening when he, Robert, and Michelle worked at the CCC restaurant when Vice President Al Gore appeared in town. Thompson spoke of how his son fed the vice president.

"Robert put his plate right in front of him."

Springsteen met an older woman, Robin Moss, through his mother. Moss was twenty-two years older than her new paramour.

On Valentine's Day, 1999, the couple tossed back a few cold ones. Their landlady, Patti Eagle, stated the next thing they did was to up and get hitched. "They just went out and did it."


Michael Scott was Robert Springsteen's good friend in Austin. Scott was born on February 6, 1974, to seventeen-year-old Lisa McClain and her seventeen-year-old best friend on the island of Yap, in the Federated States of Micronesia island chain. Yap is considered one of the most exotic islands in Micronesia and in the world. The tiny island, thirty by fourteen miles, is a closely knit, cloistered landmass, with residents who all know one another. Needless to say, the islanders immediately fell in love with little blond-haired Michael.

Michael's father did not stick around. Lisa, her parents, and some of their fellow islanders, however, took care of the young boy. Within a year, Lisa met a young man, Philip Scott, who worked for the United States Coast Guard. They met, romanced, and were married within three months. The wedding took place on February 28, 1975, in a little chapel on a hill in a Lutheran church. The ceremony was overseen by their friend who was a retired WWII combat pilot.

Michael finally had a father.

Philip Scott adopted the towheaded boy, gave him the last name of Scott, and cared for him as if he were his own.

Philip (or Phil), Lisa, and Michael enjoyed life on Yap. Michael became a water baby the minute he slipped his toes into the Philippine Sea. There were plenty of aquatic options for the family to choose from, such as fishing for tuna or swimming with dolphins. Yap is also known as the destination spot for divers to view majestic manta rays on a year-round basis.

Phil was an electronics technician for the U.S. Coast Guard. According to Lisa, one of the main reasons they married was because they both loved to travel and they both loved the water. Later in the year, Phil re-upped so they could travel to Europe. The family packed up their belongings and headed for Italy. They settled into the region of Calabria in the southernmost arch of the boot. The Scotts lived in the mountainous peninsula area until the spring of 1979 when they were transferred to the small, predominantly Hispanic town of Raymondville, located next to Harlingen, in the southernmost tip of Texas. It was quite a change from their previous exotic abodes.

The Scotts would be transferred one last time in 1980. They relocated to Austin, Texas. Lisa was pregnant and gave birth to her second son, Robert, at St. David's Medical Center.

Michael now had a brother.

What should have been a happy occasion, unfortunately, was marred by the deteriorating relationship between Phil and Lisa. What Lisa described as "really rocky on a good day" would eventually tear the couple apart. She stated that they tried to stick together for the sake of the kids, but the couple continued to grow apart.

Lisa stated that "over twenty years of being married (they would not divorce until 1996), we probably lived together two seconds." She further described the couple as "like oil and water together." Eventually Phil left to go work in San Antonio and he took Robert with him. Lisa stayed in Austin with Michael. The couple did everything in their power to make sure the brothers spent time together and that each parent had time with both sons individually.

Despite the separation, Lisa spoke highly of Phil. She acknowledged that he was a good father who treated both boys wonderfully. He was an avid Cub Scout father who enjoyed outdoor activities, especially hiking. He would take Michael out to the Philmont Scout Ranch in New Mexico, where they would venture off for a three-week backpacking excursion. If they only had a short period of time together, Phil would usually take Michael to Bastrop State Park, about thirty miles southeast of Austin. Father and son usually trekked the Lost Pines of east Central Texas, home to twelve miles of the most beautiful section used in the MS 150 benefit bicycle ride from Houston to Austin every year.

Michael's home life seemed secure despite his parents' separation. School, however, posed an entirely different set of problems. While Michael was gregarious, he experienced difficulty in school. According to his mother, Michael suffered from attention deficit hyperactivity disorder (ADHD). She also claimed that he was learning disabled because of it. Apparently, Michael was unable to stay focused on any one thing for an extended period of time, especially if it did not interest him. Though that can describe pretty much any teenager at anytime in the history of mankind, Lisa sincerely believed that his learning disability made it difficult for him to adjust. She described him as an avid reader, but a terrible writer. She also claimed that Michael's memory was extremely poor.

In 1999, that memory would be put to the test.

# CHAPTER 39

*Thursday, September 9, 1999*
*Interview Room # 2*
*Austin Police Department*
*9:08 A.M.*

Michael Scott entered the tiny interview room in the APD headquarters. He stood and looked at the sparse furnishings in the room. There was a small round table with a laptop computer on top of it, three small plastic chairs, and one wastebasket. The room was box-shaped with only one door and no windows.

Scott sauntered over to the chair against the wall farthest away from the door and sat down. He casually tossed his pack of cigarettes on the table. After a minute, he hopped up and walked over to the table to look at the laptop. The lanky, ponytailed Scott sat back down.

Eight minutes later, Detectives Ron Lara and John Hardesty entered the room. Both men were members of the newly revamped yogurt shop task force. Lara, the younger of the two, was a handsome man, with a thatch of jet-black hair. Hardesty, the older, seasoned veteran, sported a silver crew cut circa 1950s military. Lara, a twelve-year veteran, was a member of the Austin Police Department Cold Case Unit at the time. Hardesty, also a twelve-year veteran, was a detective in the APD homicide division.

When Hardesty and Lara entered the room, they laughed comfortably with Michael Scott. Once the pleasantries were out of the way, Lara and Hardesty got down to business. They asked Scott about his youth. He told them that he was born in Micronesia. His father was stationed there as part of the U.S. Coast Guard. Scott spoke of how his father met his mother on the island, how they married, and how his father adopted him. He spoke about the nuclear testing conducted on the island and how his father fought in military battles.

Scott informed the officers that his father was stationed in the United States. Once in the States, the Scotts bounced around from one military town to another. Michael was shuffled in and out of schools on a constant basis. He claimed he attended at least five or six elementary schools alone.

Scott described his wayward youth to the officers. He stated that he "was a problem child" as he got older. He talked about being arrested on The Drag, the strip of stores that line Guadalupe Drive on the opposite side of the street from the University of Texas, for possession of mushrooms. He also talked about his scholastic difficulties. Despite being very intelligent, Scott "was not a real attentive student." He eventually dropped out of McCallum High School at the age of eighteen because it was too boring.

After he dropped out of high school, he moved to Dallas, Texas, where he got a job as a roofer. After a few months there, he packed up his meager belongings and headed north for Evansville, Indiana. He worked a variety of odd jobs, about four or five of them, before he came back to Texas.

"I don't know what else I can tell you," Scott told the detectives at 9:23 A.M.

The two detectives mainly sat back and let Scott speak. Both men were calm and congenial.

Scott spoke of his current station in life. He and his wife, Jeannine, known as "Neen," and their daughter, Jasmine, had recently moved back to Austin from San Antonio, Texas. Scott had worked as a foreman at a mechanic's shop in San Antonio. He made $5 an hour. His wife, however, made good money as a field technician at Unisys, "a worldwide information technology services and solutions company," according to the company Web site. Jeannine received an offer to relocate from San Antonio to Austin with Unisys for a $10,000-a-year raise.

Just over an hour into the interview, Scott told the officers that "I have a piss-poor memory." About a minute later, Lara placed photographs of the four girls on the table in front of Scott.

"They plugged the crap out of that," Scott stated as he looked at the photographs.

Lara asked Scott if he remembered what he had done on the day the girls were murdered. Scott replied that he had been hanging out at the condominium where he was staying with his buddy Robert Springsteen. The condo was owned by Karen Huntley, Robert's father's girlfriend. She owned two condominiums at the Dry Creek Estates on Dry Creek Drive, directly off Highway 2222. The condos had a gated swimming pool and sauna in front and a large backyard that led downhill to a dry creek. Robert's father and Karen lived in one condo and Robert lived in the condo next to it. Scott moved in with Robert IV a few months earlier because he did not see eye to eye with his mother.

Scott stated that during the midmorning of December 6, 1991, he was "smoking grass."

He talked to the officers about his roommate, Robert Springsteen. "Robert used to be in a gang. Blue Bandana. He was the only white guy in this group. The rest of them were black.

"He may have been involved in the Crips.

"He was a good friend until he stole from me. He stole some concert tickets from me. Metallica. Dad worked at the Erwin Center at the time." The Frank Erwin Center is a large, drum-shaped building on Red River Street and Martin Luther King Jr. Boulevard, just off Interstate 35, next to the University of Texas campus. It is home to the University of Texas's men's and women's college basketball teams, as well as the premier venue for large-scale musical acts from country, rock, and more.

"He better pray to God I don't catch up with him," Scott threatened.

"Robert and I were kind of the potheads," he continued. "Forrest would come over . . . every once in a while, he'd show up there. We'd smoke out a little bit."

Scott returned to the discussion of December 6. He claimed he rode the city bus to the mall around noon. His story soon changed as he claimed he got to the mall in Maurice Pierce's car. It was actually Maurice's father's 1982 or 1983 Ford LTD. According to Scott, Maurice would steal his dad's car and they would go tooling around in it.

"I remember riding in the car to Northcross Mall," Scott recalled. "I smoked a couple of times that day. I remember going to the bowling alley." He referred to Dart Bowl, which is located directly across the street from McCallum High School.

"We went to the bowling alley because we both had the munchies." Scott snickered. While Scott and

Springsteen hung out at the bowling alley, Welborn went back to class and Pierce had to run some errands. The two juvenile delinquents stayed at the bowling alley until almost 3:00 P.M. They spotted Springsteen's girlfriend, Kelly Hannah, across the street.

Scott did not speak highly of Hannah. He claimed that she was not that great-looking and Springsteen "would screw anything that moved—or didn't move, for that matter." He chuckled. The three stood around and chatted for about half an hour, until Pierce came around and picked up the guys.

At 9:54 A.M., during the interview, Scott began to discuss Maurice Pierce and the purchase of a firearm. Pierce "had purchased a firearm the day before" the murders. He claimed it was a ".38 snub-nose, blue—or it was black. I was there when he purchased it. In the car. Couple of Hispanic boys. They did question them. Bought it right over by the school. Robert, me, Maurice, or another person." Scott believed the Hispanics were younger kids. The transaction took place four blocks from the school. It appeared to be a spur-of-the moment purchase. "I don't think it [was] a preplanned deal.

"We were not paying attention," Scott said of himself and Springsteen in regard to the transaction. "We didn't want to pay attention."

Scott rocked back in his chair until he leaned against the wall in the small interview room. He began to waver on when the gun was purchased. With his hands crossed in his lap, Scott said that the gun was purchased forty-eight hours before December 6. He also claimed that Pierce stole a gold Isuzu Trooper, with a bad air conditioner, the same night.

At 10:05 A.M., Michael Scott placed his hands on the girls' photos. "I think 'Reese' (Maurice Pierce's nickname) was actually looking for some grass at the time, but got a gun instead."

Suddenly Scott said to Lara and Hardesty, "I hope I'm not lying to you guys.

"We took it out and used it outside of the city limits. We went out to Lake Travis and shot it. He couldn't shoot worth shit."

Scott returned the conversation back to the night of the murders. He claimed that after talking with Hannah, they took off in Pierce's dad's car. He remembered the time to be around 3:30 P.M.

Scott drank three or four Budweisers in the car. "I used to drink like a fish," Scott admitted. "I'm an alcoholic and I know it and I don't drink anymore. I gave that up about five years ago."

Scott continued with the details. They arrived at Northcross Mall around dusk and parked the car in the back of the mall. They walked into the mall, past the movie theaters, toward the food court. They met Welborn at the tables of the food court.

"We were all buzzing pretty good."

Scott, Springsteen, Pierce, and Welborn sat around the food court, watching the nubile females as they passed by, and were indecisive as to "whether we were gonna hang out, cause trouble, or go watch a movie."

According to Scott, Hannah and a young guy, whose name he could not remember, showed up at the food court. They all sat around inside the mall for another two to three hours. Pierce only stayed for an hour and told everyone he had to go take care of some business.

Scott yawned during the interview for the first time, at 10:24 A.M.

"The only reason we went to the mall was to look at girls and play videogames. T and A. Tits and ass. Be a general pest to everyone."

Welborn took off after Pierce left.

Scott claimed that Pierce returned to the mall later that night and took him and Springsteen home.

"I don't remember anything special about that night. Other than another night of going out, getting fucked up, hanging out at the mall, and going home and going to sleep."

Scott told the detectives that after Pierce picked them up, they piled into the LTD and went to a guy's house and smoked marijuana.

"The night is when things get really vague for me," he relayed to the officers. "I smoked grass and I drank. Rob kept right up with me. He was really shit-faced by the time we got to the house." According to Scott, the boys didn't stay long.

"Maurice took us home. Smoked one-and-a-half joints. Stayed about one hour or an hour-and a half. Got back to his (Robert's) condo at ten-thirty or eleven (P.M.). By that time the world was still spinning for me." Scott claimed he watched a movie on cable television, then went to sleep around 1:00 A.M.

"I was sacked out on the couch. An itty-bitty condo.

"I woke up around ten-thirty or eleven o'clock the next morning." He claimed Rob woke up later than he did. "The boy could sleep until, like two in the afternoon.

"We usually stayed out all hours in the morning. I was really fucked up. And I needed to go home. Robert was usually trashed too."

*10:40 A.M.*

Detective Lara asked Mike if he wanted anything to drink. The interview had been going for almost 2½ hours and Scott had not drunk anything or eaten anything. He requested a Dr Pepper. As Lara left the room, Scott apologized. "I'm sorry my memory's not so good, guys. That's what I get for smoking too much grass."

One minute later, Detective Hardesty stood up from

his chair and headed out of the room. For the next seven minutes, Scott shifted around, not too uncomfortably. He stood up out of his chair and stretched. He sat back down in his chair and began to rock in it. He looked up toward the ceiling, peering intently at something. He stretched out and placed his feet on another chair. He sat up and walked around the table to look at the computer screen. He opened the unlocked door to the interview room and looked outside. He called out for Detective Hardesty, but received no reply. He walked back to his chair, sat down, and effortlessly tossed his pack of cigarettes on top of the photos of the girls. Finally, after seven minutes, Lara returned. Scott asked to go to the bathroom and was allowed to do so.

*10:51 A.M.*

Michael Scott returned to the interview room. A minute later, Lara and Hardesty returned. They saw Scott looking closely at the pictures of the girls. After a couple of minutes, he looked up from the photos and said, "This happened Friday. He (Pierce) had to have picked us up the day after."

Scott had changed his story just 2½ hours into the interview.

He had been upset with Pierce. "He put me in a stolen truck. I had enough problems to deal with." He began to talk about the joyride. "We went to one of the lakes, shot the firearms. I shot it twice. I pulled two rounds and Maurice shot the rest of them. I took a piece of limestone and chunked it out there as far as I could and shot at it a couple of times. Maurice shot at a loudspeaker horn thing."

Scott claimed they stole gas from a Stop N Go convenience store in the Barton Creek area. "Didn't get a full tank either." From there, they took off south toward

San Antonio. "I'm like, 'Hey. You want to drive to Helotes? We need to get out of the city for a while.'" About three-quarters of the way there, Pierce fell asleep at the wheel. The SUV hit the median on Interstate 35. Pierce jolted awake and pulled the vehicle over. They noticed damage to the rim of the left front wheel. Scott got out and changed the tire. "Nobody else wanted to get their hands dirty."

Scott took over and drove the rest of the way. They arrived around 11:00 A.M.

Scott claimed he did not know the truck was stolen until they came back to Austin. He then changed his story and admitted that he knew it was stolen.

Scott continued talking about the joyride. He claimed they drove to Helotes so he could see his girlfriend, Meredith Skipper, and break up with her. He told Lara that he met Skipper through the school orchestra in the summer of 1990 at a dance during UT band camp.

Scott stood up and stretched as he spoke rather cavalierly about the reason for seeing his girlfriend. "She's not that great-looking anyway. Breakup, pickup." After this comment, Lara and Hardesty stood up and left the room. Scott sat and flipped through a McCallum High School yearbook, which Hardesty had brought in earlier.

*11:16 A.M.*

Detectives Lara and Hardesty returned to the tiny interview room. Lara sat down in his chair, while Hardesty walked up to Scott. He stood just a few inches away from the seated Scott as the young man looked at the yearbook. Feeling somewhat confined, Scott moved his chair away from the hovering Hardesty. He crossed his hands and buried them into his lap.

Scott began to speak about his old girlfriend. He recalled that the guys pulled over at a convenience store so he could call her on a pay phone and get final directions to her house. He placed the call.

"Wow, you're here!" Meredith exclaimed. "Come on by."

Scott got the directions to her house.

"What did you buy when you went into the store?" Detective Lara wanted to know. Scott told him that he purchased something to drink and some cigarettes.

"What else did you guys buy?" Lara wanted to know. As he asked, Detective Hardesty stood with his right foot on his own chair and his hand on his hip.

Scott repeated, "Drinks and smokes."

The guys got back in the vehicle and drove to Meredith Skipper's home. When they arrived, Scott and Skipper headed for the nearby woods, where they talked. Scott claimed they hugged and kissed. He then broke off the relationship with her. He got back in the truck and headed back to Austin. Pierce drove the truck back. Scott could not remember what they did when they returned to Austin.

Detective Hardesty removed the yearbook from the table. He moved the photographs of the girls so they were directly in front of Scott.

"As far as I know, he put the truck back on the block."

Lara stopped Scott and informed him that the story he told them differed from the story he told Detective Paul Johnson one year before. Johnson had kept in touch with several witnesses and/or suspects that may or may not have been involved in the case. Scott was one of those people.

Hardesty moved the photos of the girls directly in Scott's line of vision. Scott became agitated and sounded defensive.

"You are not under arrest," stated Detective Hardesty. "You can leave anytime you want. You're not in trouble."

Scott did not ask to leave. Instead, he asked for a smoke.

*11:36 A.M.*

Lara, Hardesty, and Scott all returned to the interview room. Hardesty mentioned that he and Scott had a chat outside during the smoke break. He asked Scott to repeat their discussion.

"I told him, you know, if . . . if . . . if I knew who did [it]," Scott recalled, "I'd tell y'all, because I think it's wrong that those girls got killed there, the way . . . the way and fashion that they did."

"You want to tell us something that you don't want to tell us?" Lara posed.

"I don't know why," Scott answered.

"Look at these poor girls, Mike," Lara pleaded as he focused Scott's attention on the photos. "Just think of their poor parents and their families. Give them some peace."

Detective Hardesty scooted his chair closer to Scott. "You're real wound up. What are you scared of? We're talking to you as a friend. We know more than you think we know. Do the right thing. People are covering something."

"I'm not covering things up, guys," Scott informed the officers.

"You know who shot those girls."

Lara moved in closer in his chair. Scott was blocked in by the two detectives.

"Do you know what that says about you?" asked Lara.

"Either, one, I'm lying," answered Scott, "or two, I don't remember. Those are the only two options I have."

"Well, I can take out the 'I don't remember.'"

"I'm not trying to lie to y'all."

"I think you're scared of getting in trouble," Hardesty offered. "You're not revealing something you know."

"Guys, I'm not scared of getting in trouble. I'm

scared I'm not answering your questions the way y'all want answered."

"That's bullshit," bellowed Hardesty. "This thing is snowballing and it's coming to a head, this investigation. Do you know what that means? One thing it means is a grand jury.

"If you're being deceptive, that is a crime. You'll go to jail for that."

"You understand all the new technology that's been advanced for us," Lara quietly mentioned. "I really anticipate things are going to come to a close soon."

After a several-second pause, Lara curiously said, "We're telling you what you know."

"Can you think of a worse homicide in the history of Austin?" Hardesty chimed in. "Well, there ain't one. This is it."

Hardesty changed course. He patted Scott on the back and returned to the stolen truck.

"You left something out. What you bought, something very important. Just tell us what that was."

"Map?" Scott replied with a questioning tone in his voice.

"No, a newspaper."

"A newspaper," he replied as if realizing it for the first time.

"Right," stated Hardesty, who leaned over and spit into the trash can.

The detectives wanted to know who bought the newspaper. Scott told them: "Maurice probably would have been the only one with real money."

"Why is that?" Hardesty wanted to know.

"I don't know. I just remember Maurice always having money. He usually had about twenty dollars."

Detective Lara scooted closer toward Scott. "It's getting real close. It's either Robert or Maurice who bought the paper. These people are covering their ass. They're trying to cover their ass."

"Okay," Scott replied.

"Why do you think they're covering their ass?" Hardesty questioned.

"Somebody did something they weren't supposed to, or seen it."

"How do you think they're covering their ass?"

"Either lying or trying to pin it on somebody else."

Hardesty emphatically replied, "There you go."

"You got it," added Lara.

"And let me guess," Scott piped in rather dejectedly. "I'm it."

"What do you think?" said Lara.

Scott awoke with vigor. "Just hear me out, guys. Maurice is a sponge. He'll do anything to save his own ass. Springsteen's a sponge and a lying sack of shit. He stole from me. He stole from his parents. I can see Robert lying about me. And I can see Maurice lying about me."

*11:50 A.M.*

Hardesty informed Scott that "you're in the middle of this mess. You know what that does? It digs you deeper into this hole, right here, into the top of the 'get fucked' list. You don't want that, do you?"

"No," Scott replied.

"The only thing," Hardesty informed Scott, "this is bullshit," referring to the story that Scott had given them up to this point.

Lara moved in even closer toward Scott. Hardesty spit in the trash can again.

Hardesty warned Scott that "a lie becomes a snowball. It keeps getting bigger and bigger and you don't know how to get out. In a matter of weeks or months, this is all going to come to a head. And you are ass deep in it. You are ass deep in alligators.

"This is the day. This is the opportunity. This is it. These guys aren't going to hurt you. These guys are punks. None of these guys have put together a life like you have. These guys are still scum."

"It doesn't surprise me," Scott replied. "I'm more worried about myself than anything else.

"I remember some . . ."

"You remember what? Go ahead."

"I kind of remember somebody reading the paper." Scott did not continue. Instead, he continued to worry about his predicament.

"I think I've dug myself a hole, and I don't know how I've dug myself a hole."

"You know what's amazing?" Hardesty asked. "You can keep withholding all this stuff. This hole is going to get so much deeper, and then you'll be all fucking jammed up with everything, with us, with the grand jury, with the citizens of Austin. Do you know what they feel right now?"

Lara leaned in and quietly asked, "Did Maurice kill those girls?"

"No. I remember Maurice reading the newspaper."

"Did Robert kill those girls?"

"I don't think so."

"Did you kill those girls?"

"No."

"We can get this out today," Hardesty calmly added. "All those fucking years about you thinking about this." Hardesty again patted Scott, this time on the shoulder.

"I'm trying, gentlemen," Scott said. "Find the easiest scapegoat," referring to his friends. "And I'm the nice guy."

"What's fixing to come down?" Lara wanted to know.

"Y'all have figured out who done it and who was

there. Now you're just getting all your little ducks in a row."

"Michael, you're a big duck," Hardesty intervened. "You're not a little duck, you're a big duck."

Scott chuckled. "Yeah, I'm a big duck, but . . ."

*12:00 P.M.—Noon*

"You're not a very good liar," Hardesty told him. "It's this close on your mouth."

Scott withdrew his arms inside his T-shirt. "My biggest worry is that Robert and Reese fed you all a line of shit. I don't want to go to jail for something that I didn't do."

"You can forget about jail, brother," Lara said. "You'd be talking about penitentiary time."

"But you wouldn't be going to jail for something you didn't do—" Hardesty was attempting to soften the blow. Scott began to talk.

"Don't interrupt me," Hardesty sharply said. The detective put his arm in the general direction of Scott, but did not touch him.

"You're fucking going to prison," Hardesty continued.

Lara recalled the February 19, 1998, discussion that Scott had with Detective Paul Johnson. He reminded Scott that he told Johnson that he saw a commotion at the yogurt shop the night of the murders.

"That's a lie—a huge inconsistency."

Scott began to talk about being in the food court in Northcross Mall. He spoke of a "big, fat Mexican guy" who "drank a big thing of ketchup."

Hardesty was getting annoyed. "Look at me. Don't pull that cannabis head trip on me. Dig yourself out of this fucking hole. I guaran-fucking-tee you, if you don't clear this today before you leave here, you don't tell us what you know, it's going to jam your ass up."

"No doubt," added Lara.

"If you remember anything I said today, I'm not threatening you. Let's put this fucking thing to bed today."

"I know you were there, Michael," accused Lara. Scott did not reply.

"Don't stare off into space," snapped Hardesty. The detective told Scott that it "will feel good" to release the information from inside him.

"I'd like to know how I'm involved in it."

"We're talking about the nut cutting here," Hardesty said. "The big stuff. What the fuck are you afraid of?"

Scott looked down at his lap. He paused for a long period of time. Then he spoke up. "What I remember Maurice saying about it is that . . ." He paused again for a long time.

Lara leaned in and whispered something into his ear. "Something you don't forget."

"None of this stuff will you forget," added Hardesty.

"I wish that were true, gentlemen. I don't know what I'm supposed to tell you, gentlemen."

"The truth," answered Hardesty.

"I am telling you the truth."

"Are you willing to take a polygraph?" asked Lara.

Without hesitation, Scott responded, "Yes, sir, I am. I'll take one right now."

"We'll take one here in a little bit. Why don't you take a little break here."

All three men left the room for a break.

*12:36 P.M.*

Scott sat in his chair in the interview room. He flipped through the pages of his high-school yearbook. Detective Hardesty entered and walked right in front of Scott. He grabbed his chair and pulled it close to Scott.

"God, I looked like a dork in that picture," Scott said good-naturedly.

"You're involved in this thing," Hardesty told him. "We know you are."

"I don't know how I was involved."

"Yes, you do."

Hardesty stood up, patted Scott on the back again, and left the room.

*12:43 P.M.*

Detective Lara reentered the room with Austin Police Department polygraph examiner Bruce Stevenson. Stevenson was the epitome of the big good ol' boy Texan with a thick Southern drawl.

As Stevenson went about his business to prepare for the polygraph, Scott talked about different things. He wished he could call Crime Stoppers. He talked about some of the different theories about the murders.

"You'll love this one, the one I heard in school. The two girls were having an affair with a couple of police officers and the police did it. It's a load of crap." Scott chuckled.

"You think that's funny?" Lara wanted to know.

"I don't think the police did it. They wouldn't have left any evidence behind."

Scott then talked about his recreational drug use, which was not so recreational. "I have permanent tracers," he said, in reference to his use of acid.

Stevenson faced Scott and let him know that he wanted to ask him a few questions before he began the polygraph.

"Whew, I'm fucking scared," said Scott. "Let me tell you, you guys got me really scared. I'm more afraid of the law than anything else."

Stevenson proceeded to ask several personal questions—mainly, concerning his physical health. After about forty-five minutes of questions, he left the room. He never conducted a polygraph on Scott.

*1:27 P.M.*

"Michael, you know man," Detective Lara calmly stated, "we don't want to sit here and jump your shit." He positioned the pictures of the girls in front of Scott again. "Look at these girls. That is it for them, that is it. For what?"

"For twelve dollars or fourteen dollars, something like that," Scott quietly said.

"Was it worth it?"

"Not for four lives."

After four hours of discussion, Michael Scott made his first admission of responsibility in the deaths of Eliza Thomas, Amy Ayers, Sarah Harbison, and Jennifer Harbison.

"I'm trying to recall the information, guys . . ." Scott said as he began to cry softly.

Lara leaned in closer. He stood up and walked around the table. The detective leaned on the table and looked down at the young man.

Detective Hardesty quietly asked, "Whose idea was it?"

"Maurice's," came the reply. "I remember Reese saying something about needing money."

One of the detectives asked who was in the car.

"Me, Robert, Maurice, and . . . Forrest?"

All of a sudden, Scott acted as if the information had finally surfaced. It was all coming back to him. "I understand what has happened to me now.

"Maurice and Robert went through the front door. I don't remember any gunfire. They weren't in there for more than fifteen or twenty minutes," he seemed to re-call.

He did not place himself inside the yogurt shop.

"Was I at the wheel? It's possible I was at the wheel."
He claimed he did not see Pierce's gun.

Scott said that he stayed in the car and Pierce and
Springsteen came out of the store. "I kind of remember
him (Pierce) saying, 'We got what we came for.'

"'You didn't rob the place, did you?' [I asked.] And
I think he said, yes, he did.

"Why would I sit on it all this time?" Scott asked the
detectives. "Why would I keep it to myself?" The detectives did not answer.

Scott continued with his story. "They didn't tell anything they did inside. I know they love to brag." Scott
crushed the Dr Pepper can in his hand.

*1:43 P.M.*

Scott sniffled. "It's beginning to come back." But he
wanted one thing made clear for the detectives. "I didn't
do this."

Scott talked about how the plan originally hatched.
He claimed Pierce may have told him at school that he
wanted to steal some money.

Scott placed his hands on his forehead as he spoke
about his friend and roommate, Robert Springsteen. "I
was never far without Robert. And I know I was drunk
that day."

Scott talked about how Pierce drove the LTD around
the shopping center where the yogurt shop was located.
He claimed that Pierce and Springsteen were casing
the joint, but he was only along for the ride.

"I think Robert and Maurice had gone in earlier to
buy yogurt. I think I was with them." Scott recalled
going into the yogurt shop earlier in the day. "I remember eating and buying yogurt. A multiflavored one. I
think Robert got something, but Maurice didn't."

"Which one of these girls was there?" Lara asked.

"Eliza may have been."

Scott said later that night they drove around to the back alley behind the Hillside Center stores until they came up to the only other pair of double doors near the north side. "I think they just looked at each other and said, 'That one.'

"Ohhh!" Scott exclaimed as if surprised. "It had a door open. The back door was open. The back door was propped open. Metal door? It was all the way open."

Scott seemed to end many of his sentences with an upward lilt in his voice, as if he were asking a question.

Detective Hardesty attempted to clear the air. "Mike, I'm not trying to put . . . I'm not suggesting this, trying to put this in your mind. All right?"

Scott nodded and continued with his story. He claimed Pierce told him, "'Stay here and keep an eye out. Watch the car. Keep the car running.' Just sitting in the car, looking around, okay, what the fuck's going on?"

Scott returned his attention to the officers. "Y'all made a bunch of memories trigger. I don't remember a gun going off. I remember them going in, staying a short while, coming back out. I'm making sure there's nobody around.

"They run back out, got in, [and said,] 'We got what we needed, let's get out of here.'" They took off. "I don't remember if after that was done whether we went back into the mall or we went somewhere else. No, actually we drove back to the mall."

Scott asked for a bathroom and cigarette break. Before he left, however, he looked up at the two detectives. "Gentlemen, I'm sorry I lied to you. I didn't intentionally lie to you. I guess at the time I was threatened and I was scared."

"You don't have anything to be scared about," Hardesty comforted him.

The three men stood up and left the room.

* * *

*2:11 P.M.*

Ten minutes later, Scott returned to the interview room by himself. Five minutes after that, Hardesty returned and handed Scott a large slice of pizza on a paper plate. Scott only took one bite. Lara brought in another Dr Pepper for Scott.

Three minutes later, Lara also brought in a cell phone. He handed it to Scott. He needed to call his wife to let her know he planned on being at the police station for a while. He left a message on her voice mail: "Evidently I've got more information about this than I thought I did."

Lara and Hardesty returned to the room. Scott told them he could not eat his pizza "because I could have done something to stop it."

"What you can do now," Hardesty countered, "is you can put these little girls to rest and put their families' hearts at ease, finally, after eight years.

"Maurice was kind of the leader in that little group?"

"Yeah. More or less. He had the car. I was just a quiet guy along for the ride."

"What a ride," Hardesty surmised.

"We drove from the mall over there. I remember bits and pieces. At the time that this happened, I think I was terrified, and I was threatened."

"Who threatened you?"

"I think Maurice did. [He said,] 'You open your mouth and I'll kill you,' or 'You better keep your mouth shut.' Or he threatened bodily harm or death to me."

Hardesty asked about the back doors. "The door's propped partially open. I find that pretty hard to believe you didn't hear any shots."

"That's striking me as odd too," Scott agreed.

Hardesty again moved the photos of the girls directly in Scott's line of sight.

"What were Maurice and Robert's attitudes like when they got back to the car?"

"Robert was kind of distant. Maurice was more interested in getting away than anyone else. He didn't make the tires squeal. No. He just drove off. He didn't haul ass."

Hardesty asked Scott about a second gun.

"I think Maurice asked Robert if he was packing one."

"What did Robert say?"

"He said, 'Yes.'"

"Did you go in that shop with them?"

Scott said he did not. "I was not inside the shop at the time of the murders." As he denied being inside, he nervously grabbed his T-shirt and placed his Dr Pepper soda can directly on top of the photo of one of the girls.

Hardesty removed the can.

*2:49 P.M.*

"I'm scared," Scott said to the detectives. "I mean, guys, I'm scared. I don't know what's going to happen to me."

Lara scooted up in his chair so that he was only inches away from Michael Scott. "Did you go inside that shop?"

Scott muttered something unintelligible.

"What you need to do is stop minimizing your involvement. We know you were involved. We knew that before you even came over here. Don't make yourself look any more ignorant by telling us these little things. We know already."

It was the first time the officers directly implicated Michael Scott in the yogurt shop murders during the interview.

"I didn't go inside when this happened."

Hardesty moved his chair toward Scott so he was

only inches away from the young man. Scott said that he drove the car away from the scene once Maurice and Robert exited the building. He also stated he did not know if what he had said was the truth.

"This is not that difficult for you to remember," Lara told him.

"Actually, yes, it is. [I (b)]lacked it out for seven years."

"Is it possible you were inside?"

"It's possible," Scott acknowledged for the first time. His story would no longer be that of the innocent bystander who had no idea they were going to rob the yogurt shop, much less kill everyone inside. "But I did not shoot anyone."

Lara and Hardesty got up from their chairs, and without saying a word to Scott, they left the room. As the detectives left, Scott yelled out after them, "Do y'all think I did it?" After he received no reply, he buried his face in his hands.

Two minutes later, Lara popped his head in and asked Scott if he wanted a smoke.

*3:04 P.M.*

Detective Hardesty and Scott returned to the interview room.

"You mentioned something about 'no witnesses,'" Hardesty posited.

"I think Maurice said, 'No witnesses,'" Scott replied.

Hardesty changed his tactics with Scott. He played the other boys off him. "You know what kind of shitheads they are. They haven't changed. Instead of being scared about what's going to happen to you, let's try this. Get fucking pissed off at them because you should be."

"I am," an animated Scott declared. "They both ganged up against me and said that I have gone in there and got the money and pulled the trigger."

"Get fucking mad at them. That shit they're talking on you. Doesn't that piss you off?"

"Yeah, it does."

"Well, fuck them. Do something about it."

Scott sat silent.

"Just tell me what fucking happened," Hardesty laid it out.

"We parked out behind. They went inside. They did what they needed to do. We came back and drove off."

"'We came back.' You said, 'We came back.'"

"I didn't go inside."

"They came back. Is that what you meant?"

"They came back and we drove off."

"Well, fuck it. Just tell me what happened," declared a frustrated Hardesty.

Scott claimed he was supposed to honk the car horn if someone appeared in the back alley. "They went inside. Fifteen or twenty minutes later, they came back out. They jogged up to the car. They weren't in a real big hurry." Again Scott said that they drove to the mall and back to the food court.

"Where the fuck did you go?"

Scott did not respond.

*3:20 P.M.*

Detective Lara returned to the interview room. Scott and Hardesty resumed their conversation.

"I'm pissed off because these two guys have ganged up on me," Scott lamented.

"Well, fuckin' A. Do something about it."

"I didn't shoot anybody." Scott absentmindedly held his half-eaten slice of pizza. Lara told him to put it down. He tried to calm Scott down. Hardesty got up and left the room.

"Mike, I want a step-by-step process of what went down," said Lara.

"I know Forrest was there at some time." It was the first time Scott definitely pegged Forrest Welborn at the crime scene. He then said they cased the joint.

"I went in and I got a yogurt. I had a cup." Springsteen ordered first. Then Scott. Pierce waited outside in the car.

Again Scott had changed his story. His storytelling became choppy.

They checked out the store. They left and returned to the mall. After they left the mall, they drank heavily. Pierce had a gun. They cruised the Creekside and Rockwood areas. They looked at apartments. They drove around anywhere, from thirty to forty-five minutes. They drove on Anderson Lane and could see the yogurt shop.

"We didn't actually drive through the parking lot until right before it happened. We stayed on Anderson." They turned right, off Anderson Lane, into the shopping center parking lot and drove behind into the alley. He described the scene as they pulled up behind the yogurt shop.

"I think I see an open door."

Loud music emanated from the car stereo. They slowed the car down near the open back door. The front of the car faced Anderson Lane. They sat in the car for a few minutes before they entered.

"I think Maurice asked Robert, 'Are you packing?'"

Springsteen exited the passenger side of the automobile. Pierce exited the driver side. Scott stayed in the car. The two boys walked toward the back door. Scott watched them in the mirror as they went inside. He saw the door close, but not all the way.

Scott's story skipped to the aftermath. He now claimed that he drove the car. "Maurice said, 'Let's go. Let's get out of here. Go over to the mall parking lot. Drive around on the other side.'" As he recalled the story, he fiddled with his Dr Pepper can.

"Put your Coke down," ordered Detective Hardesty. In Texas, a soda is usually called a "Coke," no matter what brand it is. "Was Forrest in the car or not? You were not that fucked up." The frustration in Hardesty's voice was apparent. The tension ratcheted up several notches when he asked, "How many people were in that damn car?"

Scott did not answer. Instead, for the first time during the 6½-hour interview, he told the officers, "I want to go home."

"You know, John," Detective Lara said to Hardesty, "we ought to just take him to the grand jury. He don't want to talk about it no more."

Michael Scott began to cry softly.

"I can't remember."

"Just be a man and tell us what happened," stated Hardesty.

"I'm trying to be a man, sir." Scott paused for a moment and collected himself. "Are you telling me I went inside?" he asked.

"I know you went inside."

*3:48 P.M.*

"Can I tell y'all what I keep seeing in my head?" Scott asked.

"Tell us what you keep seeing in your head," Hardesty said.

"I keep seeing these girls get shot."

"Come on, Mike. You're doing good." Hardesty patted Scott on the arm again.

"I remember seeing them down. I remember one girl screaming, terrified. I don't know if this is real or not, or if this—"

"Michael, it's real," Hardesty declared right in front of Scott's face.

"I remember hearing a girl scream and run off. She

runs towards the front of the door. Robert went over there and grabbed her. I remember them getting the girls down on their knees. He spun her around. We moved to where you couldn't see out the doors. Out the glass, out front."

"Did you shoot any of the girls?"

"No, sir."

"Then tell us what fucking happened!" an exasperated Hardesty exclaimed. "Do you want to live with this for the rest of your life?"

"No. I don't."

"Then get it out right now. They're fucking you over. Fuck them. Do it."

"Maurice goes to the register. After . . . they got them behind the counter. They got them down on their knees. I think they were lying down? Maurice went over to the register and opened it up. And [I remember] him asking where the rest of the money is. One of the girls said, 'There isn't any more. They've already made their drop.' Maurice got pissed off, losing his temper. I remember him pointing the gun at one of the girls. 'Where's the money?' Maurice screams. She said she doesn't know. I guess he pulled the trigger."

"Did he or didn't he? You saw this."

"He pulled the trigger. He looked at the next girl. 'Where's the money?' She said the same thing. He pulled the trigger. Kneeling on the floor."

As Scott recalled his story, he stared at his lap. Hardesty told Scott to look at him.

Scott did as he was told, looked up at Hardesty, and said, "I remember standing in the back of the store. I think he shot them in the head. Temple, if I'm not mistaken."

"Let's try this," said Hardesty as he patted Scott again, harder than before. The detective pointed to the photographs. Scott pointed at Eliza Thomas and Jennifer

Harbison. He believed they were the first ones shot. He covered up their faces.

"There's a big, fat fucking blank after that."

Time for another smoke break.

*4:08 P.M.*

Scott and Lara returned to the room. Three minutes later, Lara left. Seven minutes after that, Hardesty entered the room. One minute later, Lara returned. He grabbed his chair and pulled it right next to Scott.

"Turns out that there's three in there," Scott recalled. "I remember a lot of screaming. Rob found something to tie them up with. Maurice threw something at Robert and said, 'Tie them up with this.'

"I can't even remember going inside the place, guys. I don't remember walking through the doors."

"What were they tied up with?" Lara asked.

"I want to say extension cord. Something white. Napkins?"

"You can't tie them up with napkins," countered Hardesty.

"Give me a break," added Lara.

"Was it an electrical cord?" wondered Scott. He recalled that two girls were crying. One was in shock. He said that the first girl shot, whom he believed to be Jennifer Harbison, cried before she was killed.

"'The money's not here,' Maurice said. 'There has to be more than that. The business day is over.'" Scott continued on. "Rob is looking for a safe. He's getting stuff ready. He's got something flammable. I remember a red can."

Scott remembered Eliza Thomas began to cry. "'It's not here. The money's not here. We can't get to the money.'" Scott then painted the picture of Eliza's death.

"I start to see the hammer fall and he shoots her in the head.

"Robert is getting the place ready to burn. I don't remember what he used for the accelerant."

As for Amy Ayers and Sarah Harbison, Scott said, "They were scared and crying. One said she didn't want to die. All four were tied up."

Detective Hardesty moved his chair ever closer to the young man. He was only six inches from Michael Scott's face. "What were the girls wearing by the time they were tied up?"

"Not a whole lot. Used their own clothes to tie them up." He claimed that Pierce and Springsteen tied up the girls.

"And by the time you were done, what were they wearing?"

"Nothing."

Scott vividly recalled Maurice with the gun. "'Where's the money?' I seen the first two girls bite it."

"Where were they shot? Another gimme."

"In the back of the head. Maurice shot the first one. Robert shot the second one. The two other girls are really crying and screaming then. I looked up and said, 'This is wrong.' Maurice looks up at me and says, 'Open your mouth and you're dead too.'

"I remember one getting hit. The butt of the gun. Maurice hit her."

"Were you scared of those two boys?"

"Yeah."

The nonchalant response did not please Hardesty. He mockingly parroted back, "'Yeah. Yes, sir.'"

"At the time, yes, I was."

"You helped Robert tie up the girls," Hardesty stated.

"I think one of them told me to start kicking them."

"They're fucking nuts. They just shot two girls. What did they make you do?"

"I didn't choke one of them, did I? I don't think I raped one. I think one of them got raped. I'm trying to cut through a fog." Scott paused for a moment, and said, "I can't remember if I did it or not.

"They got her up on her hands and knees. And started going at her."

"Did you do some of that girl, Michael?"

"No. I didn't. I don't think I did. I didn't rape anybody. Robert raped one. Bent her over and got her. Went after her. I remember something about the neck.

"I didn't strangle them with a garrote, did I?" he wondered aloud.

"I remember one of them getting raped. Because Robert had an itch."

*4:43 P.M.*

The story continued to evolve. "I think they made me bludgeon them."

Detective Hardesty was only inches away from Scott. He patted him on the arm one more time.

"I'm trying to pull out of my head what the hell happened," Scott proclaimed. All of a sudden, there was a knock on the interview door. Lara stood up and left the room.

"They didn't make me shoot them, did they?" Scott asked.

"Did either Maurice or Robert make you shoot these two girls?" asked Hardesty.

"I think so," Scott stated, admitting for the first time that he had a hand in the actual bloodshed. "Maurice handed me a gun. It was the revolver. I think he made me shoot them. Quick, easy kill, in the back of the head. The head. Temple. Or back. Back of the head."

"Did he tell you to do that?"

Scott looked at Hardesty and said, "'You shoot 'em.' I said, 'No.'

"'Yes, sir. Either do it or . . . because we're all in this neck deep.'"

"What did they do when you shot them?" Hardesty asked about the girls.

"One of them flopped and the other one didn't make a noise."

Scott claimed that his buddy and roommate, Springsteen, had pressured him. "Rob was watching me. 'Do it, Mike. Do it or you're next.'" He claimed Springsteen handed him his gun. "I think Robert shot one of the girls with it."

"So, one of the girls, you're saying, was shot twice?"

"No, I . . ." His voice trailed off. Detective Lara suggested another break. All three men left the interview room.

*5:00 P.M.*

Michael Scott returned to the interview room. Three minutes later, Lara and Hardesty returned. The talkative Scott piped up again.

"He (Springsteen) may have shot one of the other girls again because she was still alive." Scott shook his head in disbelief. "I don't remember doing any of this shit."

The officers changed course again. They asked about the fire.

"I think Maurice started the fire with a lighter on a piled-up bunch of stuff. Close to the girls. Napkins. Any paperwork. Any burnables. Towels. Styrofoam cups, things." Scott started to cry. He told Lara, "I need to be in the store to tell you.

"I remember this shit is from the nightmares that I've had, dude. I was so catatonic, I don't remember."

Scott continued to cry. "I'm so afraid of what's going to happen to me."

Scott returned to the fire. "I think he piled them on

top of them, to start the fire. But that doesn't seem right." It was the first mention that the fire was started on top of the girls.

"Who started the fire?"

"Maurice did. Actually, I don't know who started the fire because I wasn't looking. I just wanted out. Maurice was carrying shit. Robert was watching."

Scott suddenly banged on the table with his hand. "I don't remember walking through that door."

He continued to talk about the girls. "I hear somebody getting slapped. 'Either shoot them or you're next.' I remember looking at this girl. I cry. I hear the gun go off. I only pulled the trigger once. I turned around. 'Here's your stupid gun.' I'm in shock by then. I hear another gun go off. I think I hear a total of five shots. I hear Maurice say, 'Get over here and help me get this stuff together to cover our tracks.' I say, 'Okay. But I ain't going to help you. I ain't doing any more. You made me do something I don't want to do.'

"I remember smelling something. Almost like a petrol smell, but not. Or oil burning. I hear, 'Let's go.' Forrest was in the driver's seat and took off."

Scott had a propensity for switching back and forth around the story. "After tying the girls, Rob said, 'Watch the front.'" He claimed Springsteen took off the girls' clothes and handed them to him to hold. Scott admitted he helped tie up the Harbison sisters.

"I don't want to go to prison. And the way it is now, I'm probably going." He claimed that he only held the girls while Springsteen tied them.

Scott pointed at the photograph of Amy Ayers. He said he did not know what happened to her.

"Maurice was upset because the girls were screaming so much. He said, 'Shut up or I'll shoot you.'" He returned to Amy Ayers. "One of the younger ones. Hitting her in the head. Being handed the gun and being told,

'Here. Shoot one.' I said, 'No, it's not right.' I remember the gun going off." Scott began to cry softly again. He admitted, for the first time, that he shot Amy Ayers.

*5:35 P.M.*

"I want to go home," Scott told the detectives. "I can't remember any more and I think I need a lawyer." He placed his head in his hands. He ran his right hand through his hair.

Neither detective acknowledged Scott's request. Instead, they suggested another break. All three men left the room.

*5:43 P.M.*

Scott returned to the interview room. Two minutes later, Lara and Hardesty returned.

"Mike, do you need an attorney?" Hardesty asked. "Are you asking for an attorney?"

"I think I better," Scott answered. "I don't know what's going on."

The detectives asked him if he would speak to Detective Robert Merrill. They told him it would only be a short period of time.

"What would y'all suggest that I do? Be honest, 'cause I don't know what to do, guys."

"I suggest you talk to the case agent," Hardesty answered.

"Well, bring it on then," Scott replied defiantly. "That's fine. Let's just get it done."

Lara and Hardesty both stood up and exited the room.

*5:48 P.M.*

Austin police detective Robert Merrill, a nineteen-year veteran and member of the homicide division for seven years, entered the room. Detective Lara also sat in on the interview.

"Are you under arrest?" Merrill asked right off the bat.

"As far as I know, I'm not," Scott replied.

"You know you're free to get up and walk out whenever."

"Yes, sir."

"Did you shoot one of the girls?"

"I know what I've told them. I cannot honestly say whether I shot one or not."

"What was Rob doing?"

"I think Rob was scratching his itch. I think he raped one of them."

"Did they undress themselves?"

"They were ordered to undress themselves."

"Did they?"

"Yeah. After a threat. Rob said it while holding a gun. Rob is controlling the girls. Maurice is looking for money. They're crying. Not talking. Just crying. One of the girls says, 'I don't want to die.' Rob said, 'Shut up. Shut the fuck up.'"

Merrill, like Hardesty had done earlier in the day, calmly placed a hand on Michael Scott.

"Is there any kind of tape or recording of what happened in there?" Scott wanted to know.

"I wish there was. It would certainly help."

"It would, wouldn't it?"

"The only tape recording is in your head."

Scott spoke to Merrill about Amy Ayers. He said he did not look at her when he shot her. He handed the gun to Maurice, who shot the next girl. Scott said he nearly vomited, but he kept his control.

"I could have run off and picked up a phone. But I didn't. That makes me just as guilty as they are."

"You need to stand up and be a man," Merrill stated.

"I'm trying to be. I never talked about any of this stuff to anybody. What's gonna happen to me?"

"I don't know," Merrill replied. The detective compared Scott to a female victim of a sex crime. He wanted to let Scott feel as if he, too, had been victimized by the other boys.

"I'd love to whack myself in the head until it all pours out," Scott lamented.

"Let's not do that." Merrill laughed.

"What I would really like to do is go back and see the facility. This may be the biggest thing that opens up the door for me. This may allow me to remember everything that happened. Because I've never been there since then."

Merrill considered his request but placed it on the back burner.

Scott spoke more about shooting Amy. "Robert said, 'Don't be a pussy, man. Do it.' I remember the girl screaming, 'We're dying. Please don't kill me.'"

"What are you going to tell your wife?" Merrill asked.

"I don't know. I'm not going to tell her anything. I can't."

"Why?"

After a ten-second pause, Scott, dumbfounded, stated, "I think I killed somebody. At the time, I was a follower. Now I'm a doer. Well, I'm an idle doer right now," he said with a sardonic sense of humor. "I don't want to go to prison."

"Do you think you deserve to go?"

"No. Well, yeah. I shot somebody."

"Somebody's dead."

"It's kind of one of those—I shot somebody, I deserve to go to prison. But I didn't do it of my own free will."

Merrill asked him if Meredith Skipper, Scott's girlfriend from Helotes in 1991, was his type.

"Hell no," Scott exclaimed. "She was fucking nuts. A psychopath."

"Well, back then, that was right up your alley," Merrill added with a touch of his own sense of humor.

Merrill switched gears on Scott. "Do you ever beat your wife?"

"My wife would kick my ass."

*6:35 P.M.*

Scott and Merrill stood up. Both men retrieved their business cards and exchanged them.

*6:40 P.M.*

Scott and Merrill continued to chat. "And say—you were there," Merrill reiterated.

"Yes, I was there."

"You participated."

"I participated."

"And you shot and you left."

"I shot and I left."

Another smoke break was in order.

*6:50 P.M.*

Scott returned to the interview room yet again. Eight minutes later, Merrill walked into the room. They spoke of heading over to the old yogurt shop location. Merrill asked Scott if he could videotape their excursion. Scott agreed. He also requested the use of a telephone to call his wife so he could let her know he was still out. Merrill retrieved a phone and Scott called his wife.

"Neen," he called her by her nickname, "I know more about this case than I thought I knew." The couple spoke for almost five minutes. His wife was suffering from a migraine headache. A calm Scott let Merrill know she was not happy and that she was afraid.

*7:06 P.M.*

Merrill moved his seat back and stood up. He started to leave the room when Scott told him, "I want to make right what's been done wrong."

"I want you to too. And a lot of other people do," Merrill responded.

"Everybody in the city of Austin."

"Well, I don't really care so much for them—"

"As for the parents," Scott interjected.

Merrill left the room.

*7:29 P.M.*

Merrill returned to the interview room.

Scott spoke about his life after the yogurt shop murders. "I stayed in Austin for a long time. I worked odd jobs. Several jobs. Then I went to Dallas. I was a bum. I bummed off my friends. I stayed there for six to eight months. From there, I went to Evansville, Indiana.

"Wanderlust. Traveling.

"And I was a janitor. I worked for Hasgos Janitorial. There for maybe six months. Then I moved back to Dallas. Back to my friend's house for four months. Then I come back to Austin. Stayed with Mom for a while. Worked for Knobby Lobby for one year."

He talked about finding his own place in Austin and meeting his future wife.

"After Knobby Lobby, I worked at Fantasy Tattoos. I was a floor manager. Sorry, Singapore John's World Famous Tattoo Arcade. Fantasy Tattoos is in San Antonio. I worked for Catering by Rosemary."

Merrill and Scott seemed to be killing time.

"I've got a kid cheerleading tonight," Merrill told Scott. "It's her first night. I wanted to watch. And I can't."

Scott and Merrill laughed. They were very comfortable with one another. Finally the two men left the room and headed over to the Hillside Center.

*8:05 P.M.*

Merrill, Agent Chuck Meyer, and Scott piled into a car and drove to Anderson Lane. There they met Doug Young, an APD Crime Scene Unit officer who had a video camera. The intention was to videotape Scott as he recalled what happened the night of the murders. According to Merrill, Scott began to remember certain specific details about the crime. For no specific reason, however, no videotape was shot of the walk-through or recollections made by Scott. Merrill elected not to have Young shoot the footage. When asked later why he did not pursue the videotaping, Merrill replied, "I just didn't."

The four men remained on-site for forty-five minutes to an hour.

*9:38 P.M.*

Scott and Merrill returned to the interview room. Over twelve hours had elapsed since Scott first appeared at the police station.

"I need to go home," Scott informed Merrill as he placed a blanket around his narrow shoulders.

"Did we beat you, slap you, kick you?" Merrill asked.

"No," came the quick, easy reply from Scott.

*9:44 P.M.*

Scott continued to speak about the night of the murders. He claimed he did not go into the bathroom at the yogurt shop, just the back doors. They took a right, walked around the corner, and saw Pierce in the car "munching on a yogurt." Scott also ate some yogurt, got back in the car, and returned to the mall. They sat at their table. Pierce and Springsteen walked around a bit. The movie theater crowd let out—not a big crowd. "Kids with their parents."

According to Scott, the boys walked outside, got into the LTD, and drove around the block again. They turned into the Hillside Center. They drove around back and pulled up in the alley about fifty feet from the back door. They got out of the car. Pierce walked inside first. Then Springsteen. Then Scott.

"I guess I'm big, mean, and tall enough—and ugly-looking—that no one would come near me."

He stated that there was one girl in the back. Cleaning. She made a noise. She screamed and said, "Hey, what are you doing back here?" Amy and Sarah sat up in the front of the store in one of the restaurant's booths. Jennifer was in the back. "She run for the front. She got to the door but did not make it out the door." All four girls were eventually moved to the back of the store. Scott went to the front of the store. He said he noticed "keys in the door."

"I heard, 'Get their clothes off,' Pierce said either to Springsteen or the girls. I'm watching at first and then [I] pick something up and start tying. I tie two sets of hands, two feets, two sets of feets. And I'm like, 'What am I doing?'

"Maurice heads to the register. Can't get the money. Girls say no. I hear a firearm go off. I don't know who is shot. Maurice loses his temper and shoots the other one.

"Gun is handed to me. 'No. This is wrong, man. This is wrong.'

"'Do it or you're next,' Springsteen said to Scott. 'You're a pussy, man, do it.'"

Scott again admitted that he shot Amy Ayers.

Sarah Harbison was still alive.

Pierce grabbed things to burn. Heard two more shots. Scott thought Sarah got yanked around and hit. He said the last gunshot sounded different.

Scott described leaving the shop and heading to the car. He claimed Welborn slid over to the passenger side. Scott ran back to the car. Springsteen and Pierce jogged back.

"My next absolutely conscious memory is getting home and taking a shower." Scott said that he "smoked a bowl or a half a joint later on. I lied in the tub and turned the shower on. Crawling into my bedroom."

*10:08 P.M.*

"I would like to go home and get some sleep and talk in the morning into a tape recorder," Scott said to Merrill.

One minute later, Texas Ranger Sal Abreo entered the room. He got Scott to talk about the sequence of the shootings. Scott claimed he was not exactly sure who died in which order. He believed it to be Eliza Thomas, then Jennifer Harbison, then Amy Ayers, then Sarah Harbison, then Amy Ayers again. He also claimed that he thought Springsteen shot Sarah.

*10:18 P.M.*

Merrill informed Scott that he would not send him home with a tape recorder. They did, however, agree to meet again the following day at 10:00 A.M.

"You probably feel like we've beaten the hell out of you." Merrill sympathized with Scott. "You're beaten up, and so are we."

"Hurt my mind emotionally, but not physically."

"It took a lot of courage, though, for you to come forward like that," replied Abreo.

"What else can I do, guys? Either tell the truth or . . ."

"Keep it all inside," Merrill offered.

"Yeah."

"That eight-hundred-pound gorilla on your back," Abreo added.

"She's getting lighter. She ain't gone yet," said Merrill. "Maybe you can get a better night's sleep than you have in eight-and-a-half years."

*10:21 P.M.*

All three men left the room.

# CHAPTER 40

*Friday, September 10, 1999*
*Interview Room # 2*
*Austin Police Department*
*10:22 A.M.*

Michael Scott returned to the interview room. He sat down in his chair and wrapped himself up in a blanket. Five minutes later, Robert Merrill walked in.

"How's your wife?" Merrill wondered.

"You don't want to go there."

"Did she yell and scream at you last night?"

"Yeah. She did. She wasn't pissed at me. She was pissed at y'all."

Merrill asked Scott to visualize what happened the night of the murders.

"I dug myself in a hole yesterday in this room and I don't know how to get out of it."

"You dug a hole when you all talked about doing a robbery."

"I think I lied to y'all yesterday. And I'm not sure if I lied to y'all or not. I don't know if this is real or not, or if this is what I convinced myself of at the time. Or if I've convinced myself of it now. I need help. I need memory clues."

Scott began to tell an even different story. He claimed he did go in, but he did not shoot anyone. When he returned to the car, Forrest Welborn was gone. "I think he got out and run off. I don't think Forrest did anything. I think he was just the watchman and he run off."

Scott continued with his new version. "I think I remember is Robert did show me a gun. At the condo. One time, before this happened. It was laying on his bed and [he said] 'Look what I got.' That's the only gun I remember him showing me. It was almost like a James Bond gun. That little thing that James Bond carried around.

"I have a mild aversion to guns. Guns are cool and great and all, but the only thing they're made to do is kill."

Merrill asked Scott if he remembered much about the girls.

"The only face that really sticks in my mind is that . . . is that pale-skinned girl." He referred to Jennifer Harbison. "The one with lots of makeup on and real dark, kind of scraggly curly hair."

Merrill asked if Scott recalled what he wore that night.

"Probably wore blue jeans, T-shirt, and denim jacket. Hair was just starting to get long. I wore a bandana a lot." He also wore a dark blue trench coat, which came down to his ankles. The coat had a hood.

"What I told y'all yesterday is the truth, but not the whole truth. I would like to go through hypnotic regression. I'm not sure if I'm a killer.

"I'm sure y'all are frustrated with me and just want to send me to the grand jury and let them send me to the sharks.

"I'm not going to do it, but I have thought about

Amy Ayers at thirteen.
*(Yearbook photo)*

Jennifer Harbison
at age seventeen.
*(Yearbook photo)*

Sarah Harbison at fifteen.
*(Yearbook photo)*

Eliza Thomas at age
seventeen. *(Yearbook photo)*

The front entrance of the I Can't Believe It's Yogurt shop. *(Courtesy of Travis County District Court)*

Firefighters entered through the front doors of the yogurt shop. *(Courtesy of Travis County District Court)*

A key was found in the lock on the front door of the shop. *(Courtesy of Travis County District Court)*

The girls had begun closing the store when the killers arrived; dining room chairs were already placed on top of the tables. *(Courtesy of Travis County District Court)*

Jennifer Harbison and Eliza Thomas worked the counter
at the shop. *(Courtesy of Travis County District Court)*

The fire's high temperature melted portions of this sink.
*(Courtesy of Travis County District Court)*

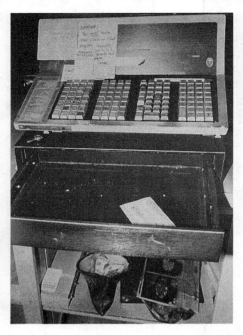

Police discovered this register both open and empty, with an open bag containing money underneath. *(Courtesy of Travis County District Court)*

This set of keys was found under the register. *(Courtesy of Travis County District Court)*

This melted telephone was found still attached to the wall. *(Author photo)*

Firefighters sloshed through an ankle-deep mix of water, ash, insulation, and blood. *(Courtesy of Travis County District Court)*

Amy Ayers's body was found in this large pool of blood, along with her clothing and change from the cash register drawer. *(Courtesy of Travis County District Court)*

Jennifer Harbison's body was located almost underneath these shelves, which melted in the heat of the fire. *(Courtesy of Travis County District Court)*

One of the girls' boots was found at the scene. *(Courtesy of Travis County District Court)*

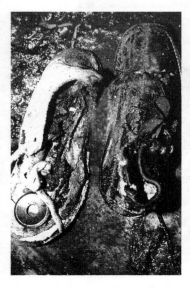

One of Jennifer's shoes and one of Eliza's, both melted. *(Courtesy of Travis County District Court)*

Texas Department of Public Safety crime scene investigator Irma Rios. *(Courtesy of Travis County District Court)*

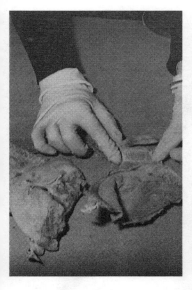

One of the girls' bras. *(Courtesy of Travis County District Court)*

A crime scene investigator lays out a burned pink sweater. *(Courtesy of Travis County District Court)*

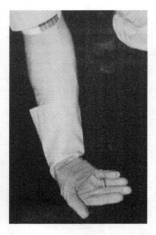

A crime scene investigator discovers a spent .22 bullet casing.
*(Courtesy of Travis County District Court)*

Ligatures used to restrain Eliza Thomas.
*(Courtesy of Travis County District Court)*

An Austin firefighter looks through the back doors. A pile of three bodies is just inside.
*(Courtesy of Travis County District Court)*

More than 1,000 people attended the funeral for the girls at St. Louis Catholic Church. *(Author photo)*

Maurice Pierce was arrested for carrying this .22 pistol one week after the murders. *(Author photo)*

Michael Scott, convicted of murder. Received a life sentence. *(Courtesy of Travis County Sheriff's Department)*

Maurice Pierce, murder suspect and alleged ringleader, was held in jail for more than three years and eventually released. *(Courtesy of Travis County Sheriff's Department)*

Robert Springsteen IV, convicted of capital murder and sentenced to death by lethal injection. *(Courtesy of Travis County Sheriff's Department)*

Forrest Welborn, the alleged lookout man, was released early on and never went to trial, due to a lack of evidence against him. *(Courtesy of Travis County Sheriff's Department)*

Michael Scott at age
seventeen. *(Yearbook photo)*

Robert Springsteen IV
at age seventeen.
*(Yearbook photo)*

Judge Mike Lynch.
*(Author photo)*

Eliza Thomas is buried at
Austin Memorial Park
Cemetery. *(Author photo)*

ELIZA HOPE THOMAS
MAY 16, 1974 — DEC. 6,

Jennifer, Sarah, and Amy are buried together
in Capital Memorial Gardens. *(Author photo)*

This monument, one
of several monuments
erected to honor the
memories of the girls, is
located at the FFA farm
where the girls used to
spend time.
*(Author photo)*

Finally Scott spoke with the officers again. He recalled the murders themselves. While the girls cried, he said, Springsteen ordered him to the back room. He described the girls as "laying down completely when we were tying them up."

Scott switched gears and spoke of the fire.

"I think I set the fire." He implicated himself for the first time. "At one time, I was a firebug."

*12:44 P.M.*

In an unorthodox move, Merrill whipped out a gun from his back right pocket and thrust it into Michael Scott's hand. It was the .22 revolver that Maurice Pierce had been arrested with eight years earlier. The detective attempted to get Scott to remember what it felt like to hold the gun in his hand. What it felt like to pull the trigger. Scott held the gun in the proper shooting manner for a couple of minutes, but he did not say anything. Merrill removed the gun from Scott's hand, held it upside in his own hand, and moved behind the young man. He quickly poked his right index finger into the back of Scott's head for a split second.

"Is this the gun?" Merrill demanded.

Scott froze up momentarily and did not speak.

Merrill just as quickly walked back in front of Scott and showed him the gun.

"Does this look like the gun you've seen before?"

"It looks like the gun I've seen before. But I'm not positive."

"Is that the gun you shot somebody with, Mike?"

"I don't—"

"Is that the gun you walked up behind somebody with and shot in the head? Is that the one? Talk to me, Mike."

"Yes."

"You did that, didn't you?"

"Yes, sir."

"We just opened some of those doors, haven't we, Mike?"

"Not really."

Merrill then asked Scott to stand up on one of the plastic chairs. He wanted Scott to imagine standing over the girls as he shot them in the back of the head. After two minutes of standing, Scott sat back down. Merrill immediately got back in his face.

"Quit being a pussy and tell me what you did! Stand up, Mike. Be a man here. We've got questions to answer."

"I'm trying to answer them."

"Answer them."

"I'm scared I killed somebody and don't fucking know it."

"I ain't buying that shit at all."

"I know you don't."

"Did you set the fire, Mike?"

"Yes, sir."

*1:06 P.M.*

Merrill reminded Scott, "You're not under arrest. Here's the door. If you want to leave—leave. If you don't want to find out what happened, you don't want to finish it, hit the door. Get out of here. All you have to do is get up and walk."

"I want to remember," Scott replied. He started to cry.

"I don't believe you now, Mike."

"You're telling me that I fucking killed four girls," Scott said as he cried louder.

"You were involved in the murder of the four girls in the commission of a robbery. Is that correct, or not?"

"I helped," he said. He paused, considered what he

just said, and added, "I was telling y'all what y'all wanted to know."

"I ain't buying that at all, Mike."

"I'm not buying it myself."

Merrill stood and left the room. Five minutes later, Scott got up and left also.

*1:33 P.M.*

Scott returned to the room, followed by ATF agent Chuck Meyer, who did not stay long. Twelve minutes later, Merrill and Abreo entered the room. The two men sat on either side of Scott as they faced him. There was a direct, open pathway for Scott to leave the room.

Scott continued to talk about the shooting. "I only shot the gun once. And I didn't want it anymore."

"I understand that," replied Merrill. "And you know what, Mike? I believe that. I always believed that."

"You scared the shit out of me."

"I meant to scare the shit out of you. Trigger points. If I could hang from the ceiling upside down and puke red ink, I'd do it just to trigger a memory for you. I'll get down on my hands and knees and pray with you. I'll stand in the chair and look down with you. I scared the hell out of you and I know it."

Calmer, Scott continued to fill in more details of the crime. "I remember a can of Zippo fluid. Out of Maurice's car. Maurice had a Zippo lighter. I was given the can to take in with me. 'Hold on to this.'" Pierce allegedly gave the can of lighter fluid to Scott. "Because it was laying down in the backseat. He said, 'Bring the Zippo fluid.' I pick it up. We went inside. The girls are gotten together.

"I . . . I piled it on top of them? I piled it up. I spread all that stuff all over it. I light it. I see Rob coming down the hallway. I was heading for the door.

"At least one of the guns is gotten rid of."

"Where?" asked Abreo.

"It was on a bridge. A real tall bridge. I get sick."

"Were all the girls dead?"

"Yes. By that time, all the girls are dead.

"I smell paper, I smell paint, I smell cotton burning. I set them on fire." Scott began to cry. "I set them on fire."

"What was the reason for the fire?"

"To destroy evidence."

"Who all had lighters to light the fire?"

"Maurice and I. He had one too."

"What does the fire sound like?"

"Like a fire. Like a fire started by an accelerant. *Whooooosh!* I remember I staggered out. I was sick. I was sick."

"What else happened to those girls before the fire was set?" Merrill asked.

"They made me rape one of them. I had sex with her."

"Was she already dead?"

"I don't know whether she was alive or dead."

"Why did they stop screaming?" Abreo inquired.

"They're gagged. But I don't remember with what."

"Were the little girls squirming around when y'all were raping them?"

"Yes."

"Was that the same girl that Rob raped? Was that the same one they made you have sex with?"

"Yes," Scott answered as he shifted his legs in his chair. "It was another one."

"Did you come inside of her?"

"I don't remember."

Scott recalled how the bodies were positioned. "Two. I keep seeing two laying down and one laying like this." He pointed his fingers in the universal symbol for "peace." He crossed the peace signs over each other at forty-five-degree angles. The peace signs appeared to resemble the legs of the victims.

"And the other one is what?"

"Is . . . is . . . is laying on top. When I . . . when I shot—no. He told me to pile them up and burn them."

"Who told you that? Who's the son of a bitch that told you that, Michael?"

"Maurice did. I pulled one on top of the other. I threw all the stuff on them." Scott said he squirted the lighter fluid. "I lit the fire. I remember seeing the smoke and the nasty smell. I ran out.

"I want them to fucking go to prison for what they made me do."

Scott skipped around back to the gun. "I didn't see which one was thrown. I was too busy puking my guts out."

He recalled shooting the gun.

"Yes. I shot. White light. This is what I saw. I shot, white light. Revulsion. I don't want this anymore."

"When you raped this girl," Abreo asked, "when you had sex with her, was it from the front, the back?"

"From the front."

"Did you have a hard time getting an erection and maintaining it?"

"Yes."

"How many times had you tried to rape that girl?"

"Twice."

"Were you angry at her?"

"No, I was angry at Robert and Maurice."

"Was she crying, Michael? Was she saying anything?"

"She could not. She was gagged."

"What did she have in her mouth?"

"I remember white. A bra?"

"Is that what it is or not?" interjected Merrill. Scott did not answer.

"You're having a hard time maintaining an erection

to do what you need to do," Abreo recounted, "because those other guys won't get off your back. Those other bastards won't leave you alone. Is the girl you raped the same one that you shot?"

"Yes."

"Where did you shoot her?"

"I shot her in the head. I had her on the ground facing—I had to have shot her in the head. Right in the face."

"In the face," repeated Merrill. "You've got to pull that trigger, Michael. You will not be able to get rid of all that screaming, all the smell of the lighter fluid, all the smell of burning flesh."

"I remember I shot her in the head." Scott started to cry again. "I pointed the gun and I closed my eyes and I pulled the trigger."

Smoke break. All three men left the room.

*3:06 P.M.*

Scott returned. Three minutes later, Merrill and Meyer entered the interview room.

Scott spoke again.

"I remember Robert off to my right. He had the Hispanic girl (possibly referring to the dark-skinned Eliza Thomas, who was not Hispanic). He had her up on her—he was fucking her from behind. I remember her giving him a hard time. She's fighting. She's moving."

"And you're trying to get your wanger up to have sex with this girl?" asked Merrill.

"Yes. And I can't do it."

"You bump her, but you don't get it in?"

"I don't get it in.

"He does her. I want to say he shoots her in the back of the head. It wasn't Maurice who handed me the gun. It was Robert who handed me the gun. He hands me the gun. I look at the gun. I point at her head and I close my eyes and I shoot. I open my eyes and I see red."

The conversation returned to Scott's current status. "There is no point in me running," Scott assured the officers. "There is no place in this fucking world that I can hide from y'all. If I wanted to, I can disappear. I can disappear into the woods, if I wanted to. That's not what I'm going to do. There's no point in running."

"You've been brutalized here for a couple of days here," Merrill told him.

"Yeah, but that's y'all's job. And it's what I deserve right now. I have no animosity for you guys."

*3:28 P.M.*

The interview ended and the lights were turned out in the room.

# CHAPTER 41

*Wednesday, September 15, 1999*
*Interview Room # 7*
*Charleston Police Department*
*Charleston, West Virginia*

Detective Robert Merrill tracked down Robert Springsteen IV in Charleston, West Virginia. He located Springsteen's supposed address. He, Detective Ron Lara, and Sergeant John Neff hopped on a plane with the intention of questioning Springsteen in regard to the yogurt shop murders. They arrived on September 14.

The following morning, Merrill contacted Detective Eric Hodges, of the Charleston Police Department (CPD). Merrill and Hodges drove to the 900 block of Bridge Street and got out of Hodges's unmarked police car, walked up to the front door and knocked.

No one answered.

The detectives decided to contact the local Kroger grocery store where Springsteen worked. They asked for Springsteen's most current address. The two officers got back in the vehicle and drove over to the 2200 block of Falcon Street. Again they got out of the car and walked up to the front door. Merrill had a gun secured away in his fanny pack.

They knocked on the door.

Springsteen answered the door. Not the front door, where the knock came from, but rather the side door.

The officers walked around to the side of the house. They introduced themselves to the young man. They asked if he would talk with them at the police station. He agreed.

Springsteen was dressed in a dark button-down shirt, a "wife beater" undershirt, a dark baseball cap, and a belly pack. He used the rest room and called his wife. After he spoke to her, he came outside and left with the two officers. He was not under arrest, nor was he handcuffed.

The three men arrived at the CPD and went inside. They entered the elevator and rode it to the second floor. The officers asked Springsteen to wait in the lobby, which he did, unattended, for almost fifteen minutes.

Merrill eventually returned to the lobby and asked Springsteen if he would follow him into the interview room. Springsteen readily agreed. Merrill, joined by Lara, entered the nondescript room. Springsteen joined them.

The officers immediately told him they wanted to interview him in regard to the yogurt shop murders. He nodded his head.

The detectives inquired about Springsteen's background. He had two stepchildren and a stepgrandson. He and his wife, Robin Moss, lived in a 109-year-old cabin. He worked in chemical plants. He was born in South Heights, Chicago. His parents were divorced. He told the officers that he liked to "fish, hunt, PlayStation. A game called Mud. Zork. Beyond Zork."

Springsteen said his grandfather had retired from

IBM. His father was a contract computer programmer. "Uncle owns his own consulting company out in Tase Valley. My other uncle, he's the head of the auto CAD design department for corporate K mart."

He told the detectives that he did not have many friends in West Virgina. His best buddy was a man named Roy Rose. Actually, Rose was his only friend. He recalled how he and his wife celebrated their wedding anniversary with Roy and Charlene Rose on Eastland Lake. The Roses had rented a boat for their anniversary.

"How long will this take, because I've got another job to go to?" Springsteen asked.

No one answered him. Instead, the detectives asked Springsteen if he remembered being brought in for questioning about the yogurt shop murders, which took place on December 6, 1991, after Maurice Pierce had been arrested for carrying a gun at Northcross Mall.

"Yeah, they put me in cuffs. Put me in a cruiser. Took me down and questioned me," Springsteen responded in a light voice tinged with a hint of a southern drawl. "They asked me this and asked me that. Four hundred fifty questions."

Springsteen informed Merrill and Lara that it would be easier for him to write things down than to say them. "I'm specific learning disabled. My brain operates backwards of the way a normal left-right thinker does. I think the opposite, so I do everything backwards. It's like trying to explain neon blue to a blind person. If you gave me a set of six numbers, I could only remember two." He informed them he took Ritalin.

The detectives asked Springsteen what he knew about the yogurt shop murders.

"I hadn't heard nothing about it. Because I pretty much kept to myself and didn't have very many friends. Forrest was a pretty good friend of mine. I met

Maurice through him." He claimed he did not hook up with Welborn or Pierce that night.

He spoke of three other friends of his: Tom Powe, a different guy named Mike, and his girlfriend, Kelly. He could not remember her last name.

Springsteen described an uncomfortable home life with his father and his father's girlfriend, Karen Huntley. He claimed Huntley would only buy bread and hot dogs and that there was never anything to eat. He said he did not get along with Huntley, so he decided to move back to West Virginia. He broke up with Kelly before he moved back.

Lara turned the focus of the interview to the night of the murders. He asked Springsteen to tell them what he did on December 6, 1991.

Springsteen said he went over to Welborn's house near the McCallum High School campus. Pierce stopped by and picked up Welborn and Springsteen. He dropped them both off at Northcross Mall. "We dicked around for a little bit." Around 2:00 P.M. or 3:00 P.M., they went into one of the arcades in the mall. By this time, Michael Scott had joined them. He believed Powe might have been with them as well.

"We ended up going to *Rocky Horror Picture Show* that night." Springsteen claimed he attended the cult favorite audience-participation midnight movie at the Northcross Mall movie theater twice a week, every week. When they arrived at the theater, he believed Pierce had to go to his sister's house. Welborn left with Pierce in "an '82 Texas State Ranger or Caprice. It was a real nice ride."

Springsteen backed up to when they first arrived at the mall. He believed they arrived at 3:00 P.M. or 4:00 P.M. Pierce and Welborn left around at 5:30 P.M. or 6:00 P.M.

Springsteen and Scott were sitting outside, watching the waitresses from the local Hooters restaurant, when Pierce and Welborn came "screaming down, more than twenty-five miles per hour, through the mall" parking lot.

"'Man, what the hell are you doing?'" Springsteen asked Pierce.

Pierce said there were some Mexicans who threw rocks and bottles at his car, three to five of them. "We never found them," Springsteen told the detectives. "Six or six-thirtyish. Fooled around for one to two more hours."

Springsteen sat comfortably in his chair. He gestured animatedly with his hands as he told his story. He stated that he and Scott went back to the mall around 8:00 P.M. They played video games in the arcade from 8:00 P.M. to midnight. Welborn and Pierce were supposed to return sometime between 11:00 P.M. and midnight. They intended to go to a party; however, Pierce never showed up, Springsteen claimed. Springsteen stayed and watched *The Rocky Horror Picture Show.* He left and went home to Scott's mother's house. He arrived at 1:30 A.M. He stated that an older white man, about forty-five, with long white hair, drove him and Scott home in a tiny Suzuki. The boys stayed up late and watched *Robin Hood: Prince of Thieves,* starring Kevin Costner.

Springsteen told the officers he was not aware of the murders until he had been brought downtown to be questioned by Detective Paul Johnson more than a week later.

Lara began to notice some inconsistencies in Springsteen's story. He pressed him on it.

Springsteen blamed his faulty memory on years of drug usage. "I followed the Dead for nine months, from seventeen to eighteen. I've done horrible things to my body, which I'm regretting now with asthma. Acid. Pot. No heroin or crank."

Springsteen talked about the joyride to San Antonio

the night after the murders. His girlfriend, Kelly Hannah, supposedly went with them. He claimed he bought a copy of the Sunday *Austin American-Statesman* from a 7-Eleven convenience store off Highway 2222, where he bought a paper twice a week. He also admitted to reading the newspaper during the trip.

"Hell, I ain't got no reason to lie to you guys." Springsteen shifted around in his chair as if agitated. Lara scooted his chair closer to him. "To tell you the truth, I really don't know what I know anymore."

"Well, that doesn't make you look very good," Lara replied.

"No, it doesn't." Springsteen nodded his head in agreement.

"You don't forget the truth. But you do forget intermittent lies."

"I can tell you two things. I do not know, have never known, whether Maurice or Forrest were involved in that. I'm talking about the murders."

"What would you say if we told you that *The Rocky Horror Picture Show* was not showing that night?" Lara asked.

"I would be surprised."

"Why would a sixteen-year-old buy a paper?"

"Why would an eight-year-old boy buy a gun and kill somebody?" Springsteen countered. "The strangest things happen all the time."

Springsteen shifted in his chair again. He said, "Let me be frank with you guys. If I'm being accused of something, then I would like a lawyer present. I would like this to come to an end. One way or another."

"You're free to get up anytime you want," replied Merrill.

Springsteen did not get up, so Merrill asked him about Scott. Lara stood up and exited the interview room. Merrill told Springsteen they had been speaking to

Scott. Merrill also told him they were talking to Pierce. The detective said both young men told quite different stories from Springsteen's.

"In my opinion, I think Maurice was the liar, but Forrest would do whatever Maurice told him to do," Merrill informed him.

"Of the four guys, you're the only one whose story is not the same as theirs. Mike Scott said, 'It was an awful, evil thing,' as a matter of fact.

"We don't believe Maurice. We believe Michael.

"Who called the shots?" Merrill demanded.

"Maurice," Springsteen answered without hesitation.

"Maurice said it was you."

"I know nothing more than what I told you. I was never in the yogurt shop. Never. Ever. I wish you guys could give me a lie detector test and ask me all these questions. I've never been there. I don't even think I've been within one hundred yards of it ever."

"People are getting things off of their chest now," Merrill said. "Getting the weight of the world off their shoulders, and they're telling everything they know about that night. And they are telling, you were with them the entire night."

Merrill asked Springsteen if he ever owned a gun. The young man said he saw Pierce with one in a shoe box under Pierce's father's bed. It was a .22.

"I was like, 'Oh, it's a cool gun.'"

Lara informed Springsteen that he could light up a cigarette in the interview room. The young man did so immediately.

As Springsteen attempted to calm his nerves with nicotine, Merrill moved in for the kill by saying that Springsteen knew more than he was saying. Springsteen looked at Merrill with a menacing stare as he blew smoke out of his nostrils like a snorting bull.

"If I was there and participated," Springsteen responded, "I would think that I would be a pretty fucked-up person. I probably couldn't hold a job. I couldn't be married, have a wife."

Merrill commented that Springsteen had seven jobs in the last five years. The detective said that he had one job in twenty years. He then mocked Springsteen's current job as a stock boy at Kroger.

"My life's not wonderful," Springsteen defended himself. "It's not horrible."

"Michael Scott says you were as big a victim as he was. That Maurice was the leader."

Springsteen just nodded his head and continued to smoke and to glower.

Lara claimed there were witnesses who saw him in the yogurt shop on the day of the murders.

"I don't eat yogurt, to tell you the truth."

Lara mentioned to Springsteen there were all sorts of new advances in technology that could help determine a person's DNA.

Springsteen sat quietly. He responded by saying, "You both seem like real nice knockout guys and have been real friendly and kind."

"Well, thank you," Lara responded. "You seem like a nice person too."

"But I was not in that store—"

"It's time to get it off your chest," Merrill interjected. "Off your shoulders. 'I'm ready to be a man and say what happened.' I've talked to good liars in my life. You're not one of them."

"I never have been. That's why I don't lie."

"You are now."

"If you believe so," Springsteen defiantly replied.

"I believe so. I'm going to sleep great tonight when I go home and go to bed. I don't hear screams in the middle of the night."

"I don't either."

"I don't see that picture."

"I don't either."

"Did you shoot one of them girls?" Merrill pressed.

"No, I did not."

Detective Lara moved his chair in even closer toward Springsteen, who looked the detective directly in the eye.

"I can't take responsibility for something I didn't do."

"You let us know how you want to play," Merrill said. "It don't matter to me."

"I guess you guys need to tell me what my options are."

Merrill mentioned the screaming of the girls again. Springsteen sighed and rolled his eyes.

Merrill showed him the photographs of the four girls. Lara got right in his face and told him Sarah reminded him of Scott: "The way her eyes and nose are."

Merrill stood up and left the room.

Lara asked Springsteen, "Is it possible you killed those girls?"

"I guess it's possible," Springsteen replied rather arrogantly. "Anything's possible."

"Is it possible that you were present there while this took place?"

"No."

"You just told me anything's possible," Lara retorted as he hovered about twelve inches from Springsteen's face.

"It is possible."

"Is it possible that you were there?" Lara asked again. "Is it possible that you killed one or two or more of those girls?"

"It could be."

"Is it possible that you were involved in the planning?"

"Yes."

"Maurice and you were casing?"

"I guess it's possible. Yes."

"What would not be possible?"

"I guess nothing."

"Is it likely you were involved in the murders?"

"It is not likely."

"You're not even upset that someone implicated you in this," Lara said. "You're sitting here thinking very hard." At that same moment, another man entered the interview room.

"This is Special Agent Meyer," Lara informed Springsteen.

After some discussion with Chuck Meyer, Springsteen said, "I've gone as far as I can go. What are our options now?"

Neither officer responded to his query.

"My wife has really changed me." Springsteen broke the silence. "I guess she's made me become more of a man. She repossesses people's houses. Her and my mom were best friends. Her ex-husband went to prison."

Meyer sat in front of Springsteen, off to his right side. Merrill returned to the room and sat in a chair located by the door. The men had Springsteen somewhat cornered. Springsteen seemed unfazed as he calmly smoked his cigarette, with his head tilted to the left.

"We know you were at the yogurt shop," Meyer informed Springsteen.

"Prove it," he replied as he looked Meyer in the eye.

"We have."

"Then I need to go into recursive psychotherapy or be hypnotized or something."

"Well, if I knew what that was, I'd get you some of that." This remark made Springsteen and Merrill laugh.

"Judging by all these statements, you're the key," Meyer suggested. "And I don't think you are. But you may be. You're the only one that can straighten it up. We've got, like, four people that know you were there."

"I don't specifically remember going into the yogurt shop," Springsteen responded. "It's possible that I may have went in. We can sit here for ten hours having this same conversation."

Springsteen began to provide more details. He claimed he sat in the backseat of Pierce's dad's car because Pierce and Welborn were "buddy-buddy." He described Pierce's dad as "kind of weird. I thought he was mean. Not really strict. But like mean and gruff and kind of maybe abusive or violent. I didn't associate with his dad or go over to his house.

"I don't know if I was in the yogurt shop or not. I don't think I was."

"Are you sure, because every now and then I see a little tear in your eye," Merrill stated. "A little tear."

Springsteen quietly shook his head no.

"You remember exactly what happened in there. You're trying to search for a way out of this, and right now, there ain't none."

"Then what's our options?" Springsteen looked exasperated. "That's what I'm trying to explain to you. If I was there and I partook in this, I would remember these things." His voice rose in volume as he spoke.

"And do you remember these things?"

"No, I don't. No, I don't."

"You're the coldest guy I've talked to in my life," Merrill told him. "Are you a cold-blooded murderer?"

"No, sir. I'm not."

"I think you are. I think Maurice is absolutely true about you. You're the coldest guy I've ever talked to."

"Then let's take whatever actions we need to take."

"We don't want to go there."

"Maybe it's possible that I was there. Maybe, whatever. Whatever. Whatever. Obviously, you guys have got some maturity or something that I do not have."

"It's not a crystal ball, it's just the facts," Meyer reminded him.

"Then you guys' facts are wrong. Because I know in my heart and in my head that I had nothing to do with that. I was not in the yogurt shop. I can guarantee you that."

"How can you guarantee me that?"

"I can't. Never mind." Springsteen lowered his head into his hands and rolled his eyes. He sat in his chair for several minutes before he spoke again. He tried to recall any memories from that night.

"I still keep coming up with the same thing. I'm not really remembering anything. It's kind of like little fragments. I'm trying to piece it together is what I'm trying to do."

He called Pierce "a big bullshitter. He talked about stealing cars or tires. Like B and E. Break into somebody's house and take their stuff and pawn it. I never perceived Maurice or myself or Mike or any of us as violent people."

"It would be a total shock to you, had something violent happened that night, wouldn't it?" Merrill asked.

"Yes, it would have."

"And you would be just as much a victim as anybody else. Because that's not what you thought about."

"True."

Springsteen spoke of the robbery plans hatched by Pierce. "I'm not going to say no anymore, because you guys have a really compelling case and I'm starting to remember a few things, here and there."

"If you haven't figured it out, Maurice blames you," Merrill told him.

"Oh, I'm sure."

"But we don't believe him. But we've got to hear it from you. I don't think you walked into that door expecting anything of what happened."

"No. As a matter of fact, I think I got the hell out of

there. To tell you the truth about the fact of the matter, come to think of it." It was the first time Springsteen admitted being inside the yogurt shop. He sat calmly as he said it.

"Got in the car, parked, got out of the car, went inside, went to the bathroom, come back out, Maurice is at the counter, I was walking out. I mean, I was like headed out of the shop anyway. Out the door. Heard somebody scream. I turned around. And all hell just broke loose.

"Maurice standing there with a gun in his hand. He said, 'Give me the fucking money or I'll fucking kill all of you,' or some dumbass shit like that. I said, 'Man, this shit is getting fucking deep,' or 'I'm fucking out of here,' or 'I don't want nothing to do with this.'

"Maurice was at the counter. I don't think Forrest was close to him. I think maybe he was inside, kind of a couple a feet away from me. Another five or ten feet past that was the counter, where Maurice was at. And I don't remember where Mike was. I was basically like 'I don't fucking believe this. I don't want no part of this.' And I left. I went out of the store."

Springsteen relayed that the girls were "freaking out." He added, "That is the closest to a cluster fuck I had ever seen. I guess I was a coward and I got the hell out."

He spoke about weapons. "I like guns, I like collecting guns. It's not a toy."

Springsteen returned to talking about the murders. "I don't remember if Mike was inside with us or not. There was just so much going on. I went outside. I stood by the car."

Springsteen said he was surprised by Pierce's actions. "This guy who's supposed to be my friend standing there with a damn gun. Done fired a round. I don't know whether anybody had been hit. 'This is crazy. This is fucking bullshit. Fuck you, guys.' There were more gunshots. They were muffled. I believe I heard five. I was thinking, 'I've got to get the hell out of here. This is not a good place for me to be. I need to get as far as hell away from here as I can.'"

Springsteen said Scott was right behind him. "'What are we gonna do? Maurice is fucking crazy.' Scott said, 'Damn straight. He's a fucking lunatic.'

"Maurice said he just scared them. Me and him almost got into it. But I didn't want to be shot."

Springsteen talked about disposing the gun. "There was a bridge by a river behind the yogurt shop. Threw the damn gun in the stream. A little bridge."

"Did Mike get out?" Merrill asked.

"I think so."

"What did he do?"

"I think he threw up. I think I threw up too."

"That's called the 'Oh Shit' factor," Merrill informed Springsteen.

"We drove back to the yogurt shop and [we saw] all the police and ambulances. Then we left immediately."

"Do you feel better?" Merrill asked.

"Thank you, guys." Springsteen nodded in compliance. "Yeah, I really do. You guys really helped me get past that."

"I guarantee you, tonight you'll sleep better than you ever slept in your life. This has to be eight years of hell for what you saw."

"I feel kind of bad. But you know—"

"Sure you feel bad. You were involved in something that was terrible."

"I really wasn't. I didn't ask for that. I didn't want that."

Lara returned to the interview room.

"We had a little breakthrough, Ron," Merrill told his fellow officer.

"At times, I don't recall," Springsteen continued. "It was such a cluster fuck."

The three men took a break.

\* \* \*

The three men returned to the interview room. Springsteen began to recall specifics of the crime. He stated that he came through the front door. He also claimed he never saw Pierce shoot anyone.

"You know, when it come down to, I guess, telling time for me, I was out the door."

"You told time," Lara replied.

"Yeah. I wasn't running to beat all hell, but I was going at a decent rate."

"When you were going out the door, did you remember grass?"

"I did. Within fifteen or twenty yards."

"Do you remember going in the back?" Merrill asked.

"I think, I don't know."

"When you came out of the bathroom, what did you see? Did Maurice tell you what to do before you went in?"

"I think he said something about, seeing what's in the back, going in to the back, stay in the back."

"Did this bother you? Did you lay in bed at night thinking about that shot? Do you ever lay in bed thinking about what happened to you and Mike? Did you ever cry for those girls?" Merrill quietly questioned.

"I cried a lot." Springsteen repeatedly nodded his head. I need to get over this," he continued. "I'm trying. It was so catastrophic that day. He was mad at me, yelling and everything, nothing about nothing. I know I was in the yogurt shop, but I don't remember all the details. Everything is so fast. I feel like I'm losing reality here."

"When you came out of the bathroom, did you see a door?" Merrill prodded.

"That would be the back door. At some point in time, we had come through and opened up the back door so we had a way to get in. I put a pack of cigarettes—I mean, like, an empty pack of cigarettes, folded up, down there to keep it from shutting all the way, down at the bottom.

"I guess I accomplished my part of the mission."

Afterward, they sat outside the movie theater for forty-five minutes to an hour before they returned to rob the yogurt shop.

"Mike was the lookout. Maurice was the man of action: 'Get the money, get the money.'"

"When you went back the last time," Merrill asked, "how did you get in?"

"The back door."

"Who was at the front door."

"Mike." Springsteen did not remember if Welborn went in.

"Were you issuing orders?"

"No, sir."

"Who was issuing orders?"

"Maurice."

Springsteen claimed he was in the back of the restaurant. He heard a shot and walked up to the front. He changed his story and said he saw a girl get shot. He noticed the other girls were screaming and crying.

"What was happening to those girls before they were shot?"

"He was messing with them. I think that Maurice and Forrest just started attacking this chick. Like trying to get her clothes off her, just going crazy."

"Did her clothes come off?"

"I remember her shirt coming off."

"What else came off?"

"They started to pull, trying to pull her pants down, but her shoes, they were messing around this area. I think he said, 'Come over here. Fuck her. Screw her,' something like that, but I said, 'No, man, I don't want to do this.'"

Springsteen said that Pierce pistol-whipped one of the girls. He claimed Pierce told Springsteen to hold one of the girls.

"Hold them for what?" Lara asked.

"So he could rape them, like 'Get the hell over here and hold them down.'

"He wanted me to kill a girl. I was like, 'No way, man, I can't do it.' He wanted me to shoot her in the back of the head."

"Did you?"

"No."

"Don't lie to me now," Merrill piped in.

"I didn't do it."

"Did Mike?"

"No."

"Who killed these girls?" Lara asked.

"Maurice did."

"How many guns were there?"

"Just one."

"No, come on, how many guns were there? That's a gimme."

"Maurice had the twenty-two and Forrest had the three-eighty."

Lara pensively asked Springsteen, "What did they make you do?"

"Shoot her." For the first time, Springsteen admitted shooting one of the girls. "He wanted me to shoot her in the back of the head, but I did not want to shoot her."

"Was she already down?" Merrill inquired. "Was she still up? What happened?"

"What was she doing when you shot her?" Lara followed up.

"Crawling," Springsteen softly spoke. "It was unreal. Crying and screaming."

"Did she talk to you?" Lara asked.

"If you call screaming talking, I guess."

"After you shot her, what happened?"

"I threw the gun away."

"She wasn't dead yet, was she? You fucking know if you fucking raped her, just say it."

"I stuck my dick in her pussy and I raped her."

"Is she dead yet?" Merrill posed a question.

"No, she wasn't dead yet."

"Describe the position. Faceup or facedown?"

"I'm thinking [she] was lying on her stomach."

"Kind of on her stomach, is that what you said?"

"Like, yeah, kind of like this." Springsteen stretched his right arm up and over three different ways. The final pose he struck was with his arm stretched out and lying underneath his chest and sticking out.

"How did she die?"

"Maurice came up and shot her again in the head." Springsteen pointed his index and middle fingers toward the back of Lara's head. He did not look as he reenacted the pulling of the trigger.

"You fucked her," Lara plainly stated.

"Yeah."

"Did you fuck her anally?"

"No."

"Did you have an orgasm?"

"I don't know."

Merrill intervened, "Was your wanger hard?"

"No more than a couple of minutes. That's why I don't think I had an orgasm; by this time, it was all fucked up more than anything I've been through."

"It was pretty bad, wasn't it?"

"Worse."

"How did that little girl die?"

"Maurice was angry with me because she wasn't dead. I didn't shoot her right, and I think he said, 'Now, goddamn it, you can't do nothing, you can't even fucking shoot her.'"

"That piss you off?"

"Yeah, I guess."

"Did Maurice have sex with one?"

"I'm sure he did."

"Did Mike?"

"I think he tried, but I don't think he could."

"He couldn't get his wanger up?"

"Yeah."

The officers paused for a moment. Eventually Merrill asked Springsteen, "Do you feel better?"

"Yes, I do, but I don't. I feel worse. To tell you the truth, I'm scared to death."

Merrill asked Springsteen whether he thought he was under arrest.

"Should I have a lawyer?" Springsteen asked Merrill. "I don't know nothing about nothing."

"If you want a lawyer."

"I don't know what to do. I don't want to get railroaded. I'm sure you probably wouldn't do it on purpose."

"Well, how could I railroad you?"

"Well, you know."

"Go tell your wife, tell her that you fucked up. Did you tell anybody else about this?"

"No."

"Ever?"

"No, not a soul. Not even God."

"God knows."

After a few minutes, Merrill read Springsteen his Miranda rights.

"I want this interview to be over so I can go home and talk to my wife," Springsteen declared.

"Are you invoking your right to your attorney?"

"Yes, sir."

"Get out."

Springsteen stood up from his chair. He leaned over and picked up some trash.

"Just trying to clean up my mess."

# CHAPTER 42

*Wednesday, October 6, 1999*
*City Hall*
*Austin, Texas*

Three weeks after Robert Springsteen confessed to the yogurt shop murders, the police went into action. Officers were staked out in four cities: Charleston, West Virginia, for Springsteen; Buda, Texas, for Michael Scott; Lewisville, Texas, for Maurice Pierce; and Lockhart, Texas, for Forrest Welborn. All four young men were arrested without incident.

Mayor Kirk Watson announced the arrests in the yogurt shop murders to his constituents of Austin. The mayor spoke of defining moments in a person's life—both positive and negative. He also spoke of defining moments for a community. He reiterated how wonderful were the innumerable positives the city of Austin had to offer. He also spoke of the significance of growth for a city and the unfortunate side effects that often accompany such change.

"There has probably been no other single event in

our community that has made us feel less like a sleepy college town than the murders of four young girls in December 1991.

"How could something so horrific, so unexplainable, happen here?"

Mayor Watson expressed his sympathies for the families of the victims.

He praised the efforts of the Austin Police Department, which may have solved the "crime that has haunted our very souls."

The mayor spoke of the effect the murders had on the city. "On December 6, 1991, we, as a city, lost our innocence. Today we regain our confidence. Today, as a community, we can, hopefully, finally begin the process of healing."

Watson spoke of Austin's lowest crime rates recorded just one year earlier. Despite that information, the citizens of Austin could not feel comfort until the yogurt shop murders were solved. "Our very lives were shaken by that unspeakable act of violence. When four young girls lose their lives, it defies reason.

"These four girls belonged to this community. I know the community grieved along with the families of Sarah and Jennifer Harbison, Amy Ayers, and Eliza Thomas, and have continued to ask, 'What happened?' and 'How could it happen?'"

Mayor Watson spoke about how the families never gave up hope "that one day we will know the truth." He commended all the departments responsible for the arrests of the four young men and for, hopefully, providing answers to everyone's questions.

"I'm very proud of our Chief (Stan Knee) and these people. You make us able to say, 'Sarah, Jennifer, Amy, Eliza—we did not forget.'"

# CHAPTER 43

While Mayor Watson reminded everyone that the girls would not be forgotten, most people did not even know who the alleged killers were.

"The names just don't ring any bells," 1992 McCallum High School graduate Jeremiah Dye told the *Austin American-Statesman*. Similar sentiments were echoed by another McCallum graduate, Blair Edgar: "I probably never even had a conversation with them, but the fact that I recognized them is pretty creepy."

Former McCallum principal Penny Miller was shocked when she heard the news: "None of us can believe that kids can keep a secret like that for that long."

Of those who did know the boys when they were younger, most were stunned by the charges. Danny Decker, one of Robert Springsteen's teachers at Cabell Alternative Education High School in West Virginia, stated, "I never saw a violent side, a dark side. Robby was a neat kid." Decker did not say that Springsteen was angelic. "Maybe robbery, I could see. But to sit and plan the murder of four girls? I just don't see it."

Decker also recalled Springsteen as an individual

who "march(ed) to the beat of his own drummer. Everyone turned left and Robby turned right."

Decker also spoke of Springsteen's difficulties with his stepfather, Brett Thompson. She believed the two "clashed violently." The teacher mentioned that Robert would visit her eighty-acre farm in Sissonville to escape the stress of home life.

Despite Springsteen's aggressive tendencies, Decker believed that he was "probably the most compassionate child I saw, as far as petting the dogs, walking the horses. There were absolutely no signs of anything."

Decker feared the worst for her former charge.

"I'm afraid Texas is really going to do him in."

Many people who knew the boys as adults were just as surprised. Jackie Loveday, a neighbor of Maurice and Kim Pierce's in Lewisville, stated, "It comes as a big shock when you've been around them. My daughter plays with their seven-year-old all the time." She spoke with Pierce on that Tuesday. He had been getting a sprinkler system put in his yard. Pierce told her, "Since we're buying the place, we might as well put some money into it."

Loveday's mother, Juvine Graham, had a different attitude. "That house has always been nothing but trouble. There's always someone fighting."

Other neighbors had a different opinion of Pierce.

"He's innocent as far as I'm concerned," eighty-one-year-old neighbor Jane Akin told the *Lewisville Leader*. "I don't think he did a darned thing."

Pierce also impressed people on the other end of the age spectrum. Eighteen-year-old neighbor Paul Herman said, "He was never the kind of guy that looked suspicious. He always seemed pretty friendly to me."

Akin said Pierce taught his daughter how to ride a bike. She could not envision such a loving young man as a brutal killer.

"It's such a horrible thing that happened, and I hope

they catch who did it. But there's no reason to think he did it."

The families of the suspects obviously did not believe they were responsible.

"My son did not do this," wrote Robert Springsteen III in an e-mail to the *Charleston Daily Mail* from his home in Mesquite, Texas. "My understanding of this goes beyond that of a father's concern for his son.

"Austin police have known the whereabouts of my son since 1991 and detectives have been in contact with my son several times since the murders and he has always been cooperative."

Springsteen III expressed his sympathies for the girls' parents and asked the media to "control the temptation for ambush and buffalo stampede tactics."

# CHAPTER 44

*Thursday, October 7, 1999*
*Austin, Texas*

It was a familiar setting for the parents of the slain girls: a cluster of news reporters, a bank of microphones, and bright lights. They hoped this particular setting would differ from previous press conferences. They hoped this time the police actually had the right people in custody.

Pam Ayers stated, "I don't think it will be real to me until we actually see the men and have an indictment in the case." She continued, "I know this is real. It's really happening. But yet, it seems it's not real either." Her voice quivered. "It's an unreal story."

The surrealism struck Barbara Ayres as well. The former Mrs. Barbara Suraci divorced husband Skip the previous year. They drifted apart since the funeral and his subsequent law school career. Barbara was so angry with her ex-husband that she went back to using her maiden name, Ayres. She said she was inspired to do so after a dream she had where she spoke to her deceased father. In the dream, he told her he was happy she would use the Ayres name. Barbara was happy too because she wanted to distance herself from her former husband. She also wanted to disappear from the public eye for a while.

The arrest of the four young men, however, would pull her back out.

"They're just people," she said of the suspects, "and I don't know who they are, and until I see them, face-to-face, I don't know how I'm going to have that feeling."

She spoke of how difficult it would be to have that initial confrontation. "When you have to look at someone who may have killed your children, you kind of have to wait until that happens until you can know."

One reporter wanted to know how the parents felt about the fact that police had questioned the boys one week after their daughters' murders. The parents were not aware that happened. Bob Ayers, Amy Ayres's father, however, was not upset. "It's water under the bridge. Why get upset about it now? Let's just take what we've got right now."

James Thomas, Eliza Thomas's father, backed up Ayers. "It's been gratifying to know that the investigation has continued."

The sentiment was continued by Barbara Ayres. She had nothing but praise for the Austin Police Department. "We have been taken care of emotionally and have shared this process, this grieving process, with so many people here in Austin, in the state of Texas."

Ayres's main concern, however, was that the judicial process be allowed to follow its own course without too much outside interference. She stressed the importance of fair trials for the suspects.

"It is important these young men get all they deserve in our judicial system, so that we never have to go back through this again, and don't want to have to go through the appeals, and their families are spared as much as possible," Ayres requested.

"We don't want to have the wrong people. We don't want anybody railroaded.

"We do want justice."

# CHAPTER 45

Barbara Ayres sought justice for the suspects. The court system, however, would not make life easy for them. Michael Scott was being held in Travis County Jail without bail. District Attorney Ronnie Earle stated that Robert Springsteen IV, who was being held without bail in West Virginia, would be extradited to Texas immediately. Judge W. Jeanne Meurer set bail for Forrest Welborn at $1 million and $1.5 million for Maurice Pierce.

Both Scott and Springsteen were staring at capital-murder charges. They could receive life-in-prison sentences or be sentenced to death by lethal injection.

Welborn and Pierce, who were minors at the time of the murders, were facing possible life-in-prison sentences. Earle stated he would seek to have them tried as adults.

*Monday, October 11, 1999*
*Kanawha County Circuit Court*
*Charleston, West Virginia*
*9:00 A.M.*

Going into the hearing for the extradition of Robert Burns Springsteen IV, Kanawha County prosecutor Bill Forbes relayed his biggest fear.

"It's very common for a murder suspect to get a bond here."

Forbes noted that most extradition hearings go on without a fight. "There's virtually no defense for extradition in this state, except for mistaken identity." He explained that most defendants waive extradition to save their financial coffers for the big fight. The magnitude of the charges levied against Springsteen, however, could inspire him to fight extradition, Forbes reasoned.

"He could be here anywhere from six months to a year, or he could be out of here next week."

Forbes also mentioned there was no death penalty in West Virginia. He sounded less than sympathetic to Springsteen's plight of extradition to Texas, infamous for its strong stance in favor of the death penalty.

"If I can't kill them here," the colorful attorney quipped, "maybe I can help kill them in Texas."

At 9:00 A.M., Robert Burns Springsteen IV arrived in the courtroom of circuit court judge Charles King. He was represented by attorney David Bungard. Forbes appeared on behalf of the state of West Virginia. They were joined by John Bencheri, Eliza Thomas's uncle, who drove almost ninety miles from Marietta, Ohio. He carried a high-school photograph of Eliza with him.

"We would challenge any extradition to the state of Texas," Bungard informed the judge. He cited the potential death penalty punishment by the state of Texas. He also suggested that Springsteen was not the killer.

Judge King granted a follow-up hearing for November 4. It would take place after Texas governor George W. Bush issued a rendition warrant to West Virginia governor Cecil Underwood.

Forbes stated afterward, "We're in a situation in this

state where it's very simple for anybody to delay anything for a long time." Forbes, nonetheless, believed it would be "pretty cut-and-dried that he will go back" to Texas.

"Every day you're not on death row is a good day."

# CHAPTER 46

*Wednesday, October 20, 1999*
*Charleston, West Virginia*

For Roy Rose, a sickness-free day was a good day. Robert Springsteen's best friend suffered from a number of maladies, some of which included chronic hepatitis C, fibromyalgia (a syndrome characterized by chronic pain in the muscles and soft tissues surrounding joints, fatigue, and tenderness at specific sites in the body), insomnia, and depression. The thirty-eight-year-old was a veritable walking pharmacy: Prozac, Valium, Elavil, Serzone, Klonopin, Darvocet, Tylox, Soma, Skelaxin, Ambien, and Restoril were some of the drugs he ingested to deal with his various medical problems.

The sickly Rose played an integral part in the Springsteen scenario. Rose was brought in to the Charleston Police Department on September 16, the day after Springsteen confessed to murder. Austin police detective Ron Lara requested Rose's presence and proceeded to ask him several questions about Springsteen. In the interview, Rose claimed Springsteen bragged to him about the killings. As a result of the interview, Austin officials wanted to fly Rose into Texas so he could testify against Springsteen.

Rose was a reluctant witness, to say the least. Through his attorney, John Hackney Jr., Rose claimed that the Austin police used "heavy-handed" tactics to elicit the statement. He specifically implicated Lara as the main progenitor of the questionable interrogation methods. Rose claimed that they would not let his wife enter the interview room, they turned off the air-conditioning in the room, and he was surrounded by four or five police officers.

When Lara asked Rose if he knew if Springsteen was involved in the killings, he responded that his friend mentioned that someone wanted to speak with him about the crimes. He claimed Lara, who sat in a chair with wheels, rolled up toward him and got right in his face. Lara allegedly refused to believe Rose did not know anything.

Rose became worried. He informed the officers of his various medical problems. One of the officers responded there was no problem—he was not impaired in any way. He just needed to keep talking.

Another officer asked Rose if he had ever been to Texas.

"Yes, I was born there," he responded.

"Well, you're about to go back at this time for a jail or prison sentence for withholding information," the officer threatened.

"Is it possible that Rob committed a robbery?" Lara asked.

"It's possible," Rose guessed.

"C'mon, Roy, we know you know that Rob told you he was in a robbery, that he told you all about it." Lara asked again, "Could he have committed a robbery?"

"Yeah, I guess so."

"Was he with anybody?"

"I really don't know about any of this."

"Yeah, you do! Yeah, you do!" Lara hollered. "We know he bragged to y'all about it."

Rose claimed that he became scared. He also claimed that he began to parrot back what the police officers told him. He said they shouted at him until he told them what they wanted to hear.

"Could this robbery have been botched?" Lara asked.

"It could have."

"It was going wrong," Lara assumed. "Rob had to do something, didn't he?"

"I really don't know anything about that," Rose pleaded on the verge of tears.

"Your best friend is bragging about this in great detail," Lara snapped in a harsh tone, according to Rose. "Now tell us what really happened."

"He shot her in the ear."

According to Rose, the detectives supposedly laughed.

"That's not it," Lara stated. He asked Rose if he knew anything about a rape.

"No, I don't know anything like that."

"Rob bragged about this so much we could hardly get him to shut up and leave. So just tell us. You're only making it harder on yourself."

"Yes, it could have happened," replied Rose.

"Did Rob shoot her first or rape her first?"

"After he shot her, he raped her." Rose claimed his story was eventually changed to anal rape and shooting the girl in the back of the head afterward.

Lara allegedly wanted to know what the other guys were doing at the scene.

"Ransacking the place," Rose responded.

"Were there any other employees working?"

"A couple of other girls around twenty years old, and maybe a guy."

"What did the other guys do with the other employees?"

"They were tied up."

"Were they gagged?"

"With their own clothes."

"Rob was really excited about telling you everything," Lara stated. "What did they do before they left?"

"They stole some cigarettes and ran out."

"Out of an ice-cream shop?"

"A convenience store," Rose stated. He later said Lara twisted his words until the crime scene became an ice-cream shop.

"What did they do before they left the scene?" Lara allegedly asked again.

"I don't know."

"Didn't Rob say he torched the place?" Lara bellowed in a loud voice.

Rose claimed he "gave in to this idea that yes, Rob said he torched the place."

"What did Rob tell you he used to do it with?"

"A cigarette lighter."

"That's wrong. C'mon, Rob told you this."

"A bomb," Rose changed his story. "Gasoline. Lighter fluid. They torched the place [and] they ran out and down the street."

Rose complained about the commotion inside the interview room. He said detectives kept coming in and out of the room and they received continuous pages on their pagers. They also continually interrupted him.

The commotion led to confusion, Rose claimed. He claimed Lara would yell at him when he did not say something appropriate. Also, he claimed Lara called him a liar and slammed his hands down on the table scaring Rose. He also claimed they threatened to put him in jail if he did not tell them what they wanted to hear.

"At some point in all this, I began saying anything I thought would get me out of the room," Rose confessed.

"The statement given on September 16, 1999, was coerced, is false, and I cannot stand by it."

Because of the alleged coercion, Rose defiantly declared he would not testify in Texas against Springsteen. His attorney, Hackney, stated, "While Springsteen is his friend and acquaintance, he's saying Springsteen didn't tell him anything to lead him to believe he was guilty of this heinous crime." Hackney added that his client was "not a material witness." He also relayed information that Rose had been readmitted to the local hospital for heart problems.

Rose's wife, Charlene, defended her husband by saying that he had taken morphine before he was questioned by Austin officials. "He was taking narcotics—prescription drugs—at the time they questioned him, and he didn't care." She was upset at what she believed was a three-hour intense intimidation session. "He did eventually tell them what they wanted to hear and signed a statement. They basically fed information to him."

The common refrain of coercive police tactics in the yogurt shop case had once again reared its hideous head.

Despite Rose's protestations that he would not testify against Springsteen, he had no say in the matter. The Travis County District Court had already secured a subpoena to make sure that he would be compelled to testify.

# CHAPTER 47

*October 20, 1999*
*Office of the Governor*
*Austin, Texas*

In an official press release, Texas governor George W. Bush sent a formal request to Governor Cecil Underwood of West Virginia for the extradition of Robert Springsteen IV.

"I hope the extradition will take place as quickly as possible so Robert Springsteen will be brought to justice for a crime he allegedly committed in Texas," said Bush.

*Thursday, October 21, 1999*
*Ninety-eighth Judicial Civil District Court*
*Austin, Texas*

Maurice Pierce and Forrest Welborn appeared before Judge W. Jeanne Meurer. The ever-present Detective Ron Lara was also in attendance.

Lara testified that the Austin Police Department had garnered confessions from Michael Scott and Robert Springsteen. Within those confessions, Lara stated, was information that implicated both Pierce and Welborn in the murders as well.

Lara also testified that the detectives attempted to trip up Welborn during the interview process of Scott. He informed Judge Meurer that a surprise meeting between Scott and Welborn took place outside the former location of the yogurt shop.

"We decided," Lara testified, "if he was taken over there, he'd remember some events." Welborn had no idea that Scott would be present at the crime scene location. Lara stated that the meeting did not work, and they gathered no new information from Welborn.

More information was made public in regard to Pierce and Welborn and their potential involvement in the murders:

- Potential crime scene evidence had been sent to the state crime lab to possibly match the suspects.
- Welborn fled the scene but was picked up by the other three boys after the murders.
- All four boys were questioned soon after the murders.
- Pierce took a polygraph in 1991; however, the results of that test were missing.
- Pierce and Welborn were warned weeks ahead of time that they would be arrested.

Prosecutors claimed both young men had troubled pasts. Mention was made that Welborn had made bomb threats at a school and Pierce had been suspected in stealing a car.

Guillermo Gonzalez, the attorney for Pierce, and Robert Icenhauer-Ramirez, the attorney for Welborn, argued that neither man had a serious criminal record.

Pierce had a conviction for driving while intoxicated. Welborn had one charge of driving without a driver's license.

Gonzalez and Icenhauer-Ramirez also requested that Judge Meurer lower the bail for their clients. The attorneys mentioned that neither man fled over the previous eight years, despite the fact that police questioned them intermittently during that period of time. Gonzalez also mentioned that after they were warned they would be arrested, they did not flee. "They weren't going anywhere. They hadn't gone anywhere for eight years."

Judge Meurer agreed with the defense attorneys. As a result, she lowered the bail amount for each man. Bail was reduced for Welborn from $1 million to $375,000. For Pierce, the judge lowered bail from $1.5 million to $750,000.

Neither the Welborn family nor the Pierce family believed they would be able to raise the 10 percent of the total bail amounts to get their boys out of jail.

*Friday, October 22, 1999*
*Springsteen-Moss Residence*
*Charleston, West Virginia*

Robin Moss was afraid. Robert Springsteen's forty-six-year-old wife was attempting to cope with the reality that her husband of less than two years would have an extradition hearing in two days. A hearing that could possibly send him to Texas, the state with more executions than any other in the United States.

According to the United States Department of Justice (DOJ), the state of Texas executed thirty-five individuals in 1999. Virginia was the state with the second-highest number of executions at fourteen.

The number of executions in Texas had increased dramatically in the preceding two decades. Texas executed 297 death row inmates from 1930 to 1977. From 1977 to 1999, the total number of executions was 199, well on its way to surpassing the previous forty-seven years.

"We have been picked up out of reality and dropped into a nightmare," declared Moss.

Not only did she not believe her husband committed the murders, she did not believe he willingly confessed to them either.

"He'd been terrorized," Moss said when her husband returned home from the interview. "He was crying, pale, absolutely sick. I think they frightened him to death." She had hope, however, when no arrest was made in the immediate week after the interview. She claimed that her husband did not hit the road because "he didn't think they'd ever be back."

Moss was realistic about the possible extradition: "This is my husband's life. It is fragile and it is out of our hands."

# CHAPTER 48

*Monday, October 25, 1999*
*Kanawha County Circuit Court*
*Charleston, West Virginia*

The life seemed drained out of Robert Springsteen as he entered Judge Charles King's courtroom. He was dressed in a prison-issue orange jumpsuit with a brown corduroy jacket draped over his shoulders. The clinking of shackles could be heard as he slowly shuffled toward the defense table. His ankles were bound together, as were his hands. He was joined by his attorney, David Bungard.

Bungard immediately informed Judge King he intended to file a petition that would challenge evidence used to support an arrest warrant for his client. Specifically, the statement he gave to police wherein he implicated himself in the murders.

"I'm not going to turn this extradition proceeding into a civil trial," Judge King informed Bungard. "I think this only serves one purpose—delay, delay, delay.

This is not a big deal and I'm not going to let it become one."

Nonetheless, King granted the request and tentatively scheduled a follow-up extradition hearing to take place within a month's time.

# CHAPTER 49

Robin Moss was determined to make a last-ditch effort to keep her husband out of Texas. She wrote an impassioned plea, which was posted on TexasJustice.com, the Web site created by Robert's stepfather, Andrew "Brett" Thompson, which he designed to point out the flaws in the case against his stepson. Moss's letter provided an excellent overview of what many believed were the difficult issues in the case.

Moss wrote of the devastation wrought on her family by her husband's arrest. "We have had to seek help from officials and professionals whom we must entrust with Robert's life. West Virginia appears to be ready to hand over one of its own to a state wanting to kill him without questioning anything."

Moss believed her husband was in trouble simply because of "his naive cooperation with the Austin police on September 15, 1999." She continued by placing the blame on police, the legal system, and the media. "We presumed there were checks and balances in place to protect innocent people and that our patience and trust in the justice system would prevail. We have been amiss in those beliefs and presumptions. Instead, we find Robert is treated as if he had already been convicted by virtue of negative media coverage immediately following his arrest."

Moss directed her skepticism toward the Austin Police Department. "It is well known that Austin developed a 'special unit' in August of this year to 'solve' the Yogurt Shop Murders. The unit's directive was to put the murders to rest by the year 2000. Strangely, they were able to unravel this eight year old murder in weeks without the help of new evidence." She also referenced the previous confessions in the case. "It is also common knowledge," she stated, "that the Austin police, in their zeal to satisfy public outcry for not having found the perpetrators of the horrific crime, have previously attempted to coerce statements from innocent individuals through suspicious practices."

Moss wrote that she used to never pay attention to injustices within the legal system. "Those situations did not directly affect my life, so I, like many of you, had no interest in further investigation in the facts surrounding the allegations. I had been lulled into believing that only guilty people had to worry."

Moss warned people that they need to be aware that what happened to her husband could happen to any one of them. "You may take for granted that you are not at risk for something like this to occur in your world. Perhaps you feel safe in the normalcy of your life as we once did. Maybe you won't know the fear of having the one you love snatched ou(t) of your life without warning or justification."

Moss concluded, "I used to feel safe too. The truth is, my husband is innocent. He is a good person who has been caught in a nightmare. We, his family, are overwhelmed and helpless."

# CHAPTER 50

One of the last people anyone expected to show up at the courthouse steps for Robert Springsteen's extradition hearing was Erik Moebius, the same man who posited the theory that the yogurt shop murders were part of a large conspiracy, and who had been disbarred from the state of Texas in 1995 for misconduct. Moebius claimed he now represented Robert Springsteen.

One problem. He didn't.

Apparently, Robert Springsteen III, Robert's biological father, hired Moebius to represent his son. Springsteen's family in West Virginia, however, claimed Moebius had nothing to do with Robert's case. Regardless, Moebius made sure his presence was felt.

The previous Monday morning, Moebius, armed with a fifteen-page legal brief requesting a change of venue for extradition hearings from local court to federal court, had rushed into Judge King's courtroom. Three days later, U.S. magistrate judge Jerry Hogg denied the petition for removal. "None of the bases for accepting jurisdiction in this court are valid and that no credible legal authority was cited."

"We're neither surprised nor upset by the ruling," proclaimed Moebius. "The most important thing is to keep the boy in West Virginia." He spoke of Judge Hogg's ruling, "In effect, he stated we need more law to point out where we can take jurisdiction. And we have more law." His strategy was simple: "We will literally be flooding that court with affidavits and case law."

These assertions came as a surprise to Robert Springsteen's state court attorney, David Bungard.

# CHAPTER 51

*Thursday, November 4, 1999*
*Rose Residence*
*Charleston, West Virginia*

Charlene Rose walked into her home after a hard day's work. She expected to be greeted by her husband, Roy, but he was nowhere to be found. Charlene noticed something on the kitchen table.

It was a note from her husband: "The police took me to court and to jail—9 *a.m.*"

Unbeknownst to Charlene Rose, her husband was taken away by two Charleston police detectives. They had a warrant for his arrest for contempt of court. Rose was taken to Kanawha Circuit Court, where Judge King ordered him behind bars at the South Central Regional Jail. The judge required that he remain there until he boarded a plane and was flown to Austin.

"I guess I'm lucky they let him write that," Charlene Rose said.

"They are taking this terminally ill man on chemotherapy and treating him like this?" Charlene pondered. "I don't see what the big hurry is."

John Hackney Jr. filed a writ of habeas corpus on behalf of Roy Rose. The writ stated that Rose's medical condition would make it near impossible for him to fly to Texas. Apparently, Rose's heart problems had been upgraded to a possible heart attack. Dr. Jon Murphy also included a letter in the writ that stated, "I feel strongly that this travel and stressful interrogation will cause deterioration in his delicate medical condition."

Charlene Rose was afraid for her husband. She was also pissed.

"If anything happens to my husband," she stated defiantly, "there's a lot of people who are going to be sued."

*Monday, November 8, 1999*
*Kanawha County Circuit Court*
*Charleston, West Virginia*

The second time Roy Rose appeared before Judge King, he was decked out in a prison-issue orange jumpsuit. He was also shackled with chains on his ankles and wrists. He wore shower shoes with no socks. The temperature outside was thirty degrees.

Judge King would make a determination that morning about what to do with Rose.

Charlene Rose testified on her husband's behalf. She reminded the court of her husband's poor health. Rose's cardiologist, Dr. William Harding, also testified on his patient's behalf. He asked the judge for a few accommodations to make life a little easier for the sickly Rose. One request was that if Rose was to be transported to Texas on a plane, he be given plenty of room to move around.

"He's a free man," stated Judge King, "not a prisoner. In fact, he will be staying in a hotel in Austin."

The reality, according to Charlene Rose, was that Judge King signed an order that would place her husband in the Travis County Jail, not the Four Seasons, when he arrived in Austin. In fact, as soon as the judge signed the forms, Rose was whisked away to a small private plane with the propellers practically spinning.

Rose was not allowed to move around on the flight. The officials also forgot to bring his medication.

When Rose arrived in Austin, he was driven past the Marriott, the Westin, and a La Quinta and directly to the Travis County Jail. Once imprisoned, Rose received none of his medication. According to his wife, guards opened his cell door every twenty minutes and flicked his lights on and off repeatedly and did not allow him to sleep.

Detectives also allegedly spoke to Rose for several hours over a period of two days about the case. Threats were made. He was told either testify or be put in prison. Rose, of course, agreed to testify.

When Rose eventually returned home to his wife in West Virginia, he did not tell her what he said before the grand jury. He was afraid to do anything wrong for fear that the Texas officials would come banging on his door again.

On November 13, 1999, Charlene Rose sent an "open letter" e-mail that was posted on TexasJustice.com. In it, she described the treatment her husband received and how they both feared for their lives. She summed up their mental states as:

> *My husband and I used to have a normal life. Now we both feel that things will never be the same. We are afraid of the police and the legal system that is supposed to protect us. We do not feel safe in our house.*
>
> *We pray that if my husband is ever compelled to Texas in the future that he receive proper noti-*

*fication and be protected from the Austin Police Department.*

She ended the e-mail with support for Springsteen: "We both continue to believe Robert Springsteen is innocent."

# CHAPTER 52

*Thursday, November 18, 1999*
*Kanawha County Circuit Court*
*Charleston, West Virginia*
*9:00 A.M.*

Ten days earlier, Robert Springsteen's legitimate lawyer, David Bungard, filed seven motions to keep his client from being extradited. Bungard focused his arguments on the criminal code differences between West Virginia and Texas. The main focus being that West Virginia did not execute the death penalty, while Texas did.

In the intervening ten days, Robert Springsteen found support from one interesting group. The Bar of England and Wales Human Rights Committee (BEWHRC), an international human rights organization, filed an amicus, or "friend of the court," brief on the suspect's behalf. The group did not argue for Springsteen, but rather against the death penalty. They cited that international law prohibited the execution of anyone who was under the age of eighteen at the time of the criminal act.

Bungard echoed these sentiments. In his motion, he wrote the imposition of the death penalty upon Springsteen "would remain so offensive, it would shock the conscience of the people of this state."

There were plenty of people in the courtroom who opposed the beliefs espoused by BEWHRC and Bungard. Namely, Eliza Thomas's uncle John Bencheri and Mark Harbison and Fred McClain, uncles of Jennifer and Sarah Harbison. The three men were adorned with black-and-white "We Will Not Forget" buttons.

Thus, the stage was set.

Bungard repeated his argument. Judge King, however, was reticent. He stated he did not want West Virginia to become a hideout haven for individuals who wanted to avoid capital punishment.

"What you're saying is our citizens can go to other states, rob banks and kill people, and then come back here without facing the death penalty?" the judge questioned Bungard. Springsteen's attorney argued that his client should be eligible only for the maximum possible punishment in West Virginia, which is life without parole.

King did not bite.

Extradition was granted.

A few hours later, Springsteen, clad in his orange jumpsuit, was led by a Texas Ranger onto the tarmac at Yeager Airport. The shackled suspect was guided toward a small turboprop plane used to fly him back to Texas. A crowd gathered behind a chain-link fence to watch the spectacle. He looked up as the Ranger double-checked his restraints and noticed the crowd. Springsteen gave them a big thumbs-up sign.

Robin Moss was eager to give the entire proceeding an entirely different finger. Springsteen's wife could not believe what had just occurred. She was terrified for her husband.

"I'm no longer a believer in the justice system," she told reporters gathered around her after her husband was flown out of the state. "They can do virtually anything they want to do. There's no way he's involved in something this horrendous."

# CHAPTER 53

*Monday, November 29, 1999*
*Ninety-eighth Judicial Civil District Court*
*Austin, Texas*

Forrest Welborn and Maurice Pierce both appeared before Judge Meurer for a hearing to determine whether they should be tried as adults or minors.

In the state of Texas, a person who is under the age of seventeen when a crime is committed cannot face the death penalty. Pierce was sixteen and Welborn was fifteen at the time of the yogurt shop murders. The determination of the hearing would be whether or not they could have been considered adults at the time of the murder. If they were found to be so, each young man could face a maximum sentence of life in prison. If they were not to be certified as adults, all charges against them would be dropped because suspects over the age of eighteen cannot be tried in juvenile court.

The atmosphere was more like a capital-murder trial than a juvenile-certification hearing.

Detective Robert Merrill testified against the two

suspects. He stated Pierce was called the "mastermind" of the crime by Michael Scott and Robert Springsteen in their confessions.

Robert Icenhauer-Ramirez, the attorney for Welborn, and Guillermo Gonzalez, the attorney for Pierce, had harsh words about the investigation. Icenhauer-Ramirez stated police used "terrible and deplorable investigative techniques" to garner information. He also cited a lack of evidence when he claimed the officers had "no reasonably trustworthy information" that would implicate Welborn.

Merrill continued to testify to the specific details of the crime. It was the first time the information was released to the public.

Some of the details Merrill mentioned were:

- Pierce came up with the idea to rob a store.
- Pierce bought yogurt from the girls while Scott and Springsteen propped open the back door.
- The boys returned to Northcross Mall and waited for it to get dark.
- Pierce told Welborn to wait in the car and serve as a lookout.
- Pierce, Scott, and Springsteen entered through the propped open back door.
- They noticed a single key in the front-door inside lock.
- The boys told the girls to disrobe.
- The boys tied up the girls' hands and feet with their own undergarments.
- Pierce attempted to ransack the cash register. When he saw that there was very little money in the drawer, he demanded one of the girls show him where the money was kept. When she said there was no money available, Pierce shot her in the back of the head, execution-style.

- Pierce then turned to the second girl, asked her the same question, got the same response, and shot her in the back of the head.
- Pierce ordered Springsteen to rape one of the girls, which he did.
- Scott attempted to rape one of the girls but could not achieve an erection.
- Pierce threatened Scott to kill the girl or he would be next—Scott complied.
- Pierce told Scott to shoot Amy Ayers, which he did. She did not die, however, so Pierce shot her again. She crawled away, so Pierce strangled her.
- Scott hauled the bodies together in a pile and set them on fire.
- Welborn took off and was later picked up by the boys.
- They drove to a bridge and threw away one of the guns.

The shocking details made some in the audience gasp. The parents of the girls audibly wept as Merrill described what happened to their daughters.

"'The girls were crying and whimpering. They were begging us not to kill them. They said that they didn't want to die,'" Detective Manuel Fuentes read from Scott's written statement.

Afterward, Pam Ayers told reporters that she did not know all of the details as to how her daughter had been killed. Barbara Ayres added, "As horrible as it was, we had to hear it. They suffered it. Now we're finding out, it's as bad as we could have feared."

On the other side of the aisle, Bill Pierce, Maurice's father, believed Merrill's testimony cleared his son. He believed Merrill's admission that the confessions had changed and shifted throughout proved his son's innocence. Basically, Scott and Springsteen lied; therefore, their entire confessions were deemed untrustworthy.

"We know that he had nothing to do with it," the elder Pierce believed.

Barbara Ayres, on the other hand, felt quite the opposite: "We've got the right ones. It's all right that it took eight years, as long as we've got the right ones."


The second day of the certification hearing was a day of videotapes. Parts of Scott's taped confession were played before the court. Also, a taped interview between Welborn and Austin police detective Douglas Skoulat was played. It was recorded during the same time frame as the Springsteen and Scott confessions.

Skoulat attempted to get Welborn to confess to being the lookout.

"You hear it every day in your head," the detective said to the long-haired Welborn during the interview. "You know you could have stopped it. Did you want it to end? Did you? Did you?"

"I don't remember," replied Welborn.

"Bullshit, you do remember," insisted Skoulat. "You can hear those bloodcurdling screams. You can hear the gunshots. You're hearing [them] right now," he dramatically stated. "You're hearing those girls scream and cry. You're never going to forget it."

Welborn sat silent for more than twenty minutes. He asked if he could leave. Skoulat ended the interview.

On Thursday, December 2, Detective John Hardesty testified about the joyride the four boys took the night after the murders. He also admitted that the detectives had no physical evidence that implicated either Welborn or Pierce.

The day before, however, Austin police detectives served search warrants on all four young men. The objective of the warrants was to collect blood and hair samples from each one. Apparently, there was evidence collected at the crime scene that may have matched any or all of the suspects. The evidence was given to Detective Paul Johnson.

Thursday remained a busy day outside the courtroom at the certification hearing of Welborn and Pierce as well. Bob Ayers declared he would seek to change the law for teenage murder suspects.

"If you're grown up enough to pull the trigger, you're grown up enough to stand trial." Ayers said even if the young men were not certified as adults, he would still push to change the law so a murder suspect from the age of fourteen to seventeen would automatically be charged as an adult. "We are going to live on the steps of the Capitol to get the law changed."

Meanwhile, Joe James Sawyer, Robert Springsteen's new lawyer, began to work the media. He was upset with the poor quality of the interview tape used in the confession of his client. The audio was marred by heavy static, which made the tape nearly unlistenable.

"Let's just say these geniuses [in the Austin Police Department] have proved once again how inept they are in investigating one of the most famous murders in Texas history."

Sawyer believed the police purposely mangled the recordings. "This is the single most important interview they're going to get," Sawyer exasperatedly stated, "and they botched that. I think it was a deliberate botch. We're now going to have an impaired recording."

Sawyer explained the significance of the turn of events. "Guess whose memories we're going to have to rely on? Yeah, the cops."

Springsteen's attorney also made it clear he was ready for a dogfight. He emphasized he looked forward to going to trial.

"First of all, I believe Springsteen is innocent,"

replied the zealous advocate. "I am not interested in a plea bargain for Rob."

*Monday, December 6, 1999*

Out of respect for the families of the victims, Judge Meurer postponed the certification hearings for the eighth anniversary of the girls' deaths. The postponement extended through December 7 as well.

*Wednesday, December 8, 1999*

The hearings resumed with Sergeant John Jones on the stand. The former lead investigator spoke of why the yogurt shop murders task force questioned Pierce and subsequently wrote him off as a suspect.

Jones gave several reasons as to why he dismissed Pierce as nothing more than a disillusioned teenager seeking attention. He noted, first, that Pierce asked for and took a lie detector test. He did not, however, state what the result of the examination concluded. Jones also mentioned the results of the test had been lost.

Jones stated Pierce allowed police to search his home. Nothing was uncovered.

Jones also testified Pierce agreed to wear a wire, or recording device, in an attempt to implicate Welborn in the murders. Jones informed the court, "It was obvious to everyone that Pierce was trying to force the issue on Welborn, who appeared to have no idea what Pierce was talking about."

Jones also admitted police were unable to match the revolver Pierce carried into Northcross Mall on December 14, 1991, with the bullets found at the yogurt shop.

Bruce Stevenson, the polygraph administrator who asked Michael Scott questions during his interview, testified he had also examined Forrest Welborn back in

1997. He claimed Welborn showed deception in the test when asked if he knew who killed the girls. On all other questions about the murders, including whether or not he participated or was in the shop, he showed no deception. Stevenson testified that Welborn also passed the polygraph when asked whether or not he had ever possessed a firearm that belonged to Pierce.

# CHAPTER 54

*Thursday, December 9, 1999*
*Ninety-eighth Judicial Civil District Court*
*Austin, Texas*

"We just want him to come home," said Forrest Welborn's mother, Sharon Pollard.

She would know soon enough whether her wish would be granted. Judge W. Jeanne Meurer convened court to decide whether Welborn and Maurice Pierce should be tried as adults in the murders of Amy Ayers, Eliza Thomas, Jennifer Harbison, and Sarah Harbison.

Defense attorneys were allowed to make their final pleas for their clients. Robert Icenhauer-Ramirez reminded the judge that Welborn was the only one of the four suspects who maintained his innocence from the get-go. He also stated he believed it was the Austin police detectives who tried to plant him at the scene when they interviewed Michael Scott and Robert Springsteen.

Guillermo Gonzalez, Pierce's attorney, was much more demonstrative. He claimed that he had no doubt that Springsteen and Scott had committed the murders.

He also blamed the police for forcing ideas into the two older boys' heads about his client.

"Like rats from a sinking ship, they were offered a way out," Gonzalez stated. "And sadly, they took it."

After hearing the last-minutes pitches, Judge Meurer was almost ready to make her decision. The parents of the girls sat in the front row of the courthouse. They all held hands. Judge Meurer leaned forward to give her opinion. She concluded both Welborn and Pierce's cases would be transferred to the adult legal system despite being minors during the commission of the crime. The parents of the girls let out a collective sigh upon the news.

Judge Meurer added she would not reduce the bail for either man.

Forrest Welborn's family, however, was able to raise 10 percent of his $375,000 bail the next day. The bail money was paid in cash. Donna Sproles, Welborn's aunt, contributed the majority of the deposit. The twenty-three-year-old suspect was released from Travis County Jail later that day. He was greeted by his father, Jimmy Welborn, and sister India. Tears silently dripped down his face as he was escorted away by his loved ones.

"It was hard for him being in there and being innocent," stated India. "He hasn't been able to see his son." She added her brother would return home to Lockhart and await trial.

It would be a while before any trial began.

Assistant District Attorney Gregg Cox stated that trials would not probably begin for another year. "Justice demands . . . that this case be allowed to proceed and that a jury sees this case," Cox proclaimed. He added that the district attorney's office had every intention of trying each of the suspects individually.

Bob Ayers commented, "This hearing is nothing compared to what the trial's going to be." He declared his family needed a break. "We're going to get some rest, put this behind us, stay in touch with the DA's office and let them tell us when the first trial date's going to be and where—and then we'll start preparing."

As for the additional wait, Ayers realized the wheels of justice were not controlled at his behest. Besides, he had already waited eight years.

"There is nothing we can do. There is nothing these boys can do except let the legal system work."

Pam Ayers added, "There is no relief really for what we are going through. But it is a relief that we have crossed at least one hurdle."

Sharon Pollard could only hope her son would receive a fair trial. "If this is their evidence," she wondered, "how could he be convicted?"

# CHAPTER 55

Tuesday, December 14, 1999
Blackwell-Thurman Criminal Justice Center
Austin, Texas

Judge Mike Lynch, criminal court judge for the 167th District, announced he placed a gag order on all parties involved in the yogurt shop case.

Joe James Sawyer, Springsteen's attorney, however, opposed the gag rule.

"Anytime you abridge the First Amendment, you're walking a tightrope," the boisterous Sawyer exclaimed.

Three hours later, District Attorney Ronnie Earle, with the parents of the slain girls by his side, announced his office would officially indict Robert Springsteen IV. He added he would seek the death penalty.

Wednesday, December 22, 1999

The families of two of the four suspects held a candle-light vigil to bring attention to what some people in

Austin believed to be a travesty. Fewer than twenty-five people showed up.

Philip Scott, Michael Scott's father, wanted to know what new evidence had been uncovered that would lead to the arrest of his son.

"It is tragic enough that four young girls were murdered, but to unjustly persecute four innocent boys is also a travesty.

"Why did the APD choose . . . to believe these boys were not involved in these murders for eight years?" wondered Scott. "Things just do not add up in this case."

Jeannine Scott, Michael Scott's wife, shared a similar belief.

"Mexican nationals, Satanists, People in Black, and more have been said to have been guilty in this case. Now, why these boys? We challenge the people of Austin to consider the case not only with their hearts, but also with their minds."

Maurice Pierce's wife, Kimberli Pierce, also participated in the vigil. She stated the "confessions of Mike Scott were very clearly coerced and pressured."

The Springsteen family, back in West Virginia, could not attend.

On the advice of his attorney, neither Forrest Welborn nor his family attended the vigil.

*Tuesday, December 28, 1999*

Ronnie Earle appeared again before a bank of microphones. He came to announce that the grand jury had convened. They were to decide whether Michael Scott and Maurice Pierce would have to stand trial. Earle confidently stated the grand jury had decided there was enough evidence to go forward with the charges against both men.

Earle added he would also seek the death penalty against Scott.

Pierce, on the other hand, would not face the death penalty, due to his age at the time of the murders.

No mention was made of Forrest Welborn other than "the investigation is continuing."

# CHAPTER 56

*Tuesday, May 2, 2000*
*Bureau of Alcohol, Tobacco, and Firearms*
*Dallas, Tx*

The beginning of 2000—or what many people mistakenly referred to as "the new millennium"—found things rather quiet on the yogurt shop front. The autopsies of the girls had been unsealed and reprinted in the local newspaper. Also, the specter of Erik Moebius's conspiracy theories raised its head. Tony Diaz, lawyer for Michael Scott, met twice with Moebius to get a clearer understanding of his complex insurance-scam theory. Diaz was intrigued by the theory.

"Whenever he tells me something, it seems plausible," explained Diaz. "Whether it's true or not, I don't know. But we probably will explore it."

Robert Springsteen's attorney, Joe James Sawyer, was less than thrilled with Moebius's intrusion. "I do not pay attention to, and give no credence to, the ravings of idle minds."

Otherwise, things seemed rather sedate. That is, until several gun issues arose.

The first issue involved a federal ballistics report on the .22-caliber revolver Maurice Pierce had been arrested with back on December 14, 1991. The ATF report stated the bullets found in the bodies of the girls did not match Pierce's gun. Ballistics expert John Murdock's research indicated the bullets found inside the girls' heads were not fired from Pierce's gun.

"My client has always insisted he is innocent," said attorney Guillermo Gonzalez. "They could have done it when they put this new task force together. They could have nipped this in the bud before making arrests."

Murdock also tested two .380-caliber semiautomatic guns. Neither gun was used to shoot the bullet recovered from Amy Ayers.

The ATF report forced the prosecution to scramble. It was time to find a gun.

*Friday, May 5, 2000*
*Loop 360—Pennybacker Bridge*
*Lake Austin*

The Texas Department of Public Safety's Dive Recovery Team decided to drag the lake. Based on Springsteen's confession, Pierce had allegedly tossed the .380 automatic pistol into Lake Austin.

State prosecutor Buddy Meyer feigned ignorance about the search. "I don't know that anything's missing here."

Springsteen's attorney was incensed. "As they have throughout this case, the state finds itself, once again, groping blindly in the dark."

Indeed, the search was near impossible. Lake Austin, which is also part of the Colorado River, had experienced six floods since 1991.

No gun was found.

* * *

*Wednesday, May 31, 2000*

The third gun issue involved the confession of Michael Scott.

Tony Diaz filed a change-of-venue request for his client due to extensive and biased pretrial publicity. Within the motion, Diaz included a statement and a photograph of the interview of his client with Detective Robert Merrill. The statement professed that Merrill had used a gun to coerce a confession from Scott. The photograph showed Merrill as he stood behind Scott in the interview room with his finger pointed at the back of Scott's head while holding a gun.

Diaz failed to mention that Scott had confessed to two completely different officers, besides Merrill, more than twenty-four hours before the alleged gun incident. Diaz also failed to mention the videotaped confession clearly showed Merrill holding the gun upside down, with the barrel pointing away from Scott's head, and no finger on the trigger. The videotape also showed Merrill jabbing his finger into the back of Scott's head for a split second and then quickly removing his hand and bringing it back around in front of Scott.

Regardless, Diaz achieved his goal, which was to get the still photograph of Merrill with the gun "in the vicinity" of Scott's head out to the public. The picture was widely seen by the citizens of Austin and beyond, via newspapers, magazines, and the Internet.

Sawyer confronted Merrill about the gun during a pretrial hearing to determine whether or not Judge Lynch would allow in Springsteen's confession.

"Are you the person who crammed the gun in the back of his head?" asked the irrepressible Sawyer.

The query raised an objection from prosecutor Buddy

Meyer: "We want to try this case in court, not in the media." The objection led to an argument between Sawyer and Meyer. Finally Judge Lynch asked Sawyer to rephrase his question.

"Was Mr. Scott's statement in any way coerced?"

"No," replied Merrill.

"What would you deem to be coercion?"

"Forcing him to tell."

"If, hypothetically, someone placed a gun to the back of a person's head, would that be coercion?" Sawyer postulated.

"It might be."

"Was there a firearm present at the interview of Mr. Scott?"

"Yes."

"Did it come close to the back of his head?"

"It did."

"Did you scream at Mr. Scott?"

"Yes."

"Did you call him a 'pussy'?"

Meyer objected again.

"Mr. Sawyer, will you please get to the point?" pressed Judge Lynch.

"Your Honor, I believe I already have," replied the satisfied Sawyer.

# CHAPTER 57

*Wednesday, June 7, 2000*
*167th District Court*
*Austin, Texas*

Judge Mike Lynch was not in his office.

Had he been there, he would have received a disturbing letter. It was addressed by grand jury member Diana Castañeda, former member of the Austin School Board. Castañeda wrote that she believed the prosecution was not completely forthcoming in regard to the evidence presented to the grand jury.

"I am not convinced that the grand jury was treated in a forthright manner," Castañeda stated, "but rather used as pawns in what I assume to be a rush to judgment.

"I respectfully request that you hold a hearing . . . to determine whether the indictments returned by 147th [*sic*] our grand jury were obtained by deception or withholding evidence."

Castañeda cited no particulars. She gave no specifics of the charges she levied against the prosecutors. She did say, however, she followed coverage of the case in the newspaper.

*Thursday, June 22, 2000*
*167th District Court*
*Austin, Texas*

Guillermo Gonzalez sought to lower Maurice Pierce's bail substantially. He had what he believed was compelling evidence of the deception being perpetrated by the police officers investigating the yogurt shop murders.

Gonzalez informed Judge Lynch that Detective Paul Johnson admitted to him he knew Maurice Pierce's .22 revolver may not have been the gun used in the murders. And he knew even before Michael Scott and Robert Springsteen confessed and implicated Pierce.

Detective Johnson testified in the pretrial hearing about a ballistics test run on the bullets by the Austin Police Department ballistics division back in January 1999. The results proved to be almost identical to those reported by the ATF's May 2000 report.

Johnson testified he did not mention the test in the November 1999 certification hearings because he "forgot." He claimed he intended to include the finding in one of his reports; however, it slipped his mind.

Despite the omission, Lynch only lowered Pierce's bail from $750,000 to $700,000.

Kimberli Pierce cried as she told reporters that she still could not afford to get her husband out of prison.

"He has a family. He has a daughter. He will not run. Innocent people don't run."

# CHAPTER 58

*Friday, June 30, 2000*
*299th District Court*
*Austin, Texas*

Forrest Welborn had kept a low profile ever since he was bailed out of jail the previous December. A second grand jury took on his case in March. Their term ended the day before, on Thursday, June 29. The prosecution did not make its case in time; therefore, the grand jury did not bring charges against the alleged lookout.

As a result, Judge Jon Wisser officially dismissed all charges against Welborn.

District attorney trial chief Buddy Meyer claimed Welborn was not out of the woods just yet. "The state has no legal basis to contest the motion that has been filed here today, but Forrest Welborn still remains under investigation for the murders."

Welborn's official status changed from accused to suspect.

Everyone around him hoped the dropped charges would help him get back on the right track with his life. Ever since his arrest, he lost his automobile repair shop and was unable to find work after his release.

"This whole ordeal has been a horrible strain on Forrest and his family," stated his mother, Sharon Pollard.

Welborn's attorney, Robert Icenhauer-Ramirez, again stood behind his client. "He has always denied being there. I think this guy is innocent."

The parents of the girls were not so quick to agree.

Pam Ayers believed the grand jury made a mistake. "I just don't exactly know what his role was, but I believe he had a role in it."

Barbara Ayres added, "They don't have enough evidence to hold him now. That doesn't mean they won't have more evidence after the others are tried."

It would be almost another year before the first trial took place.

# PART III

# TRIBULATIONS

# CHAPTER 59

*Tuesday, May 8, 2001*
*167th District Court*
*Austin, Texas*

After nearly ten months of legal housecleaning, interminable delays, and twelve days of jury selection, the trial of Robert Springsteen IV began.

The defense team included fifty-five-year-old Joe James Sawyer, a graduate of the University of Texas undergraduate school and law school, a burly man with an old-school Texas twang and charm to boot. According to sources, Sawyer had a reputation for throwing back a cold one or three. His partner at the defense table was Berkley Bettis.

The prosecution consisted of Darla Davis, an energetic assistant district attorney who worked on the disappearance and subsequent murder case of Atheist leader Madalyn Murray O'Hair, Robert Smith, the assistant district attorney who requested the girls' autopsies be sealed back in 1992, and Efrain de la Fuente, who grew up as a migrant farmworker who toiled in the fields. His father gained his United States citizenship with the help of Cesar Chavez. De la Fuente was a battalion commander in the ROTC, attended college at St. Mary's in San Antonio, and was an officer in the United States Army. De la Fuente studied law at Drake University. After law school, he became a JAG officer. He later worked as a prosecutor and a defense lawyer.

The proceedings would be overseen by Judge Mike Lynch, a University of Texas Law School graduate, former prosecutor, and former defense lawyer, who became a judge in 1993.

Judge Lynch received support from court reporter Jim King, head bailiff Salvador "Sal" Hernandez, who was later voted Best Dressed Bailiff in the 2002 *Austin Chronicle* "Readers' Poll," and assistant bailiff Bob Burnett.

The pain was evident on the faces of the victims' families as they entered the courtroom. Bob Ayers spoke of how his feelings had changed over time. "I said before that I had no feelings toward them, but as I start to learn more, I'm starting to get mad."

The person Ayers was mad at entered the courtroom. Robert Springsteen, dressed in khaki pants and a button-down long-sleeved shirt, ambled in toward the defense table. He had put on several pounds while behind bars. The defendant took his chair at the table. Once seated, he looked around to see who was there to support him. The majority of his family had been subpoenaed by the prosecution, so they were not allowed to attend the trial. His one constant was his grandmother Maryjane Roudebush. After he spotted his kin, Springsteen's eyes drifted over to the other side of the aisle. There he saw Bob and Pam Ayers, Maria Thomas, and Barbara Ayres-Wilson (who had remarried before the trial), seated in the first two rows directly behind the prosecution table.

Robert Smith stepped forward to make the opening argument for the state against Robert Burns Springsteen

IV. He began by re-creating the night of December 6, 1991. He spoke of the girls at work. He mentioned how Springsteen propped open the back door of the yogurt shop with a pack of cigarettes. How the boys returned to the store and entered through that same door. He talked about how each girl was tied up and executed by the defendant. Smith's soft delivery style contrasted drastically with the despicable imagery he painted.

"Robert Springsteen and his friends left out the back door on December 6, 1991, and they have successfully eluded justice until today."

Smith spoke of the distorted crime scene caused by fire and water damage. How it was difficult to obtain usable evidence because of the destruction of the scene.

Smith discussed the states of the girls' bodies. How they were lying. Distinguishing characteristics of what was done to them. He mentioned the ice scoop and how it was used on Sarah Harbison. He spoke of how Sarah removed her boyfriend's ring before she was forced to strip off her clothes.

Smith talked about the makeup of the police homicide division back in 1991. He mentioned how severely understaffed the group was and how that led to several problems involved in the murder case.

The prosecutor detailed the different interviews conducted with Robert Springsteen, Michael Scott, Forrest Welborn, and Maurice Pierce. He covered the confessions given by Scott and Springsteen. Of Springsteen's confession, he said, "You will . . . see the complex inner workings of a guilty mind who tries to deny, to avoid, to shift blame, and ultimately to admit responsibility."

Smith looked at the jury as he closed. "There is going to be no question that he did it. There is going to be no question, when you hear all of the evidence," he said as he turned toward Springsteen, "that you are sitting in the courtroom with the man who killed Amy Ayers."

Joe James Sawyer stood before the court to give his opening remarks. He acknowledged the jurors. "I will not say 'good morning' to you. That would be obscene. There is nothing good about a morning when we begin this process of discussing the deaths of four young girls in the presence of the family and loved ones," Sawyer solemnly stated. "And maybe the only thing to say in regard to that, that is sufficient, is, 'Unto the day is the evil of the day.'"

Sawyer immediately honed in on the crime scene processing. He questioned the lack of protocol for logging in participants at the crime scene that night. He also pointed out a dichotomy in Robert Smith's opening statement in regard to the evidence.

"Mr. Smith told you two things at once," he declared to the jury. "That the fire destroyed this crime scene, and yet he was able to show you with great exactitude the plentitude of evidence that actually came out of the crime scene."

Sawyer questioned the issue of holdback information in the case. "Within weeks of this crime, the details of the crime had become almost meaningless."

Springsteen's representative also discussed the issue of the fire. "I'll tell you something else Mr. Smith didn't tell you"—Sawyer paused as he spotted a juror who seemed to waver—"and if this bores you, I'm sorry—this may be one of the key issues in this trial. How did this fire begin?" Sawyer briefly touched on how fire investigator Melvin Stahl conducted an on-site investigation, yet the state chose not to use his report in the case.

"What does it tell us, then, about the crime scene? Maybe the evidence begins to speak to us. Maybe these killers weren't so bold that they shot and strangled this girl and then took the time to build a fire on top of someone. Maybe something else happened.

"That fire may be the single most important piece of evidence for you to consider."

Sawyer also mentioned politics.

"Another component, that is, another subtext to this case, that is nasty but true, and that was the sheer political pressure to solve this case."

He also mentioned that several people confessed to the murders before his client did.

Sawyer also spoke about the possibility of police misconduct.

"Remember, remember—the police may lie. Remember that these police are going up there naked . . . with not a shred of evidence to support any accusation against this man," he stated as he nodded toward Springsteen.

Sawyer closed by saying, "This case excited our city in a very negative way. Excited our city as no case probably ever has before and, I pray to God, never will again.

"But when you sift through it . . . you begin to see a pattern of evidence that . . . points to another possibility, if not probability, if not with absolute definitude."

*1:00 P.M.*

The state hoped to open their case on a strong, emotional note. Robert Smith called Bob Ayers to the stand. Ayers spoke of life with his daughter. What she enjoyed. The things she did to make her family happy. He also spoke of December 6, 1991.

"She followed us to the door," Amy's father recalled. "We told her we loved her. She told us that she loved us, and she locked the door behind us."

"And was that the last time you ever saw your daughter alive?" Smith asked.

"Yes, sir."

The prosecution followed with Barbara Ayres-Wilson, mother of Sarah and Jennifer Harbison. Ayres-Wilson gave more emotional testimony about the last day of her daughters' lives.

Next up was Maria Thomas, mother of Eliza Thomas. She spoke of how she helped her daughter with her sick pig the morning of December 6, 1991. She also recalled how she saw all four girls alive in the yogurt shop just hours before their deaths.

Eliza's father, James Thomas, gave similar testimony about seeing his daughter and her three friends at the restaurant on the night of the murders.

After Mr. Thomas, the state called Sam Buchanan, Jennifer Harbison's boyfriend. Buchanan was a successful baseball player at Lanier High School at the time. He also had been sexually active with Jennifer Harbison. In fact, his semen had been found in her vagina at the crime scene. Buchanan talked about attending his grandfather's funeral the day Jennifer was murdered.

Next up was Sarah Harbison's boyfriend, Michael McCathern. Michael and Sarah had been dating for one month at the time of her death. The young man spoke of the ring he had given Sarah. It had a green stone in the middle, with a tractor on one side and his initials on the other side.

It was an extremely tearful beginning to what would be an emotionally wrenching trial.

After bringing the girls to life through their loved ones' testimony, Smith shifted gears. He now needed to re-create what happened that night for the jury.

He began with Dearl Croft.

Croft detailed his visit to the yogurt shop that night. He spoke about a strange encounter with a boy in a green fatigue army jacket.

The next key witness was Officer Troy Gay, now a lieutenant, the man who first spotted the smoke and fire at the yogurt shop. He was the first witness to describe the details of the crime scene. He was also the first witness the defense team cross-examined.

The final witness for the day was fire specialist Rene Garza, who described extinguishing the fire inside the shop. He also described the discovery of the bodies.

## Wednesday, May 9, 2001

The first portion of the second day of testimony covered more firefighter and police officer descriptions of the crime scene. On cross-examination, the defense team focused on the number of personnel traipsing through the murder site and the dissemination of crime scene information. Sawyer also pressed the firefighters if they recalled Sergeant John Jones's arrival at the yogurt shop with a Channel 7 cameraman and newsreader.

The second half of the day featured testimony from Texas Department of Public Safety crime scene investigator Irma Rios. She spoke at length about the processing of the yogurt shop murder scene.

Rios recalled the process of collecting evidence that night. To illustrate her testimony, the prosecution projected several graphic photographs of the girls' corpses. The larger-than-life-size views of a naked Amy Ayers and the other three girls' charred bodies caused ripples of emotion throughout the courtroom.

The families of the girls wept openly.

Barbara Ayres-Wilson looked away from the photographs of her daughters. It was especially difficult because she should have been celebrating Jennifer's twenty-seventh birthday this day.

## Thursday, May 10, 2001

Judge Lynch attempted to kick the day off on a humorous note. After the jury was seated, he asked if they experienced problems with the new high-tech facility's elevators. It was an ongoing problem ever since the building was built.

"We had a FedEx guy trying to get up here to deliver a package," the judge recalled, "and we decided he spent more time between the first floor and the eighth floor than he did from here to Dallas."

A few of the jurors grinned and nodded knowingly.

It was a nice anecdote to the grim testimony that would follow.

Smith finished up his questioning of Irma Rios rather quickly. He passed the witness to Joe James Sawyer, who immediately pounced on the fire evidence in relation to the girls' bodies.

Sawyer asked Rios if she took pictures of the floor where the girls' corpses lay after they were removed. He mentioned it was important because "you can later determine whether or not the person had been moved, whether the person was there when the fire began, [or] whether the person was there when the fire started." Sawyer pointed out a bare spot underneath Jennifer Harbison in one crime scene photograph. He surmised that that indicated she was there when the fire started.

Sawyer also asked Rios if she smelled anything unusual at the murder site.

"I did not smell anything like gasoline or any kind of accelerant." She added, "There could have been another accelerant used."

Sawyer wanted to know if Rios knew the whereabouts of the metal shelves located in the back of the yogurt shop—the same shelves upon which, arson investigator Melvin Stahl claimed, the fire began.

"The metal shelves were not collected."

"Would you agree with me," Sawyer responded, "that the preservation of those shelves would have been important . . . to help the jury determine the truth of the origin of the fire?"

Rios declined to answer fully. She claimed that she was not an arson investigator; therefore, she was not properly suited to answer that question.

"The fire burned with sufficient intensity to melt an aluminum alloy in the aluminum ladder. Did you collect the ladder?" Sawyer followed up.

"No, I didn't," answered Rios.

"Did anyone collect it?"

"No."

"So it's not available for the jury to examine or for anyone to testify about the intensity of the gases at the top of that fire?"

"No."

Sawyer continued to attempt to show disorder at the crime scene with Rios and the DPS crime scene investigative team.

"Wasn't Mr. Les Carpenter, from the medical examiner's office, on the scene demanding that you release the bodies to him and arguing about the procedures that you were following?"

"I wouldn't describe that as demanding," answered Rios. "We had a discussion about the collecting and the removal of the bodies."

Sawyer also asked if she changed latex gloves every time she took a swab. Rios stated, "Whenever they looked contaminated."

"You understand that not changing gloves between swabs in the field furthers the risk of cross-contamination," proclaimed Sawyer. "That is, if a contaminant is taken off the swab onto the glove and then you swab the second thing, that you have enhanced the risk of cross-contamination."

The picture Sawyer painted did not look good for the prosecution.

The grim testimony continued when medical examiner Dr. Tommy Brown testified. Brown performed the autopsies on the four girls on Saturday morning, December 7, 1991. He presented pictures of the autopsies to the jury as he described specific details of their deaths. He did not show the photographs to the gallery.

Brown described how each girl was shot at point-blank range. Each received a "contact gunshot wound." He described such a wound as one that "when the gun is pressed up against the scalp, the gas that comes out of the end of the gun barrel goes beneath the scalp, and there between the scalp and the hard bone, the gas expands that and splits the tissue or causes a laceration."

Brown went on to describe Amy Ayers's corpse.

"She had a gunshot wound that was located at the top of her head. . . . She also has another entrance gunshot wound in the left occipital area, which is located between the top of the ear and the back of the head.

"She also had a ligature around her neck. She had petechia, which is small blood hemorrhages all over her face but mainly around the orbits of the eyes.

"She had a bullet exit laceration of her right cheek area . . . bruise of the left lower lip area . . . hemorrhage around the right eye . . . [and a] scrape underneath her chin."

Brown stated that Amy's skin had received second-degree radiation burns.

DA Smith asked about the petechia. "What does the presence of petechia indicate to you, sir?"

"She had a ligature around her neck, and the ligature closes off the blood supply. When you close off the blood supply, then that backs up the blood and it causes petechia, or little blood blisters."

"What does that signify to you, sir?"

"Strangulation."

"Do you have an opinion as to whether or not she was alive at the time she was strangled?"

"Yes, she was alive," the doctor responded.

Smith followed up with the bullet wounds. "Now, you

described two separate gunshot wounds that you observed. Could you go through these in detail, please?"

"Yes, sir. The gunshot wound to the top of the head was five-eighths of an inch to the left of midline. The bullet went through the scalp. It hit the top of the skull and knocked a small plug, just a little bit larger than the size of the bullet, down on top of the brain. The bullet stopped there. It did not go into the brain."

The doctor testified that the first shot probably did not kill Amy Ayers. "She might have even been conscious after that gunshot," Brown added.

"Was there an exit wound associated with that first gunshot wound that you described?"

"No. I collected the bullet at the autopsy from in the skull. It's a small-caliber lead bullet."

"Could you describe, please, gunshot wound number two that you mentioned?" inquired Smith.

"That gunshot wound was located in the left temporal occipital area. It's four-and-a-half inches below the top of the head and it's three-and-a-half inches to the left of midline. It's in between the top part of the ear and the back of the head.

"This bullet was also a contact gunshot wound. [It] traveled through the left side of the cerebellum or the back part of the brain. It then struck the brain stem. It grazed across the floor of the right side of the cerebrum and it went in beneath the petrous bone, which is a bone at the base of the skull.

"When it did that, then it went down through the face and the sinuses . . . and came out in an exit wound, which is a slitlike exit wound present on the right anterior-cheek area. That was a 'through-and-through' gunshot wound."

"Did you note injury along the bullet track inside the brain itself?" asked Smith.

"Yes. It did significant injury to the cerebellum,

brain stem, and also the cerebrum and the base of the skull. It also caused some fractures of the base of the skull at various points."

"Do you have an opinion as to whether or not this would have been a fatal gunshot wound?"

"Yes, this was fatal. It would have been instantaneous because of the location of the wound track. This would have been an instantaneous death."

"Do you have an opinion as to whether or not she was, in fact, alive before she was shot with that second gunshot?"

"In my opinion, she was alive when this gunshot wound was delivered to her head."

Dr. Brown also performed a rape kit to determine whether Amy Ayers had been sexually assaulted.

"Did you note any trauma to the female sexual organ or rectum of Amy Ayers?"

"No."

"Does the absence of trauma in your experience preclude the possibility that sexual activity had occurred of some kind?"

"No."

The potential rape of Amy Ayers was a key factor for the defense's argument. Part of Michael Scott's testimony was that he raped Amy before she died.

Dr. Brown methodically plowed through the autopsy results of Eliza Thomas, Sarah Harbison, and Jennifer Harbison. He described how he believed each girl was killed. He also spoke of the damage the fire caused to the three girls.

He described the condition of Eliza Thomas's body as "seriously charred from the top of her head to the bottom of her feet. She had third-degree burns. Some people call it fourth degree, in which the charring has occurred. She had burned away the top part of her hair in the front, and her face, ears, and . . . all of her face was extremely charred."

Brown testified that Eliza's neck, chest, abdomen, genitalia, and lower legs were charred. The fire was so hot that it caused heat ruptures, or rupturing of the skin, similar to the rupturing of a hot dog that had been left too long in a microwave, around her pelvis and thighs. Her back and buttocks showed sparing, which indicated her body lay on its back while she burned.

Brown also stated that Eliza had a gag in her mouth, which was tied at the back of the neck. Furthermore, her hands had been tied behind her back with a bra.

A sexual assault examination did not indicate any sexual abuse. Eliza did have some blood in her endometrium, or the lining of her uterus, which indicated she may have been on her period.

Similar to Amy, Eliza died from a contact gunshot wound to the back of the head. She, too, was dead before the fire.

Sarah Harbison's autopsy findings were similar to Eliza's. She had been severely charred. A gag was found in her mouth. Hands tied with panties. Heat ruptures on her lower extremities. Dr. Brown also discovered "abrasions of the inner—the vestibule or the opening into the vagina."

"Can you tell us what you mean when you say an 'abrasion'?" asked Smith.

"It's a forceful scrape of the skin," answered Dr. Brown. "This is a protected area, so it did not come from a fall. This would have to be some type of external force."

"Is it consistent with a penis or a hard type of object being inserted into her?"

"A hard object."

"Would it be consistent with that metal ice scoop being inserted into her vagina?"

"It could be."

Dr. Brown described Sarah's contact gunshot wound. It was slightly different from Amy's and Eliza's. The wound was located at "the direct center of the back of the head."

Dr. Brown also noted that Sarah wore a Mickey Mouse watch on her left wrist.

The sixty-two-inch, eighty-six-pound body of Jennifer Harbison was the most badly charred, according to Dr. Brown. The front part of her hair had burned off. Her face was burned so badly that her teeth were charred. She also had heat ruptures and severely burned genitalia. Her gunshot wound was similar to her best friend Eliza's: back of the head just to the left of the midline. Also, just like her best friend, she had been having her period.

Jennifer was also dead at the time of the fire, according to Dr. Brown.

Robert Smith passed the witness to Joe James Sawyer, who asked Judge Lynch if he could approach the bench. The judge agreed and the attorneys stepped toward the judge's bench.

"You actually saved me." Sawyer sighed. "I was afraid I was going to start crying."

"You what?" queried Judge Lynch, somewhat taken aback.

"I was afraid I was going to break down and start crying. I forgot how much these girls . . ." His voice trailed off. "I'm a father."

Judge Lynch announced a ten-minute recess.

Sawyer composed himself and crossed Dr. Brown. He attempted to discern the order in which the doctor believed weapons were used on Amy Ayers. Brown stated that he would place the strangulation first, the gunshot to the top of the head second, and the gunshot on the left side of the head third. Or, you could change the order of the strangulation and the gunshot wound to the top of the head.

Sawyer asked Brown to describe what he thought happened to Amy.

"The scenario I would put forth would be that they were all in the same room at one time. Amy had the spunk to try to get the hell out of there," Dr. Brown speculated. "And I think that she—I don't know if it was because of the ligature or if she was shot and she did not lose consciousness, but she knew that she was in for some horrible times, so she was trying to get out of there."

# CHAPTER 60

*Friday, May 11, 2001*
*167th District Court*
*Austin, Texas*

The main focus for the day was the fire. David Spence, supervisor of the trace evidence section of the Southwestern Institute of Forensic Science, aka the Dallas Medical Examiner's Office, discussed various types of accelerants. An accelerant is the source of ignition used to start a fire. He explained that just because no accelerants were detected did not mean one was not used. He also testified that water tends to wash away accelerants.

The fulcrum of the case for the defense, however, was on the horizon. Robert Smith called arson investigator Melvin Stahl to the stand. Stahl was the on-scene investigator at the yogurt shop.

Melvin Stahl worked for the Austin Fire Department for twenty-five years and one week. He retired on March 1, 1997. He was hired by AFD in 1972 and worked as a firefighter for six years. He was promoted to fire specialist at Station 20, where he worked for four years. He was promoted to lieutenant in November 1981 and worked in the fire marshal's office, where he worked investigations until he retired. He had been employed by AFD for almost twenty years on the night of the murders.

Prosecutor Efrain de la Fuente elicited from Stahl that he was the first arson investigator on the scene.

"How do you work a crime scene as an arson investigator?" de la Fuente wanted to know.

"All fire scenes are treated as a crime scene until you prove that it's an accidental fire."

Stahl stated he took several photographs to assist in his investigation. He later escorted EMS inside to pronounce the bodies dead. He also helped the medical examiner remove all four bodies. In addition, he interviewed several firefighters at the location.

De la Fuente asked Stahl to explain "V shape."

"Fire will travel up, out, and down. If you set a fire in a chair against the wall, that fire is going to travel up and out until it hits something that stops it.

"If it travels up and out and hits the wall, it's going to go up until it hits the ceiling. As it continues to burn, the fire will roll across the ceiling, and that will give you your V pattern, where it travels up, out, and down.

"The inverted V, or cone, would be indicative of some type of liquid accelerant."

Stahl claimed that there was a V pattern in the cooler and shelves area.

"At any time, did you go back and relook at your findings as to where the origin of the fire was?"

"Yes, I did."

"And at whose direction was that?"

"I met with ATF agent Marshall Littleton." Stahl added he looked at photographs of the crime scene in addition to a report prepared by Littleton.

"Have you also gone back in looking at these photos

and looked at the bodies themselves in a much more detailed manner?"

"Yes, I have."

"And having gone back and revisited your initial findings, what have you concluded as regard to the origin of the fire?"

"I believe the fire originated more toward the center of the room rather than in the corner." This, of course, was a drastic change from his on-site impression ten years earlier. Stahl claimed that the combustibles near the bodies and the V pattern, which led back toward the bodies, were what convinced him to change his official report.

Joe James Sawyer was licking his chops.

"This report that you relied on in changing your opinion . . . that's dated November 17, 1999. Is that correct?"

"Yes," Stahl sheepishly replied.

"How did you get it?"

"We're not certain. I think it was through the DA's office."

Sawyer wanted to know who in the district attorney's office asked Stahl to look at Littleton's report and consider whether he (Stahl) was wrong.

"They never asked me to consider my report if it was wrong," Stahl clarified. "They just asked me to read Agent Littleton's report and to possibly sit down and meet with him at a later date." Stahl testified that he met with Littleton earlier in 2001.

"At the time that you met with Agent Littleton," Sawyer asked, "had you already changed your mind?"

"No, I had not."

"So even after you considered his report, it wasn't until you actually met with him, face-to-face, that you began changing your mind?"

"No. I did not have the opportunity to review the photographs before we met."

"Wouldn't you expect that you would find evidence if there had been a fire in the center of a room that had entrained oxygen, and if it can cause those burns— why isn't the concrete blistered? Why isn't there some spalling? Why is there no evidence of a fire there?"

"The area where it's burning, the bodies actually protected the floor. The bodies were absorbing the heat."

"In all the years until you were contacted by the district attorney's office," Sawyer drilled, "had anyone so much as questioned your findings or suggested to you that they were wrong?"

"No one suggested they were wrong," Stahl quietly answered.

Next up for the state, appropriately enough, was Marshall Littleton.

Marshall Littleton worked as a field agent in the Houston field division of the ATF. He worked for the ATF for thirteen years. Prior to ATF, he worked for ten years in the Austin Police Department. His current job with ATF was explosives and fire investigator.

De la Fuente asked Littleton how he became involved in the yogurt shop case.

"I was first called in January of 1999 to look at this fire to see what the probability of running FPE (fire protection engineering) tool on this particular fire was."

"So you were called upon to fire model the rear of the yogurt shop?" de la Fuente asked.

"Yes, sir. That's correct."

"And when you fire model, what are you talking about?"

"It is a zone-type model that makes the assumption that the room is basically divided into two zones, a hot zone and a cold zone. It will make calculations such as upper hot-gas-layer temperatures, flame plume temperatures, smoke flow through an opening.

"It does not model the fire, per se; it models the impact of the fire on its environment."

"Were you able to fire model the rear of the yogurt shop?" posed de la Fuente.

"No, sir, I was not."

"Can you tell the jurors why?"

"The model makes the assumption that a hot-gas layer is going to be able to build up, which basically means that there will not be an opening to the room of origin or above the ceiling.

"Too much of the strength of the fire," Littleton explained, "is lost to the chimney effect if there is a hole in the ceiling."

"What was it about the rear of the yogurt shop that prevented you from fire modeling?" de la Fuente asked.

"Above the walk-in cooler," Littleton described while pointing toward a diagram of the yogurt shop, "we have an opening that goes from the top of the cooler to the drop ceiling.

"We also have an opening from here that there is no header"—or something like an exit sign above a door or archway. This would not allow a hot-gas layer to build up very uniformly in this particular room. Therefore, the model itself would not be that robust."

"So, despite the fact that you were not able to fire model the rear room of the yogurt shop," asked de la Fuente, "how did you proceed in trying to determine the origin and the cause of the fire?"

"I was contacted by assistant United States attorney Jerry Carruth," who asked Littleton about the call Melvin Stahl had made on the fire. Littleton believed that "the damage that was described . . . simply did not fit all of the physics involved in this particular fire."

Littleton continued with his fire testimony. "A fire has got to burn according to all the laws of physics. One of the things you have to do is find the irrefutable facts. The irrefutable fact was, we have damage to the victims." He also mentioned an oxygen-depleted environment, a melted ladder, a melted hamper, and firefighters at the scene near the end of the flames.

"That fire is getting ready to burn itself out, which tells you that most of the things that are going to be able to burn in that area have already burned."

Littleton referred to his meeting with Carruth. The assistant attorney asked him "if a fire set in the center of the room on the victims would [it] yield the type of damage" that was seen at the yogurt shop.

"I said at the time my intuition says yes."

"So do you have an expert opinion as to where the origin of the fire started?" asked de la Fuente.

"In the center of the room."

"Also, do you have an expert opinion as to what caused the fire?"

"The open flame ignition of available combustibles." In other words, items that were stacked on top of the bodies.

The defense chose to defer their examination of Marshall Littleton until Robert Springsteen's defense. The first week of the trial had ended.

Things were about to heat up.

# CHAPTER 61

*Monday, May 14, 2001*

Roy Rose, Robert Springsteen's best friend from West Virginia, appeared in court. One problem: he did not want to be there. Rose took the stand before the jury was let in and pleaded the Fifth Amendment.

Asked if he intended to answer questions, Rose replied, "I respectfully refuse to answer that question on the grounds that it may incriminate me." His attorney, Carolyn Denero, who flew in from West Virginia, argued that if Rose testified to what he believed was the truth, it would contradict his grand jury testimony, thereby, perjuring himself.

Judge Lynch ruled Rose did not have a Fifth Amendment right and he must answer any questions posed to him.

Instead, Rose continued to plead the Fifth.

"Mr. Rose, despite the court's order, you are saying at this time that you are going to refuse to abide by the court's order?" asked Judge Lynch.

"Yes."

"At this time, you are held in contempt by the court. You will be ordered jailed in the Travis County Correctional Facility until such time as you purge your contempt."

As Rose was escorted away, he muttered under his breath, "Thank you for playing God," to Judge Lynch, followed by an unintelligible obscenity.

"Yes, sir, Mr. Rose," snapped a peeved Judge Lynch. "I suggest you conduct yourself appropriately or you will have a double contempt."

Charlene Rose, Roy's wife, commented later that she felt like she was in a Third World country instead of the United States, "where they have a dictator in charge. Where people who don't agree with the policy line just disappear."

The other important witness to appear on the stand was Detective Robert Merrill, one of the officers who elicited the confession from Springsteen. He spoke of the preparation for the trip to West Virginia and the interrogation. He spoke of his arrival in West Virginia, the coordination with the Charleston police officers, and the setup of the interrogation materials, such as the video camera and audiotape recorder.

Defense lawyer Berkley Bettis argued that the videotape of Springsteen's confession should not be omitted.

"Judge, what you have seen is an enhanced tape. That is to say, let's suppose that you had a photograph taken with a camera with a broken lens, and that that photograph was then given to someone with a computer and that computer enhancement was able to remove the cracks, the distortions, the kaleidoscope effect of the broken lens. That is what you have been listening to. What is being offered right now is [a] view through a broken lens."

Bettis went on to give what may possibly be the

longest grammatical sentence in the history of the modern Texas judicial system:

> *I am saying that it is probably within the discretion of the court as a matter of law to determine upon a proffer by a party whether any recording is or is not a true and accurate representation, but that the burden initially is upon the proponent of the recording to show that that predicate is true, and that the conclusory testimony of Detective Merrill to that effect with respect to this exhibit is insufficient to allow the court in its initial role in determining the admissibility of evidence to make that determination.*

Bettis took a deep breath. He was not finished.

> *Or, to respond more directly, clearly one hundred percent, ninety-nine percent, I think that's a—that would be reductio ad absurdum. But there again, there is some point, as I said, where the lens is broken that you are not talking about the mere weight to be given the evidence; you're actually talking about its admissibility as a true and accurate representation, and that's an initial determination to be made by the court under the proper objection when the evidence is proffered by the proponent.*

Judge Lynch took Bettis's analogy a step further. "I would analogize this to someone who caught a crime on videotape in the middle of the night. The tape is fuzzy, unclear in spots, and may not clearly delineate who did what." Judge Lynch concluded that the tape, however, "could be offered to assist the jury in whatever they did."

After the judge's denial, Robert Smith and Detective

Robert Merrill proceeded to go over videotape clips of the Springsteen interview and confession. Judge Lynch, the families of the four girls, and the jury received transcripts of the videotape so they could follow along. Springsteen had a copy of the transcript on a laptop computer. After each short clip, Merrill answered questions about what the jury saw. But before the prosecution could truly get started, the end of the workday arrived.

The following day, Merrill was the only witness who took the stand. The prosecution continued to play the Springsteen confession tape, while Merrill retold what the jurors saw.

*Wednesday, May 16, 2001*

For the third day in a row, Merrill sat in the witness stand. He continued to review the prosecution's most critical evidence against Springsteen. Smith asked Merrill if it was common for a guilty suspect to shift responsibility of a crime to another person. Merrill replied, "It's common."

Merrill also noted Springsteen was not upset when told someone had implicated him in the murders. "People tend to get pissed off when they're accused of a crime they did not do."

The state returned to playing more clips of the videotape. After several minutes of this, Joe James Sawyer objected.

"All we are doing is reemphasizing the state's greatest hits out of this tape. I object."

Judge Lynch responded, "It seems to me, like after introducing a written statement, the state could go back and question the witness about individual parts of that statement. So, I don't think it's unfair at this point in time."

Several minutes later, Judge Lynch asked Smith how much longer he would question Merrill.

"About twelve minutes, maybe fifteen," Smith replied.

"I like that exact assessment, Mr. Smith. Then I'm supposed to add in the usual forty percent lawyer factor and come up with twenty minutes?" the judge tossed somewhat flippantly.

"Yes, sir," came Smith's obedient reply.

Judge Lynch excused the jury so the defense could voir dire Merrill. The issue at hand was whether or not the police erred in not letting David Bungard, Springsteen's attorney, come into the interview room during the confession. Merrill informed the court the reason he did not stop the interview when Bungard made his presence known was because Springsteen "never made an express request to have an attorney present."

Judge Lynch agreed with the state.

Sawyer decided to focus on lies. "The one thing you do consistently in this examination is lie to him."

"Pardon me?" responded Merrill.

"Is lie to him. You lie to him throughout that interrogation, all the way through, don't you?"

"A little."

Sawyer mentioned different tactics the officers used on Springsteen during the confession: lies, getting in the suspect's face, telling him they could stay there all day, etc. "Do you think that this is a risk here that by applying this kind of pressure . . . that an innocent man could be led to make statements that have nothing to do with his guilt?"

"I don't think with this, no," replied a confident Merrill.

"With this case in particular, or at all?"

"This interview."

Sawyer brought up that Springsteen had not been Mirandized until after the confession and before he gave a written statement. "You knew perfectly well you were going to give him his Miranda rights, didn't you?"

"I did," Merrill replied.

"You wouldn't interrupt that interrogation for anything," an incensed Sawyer belted out. "Nothing was going to stop it. You weren't going to stop it at all until you had what you wanted. But you didn't have it yet, did you?"

"That's correct."

"Because we know to an absolute certainty that the moment that .380 was fired, that little girl had died."

"Yes."

"So she wasn't alive to be raped. She wasn't alive to have Maurice come and finish her off. You know that is not only improbable; it is forensically impossible."

"That's correct. But we also know the sequences are out [of order]. We know that she was choked. We know that she was shot. He said he had the .380. We know that's the bullet that killed her."

"Why didn't you keep talking? Why didn't you ask him about the choking?" Sawyer asked. "I mean, surely you will agree at the end if you had put him on the grassy knoll at the killing of JFK, he would have said he did it."

"I don't think so," Merrill calmly replied.

"He was giving you everything and anything you wanted," roared the contentious Sawyer.

"No, he wasn't."

Sawyer finished with the detective. Prosecutor Smith followed up.

"The fact of the matter is, he can call the game at any time," Smith stated, referring to Springsteen ending the interrogation. "And you made that clear to him."

"Yes, sir."

"So once somebody says, 'I want a lawyer,' you're forbidden under the law from questioning them, correct?"

"Yes."

"Do you have anything that you are ashamed of, with regard to this interview with Robert Springsteen?"

"No, sir."

Another key witness, Chandra Morgan, took the stand. She claimed she was with the four boys on December 6, 1991. Morgan, who was thirteen years old at the time, had a crush on Maurice Pierce. She claimed she and the four boys took acid in the Northcross Mall parking lot. She mentioned Pierce had already taken a hit earlier that day. She also testified she and three of the boys, excluding Forrest Welborn, went inside the yogurt shop. She said two of the boys went to the rest room.

They all left and returned to the mall, where Morgan claimed she got separated from the guys. She eventually hooked up with them again, about thirty to forty-five minutes later. Three of the guys pulled up in a car. Welborn was not there. Pierce asked her if she wanted to come with them. Suddenly she spotted Welborn walking from the direction of the Oshman's Sporting Goods store. She jumped into the car, as did Welborn. Pierce pulled the car out of the parking lot and headed south on Burnet Road. Morgan claimed she heard sirens as they drove on. She wanted to see what the commotion was all about, but the guys told her no and continued.

Morgan testified Pierce drove everyone a mile-and-a-half to Gullett Elementary School at the 6300 block of Treadwell Boulevard. She also claimed Springsteen had a gun on him.

"I saw it in his waistband. Just the butt. It appeared to be a semiautomatic."

Morgan stated she and three of the boys got out of the car. Welborn stayed inside the vehicle. Springsteen and Scott led the way to a petting zoo on the school grounds. She and Pierce followed, but veered off toward the baseball field.

Outside the presence of the jury, Sawyer expressed concern about Morgan's mental state. He asked Judge Lynch if she "is under the influence of any drug or narcotic, specifically heroin." He added, "She is moving like she lives underwater and she really is manifesting behavior that I associate with the use of an opiate—"

Prosecuting attorney Darla Davis interjected, "I have had conversations with her today and I have no reason to think that she is under the influence at all."

Judge Lynch concluded that "she looks to me like pretty much the standard twenty-two-year-old girl that walks up and down the streets of Austin all of the time. She doesn't seem to be out to lunch like a lot of people I see in my regular calling of the dockets."

Davis resumed her examination of the witness.

"Shortly after the night of December 6, 1991, did you see Maurice Pierce again?"

"Yes, ma'am."

"Did he say anything to you about being quiet?"

"He wanted me to keep my mouth shut. I think it was two or three days after the event."

"Did he ever say this to you again?"

"A couple of days after that, I believe he was arrested for a gun, and it was after that."

Sawyer elected to defer his cross-examination of Chandra Morgan until he presented his client's defense.

The next witness was Kelly Hannah, Springsteen's temporary girlfriend at the time of the murders. She testified that Springsteen and Pierce were supposed to stop by her house that night but never showed up.

Next up was Springsteen's father, Robert Springsteen III. He testified that he called the police to report his son was missing on the morning of December 6, 1991. He had not seen him since 10:00 P.M. on December 4.

He also spoke about his son's mother and how she was strict with Robert. Springsteen III believed you should give kids plenty of rope. He admitted he pretty much let his son come and go as he pleased.

# CHAPTER 62

*Thursday, May 17, 2001*

Another situation arose, which left a sour taste in Joe James Sawyer's mouth. Detective Bruce Boardman testified he interviewed Robert Springsteen and Michael Scott on December 15, 1991, the day after Maurice Pierce was arrested. What frustrated Sawyer was Boardman did not locate his interview notes until four weeks before his testimony.

Almost 9½ years later.

"In my move from homicide in 1992," Boardman attempted to explain, "I had two boxes that I carried with me from unit to unit. In my last and latest move . . . from internal affairs to the traffic office . . . I started consolidating these two boxes.

"And absolutely to my surprise, I found two eight-and-a-half by eleven legal pads, which—the first one I looked at had the name of Robert Burns Springsteen on it, the date and the time, and I immediately brought it to the attention of the district attorney's office."

Boardman's notes contained some interesting entries. The guys claimed they heard about the murders from someone named "Mace." The first mention of the guys hanging out with Kelly Hannah. And most significantly, Michael Scott used to date one of the girls.

On cross-examination, Sawyer did not take Boardman to task for the recent "discovery."

The state also questioned Joseph Wills, a friend of Maurice Pierce and Forrest Welborn's. Wills testified he saw Pierce with a .22. He also claimed he was in "the Fungus," a grassy area between Hillside Center and MoPac Freeway, where many of the so-called "undesirables" hung out and got high, when he heard gunshots. Soon thereafter, fire trucks arrived at the yogurt shop. He testified he saw Welborn walking up by Oshman's.

Wills also admitted he was currently on parole from prison for burglary.

The rest of the day's testimony covered a hodgepodge of items from a search conducted in the Fungus in 2000, which uncovered a pair of panties and a knife, to "rifling" characteristics of bullets and how certain patterns are created from a bullet and can be traced back to a specific gun.

The day's testimony concluded with two women from Michael Scott's past: Meredith Skipper and Amanda Statham. Skipper spoke of the day Scott arrived at her doorstep in the stolen Pathfinder. She indicated something seemed wrong with her then-boyfriend. He appeared uncomfortable and would not open up to her.

Amanda Statham testified that Scott admitted to the killings. She claimed she was at Scott's house and he and Forrest Welborn were talking about the murders.

"Did you hear Mike Scott say anything to Forrest Welborn?" asked Darla Davis.

"He said, 'Keep your fucking mouth shut,'" replied Statham.

"How was Mike acting?"

"Panicky."

"What was he doing?"

"He was yelling out the door to keep his fucking mouth shut."

A few days after the yelling incident, Statham claimed Scott came over to her house. While there, he admitted his participation.

"Did you ask him why he had been questioned by the police about the yogurt shop murders?" Davis prodded.

"Yes," Statham responded. "He told me . . . that he, Robert, Forrest, and Maurice had all been questioned or [were] all involved and that he had done it."

"Michael Scott said, 'I did it'?"

"He said, 'I did it.'"

"What was your reaction?"

"I said he was a fucking sick bastard and smacked him upside the head."

Statham, who was only thirteen at the time, claimed Scott told her details about the murders; however, she could not recall any specifics.

When asked why she did not call the cops and report Scott, she replied, "I thought he was kidding" and "He was a boy even my grandmother liked."

*Friday, May 18, 2001*

The state introduced several DNA experts that all said that they were unable to prove or disprove that any of the DNA found at the yogurt shop belonged to Robert Springsteen or any of the other suspects.

The other key testimony for the day came from Detective Manuel Fuentes, who took the written statement from Michael Scott. On direct examination, Fuentes was allowed to read Scott's redacted confession into the record.

On cross, Sawyer found it odd that both Scott and

Springsteen's statement had certain similarities. He asked Fuentes if he was "aware of any resonance between the two statements."

"Resonance?" Fuentes asked.

"Yeah. They begin to sound alike, look alike, that kind of thing."

"Could be because they are true."

"Yeah, could be. That would then be all the corroboration that is needed, right?"

"The truth is the truth."

"Yes. The truth is the truth."

After the attorneys finished with Fuentes, they informed the judge there were no more witnesses for the day.

Judge Lynch joked, "Ladies and gentlemen of the jury, I think the lawyers have conspired to end the day early. I'm joking, of course, but the fact of the matter is, we don't have any additional witnesses."

For that day, at least.

*Tuesday, May 22, 2001*

There was no court on Monday due to severe rain and a hailstorm, which caused damage to one juror's home. Tuesday's return to the courtroom would be the last day for the state's case.

Outside the presence of the jury, Chuck Meyer testified about serial killer Kenneth McDuff. Meyer was one of the lead detectives in the McDuff case and was present at McDuff's capture and arrest in Missouri. Sawyer asked if Meyer was aware that on the day McDuff was arrested, a witness by the name of Judy Tinker phoned in a tip placing McDuff at Northcross Mall on December 6, 1991.

The state also brought in James Ramsbottom, a former friend of Springsteen's, who claimed Rob had a

.380 firearm in 1986. Springsteen was twelve years old at the time.

Another gun incident allegedly occurred in the summer of 1991 between Maurice Pierce and Guy Schumann. Pierce supposedly pulled a gun on Schumann at a basketball court in Brentwood Park, less than 2½ miles away from I Can't Believe It's Yogurt.

Both men, Ramsbottom and Schumann, were serving time in jail during their testimony.

Sawyer declared their testimonials to be "the skunk . . . in the jury box."

Later that evening, Sawyer was surrounded by a gaggle of reporters. He mentioned the specter of Kenneth McDuff.

"For those of you who were in court today, it was evident that we think there is some strong likelihood that he is the person who committed these crimes. It would really fit his modus operandi."

Sawyer would get the chance to toss this theory into the ring very soon.

# CHAPTER 63

*Wednesday, May 23, 2001*

Robert Springsteen's defense began. First up on the witness stand was Hector Polanco. Instead of going after Polanco, however, Joe James Sawyer practically handled him with kid gloves.

"You have never used coercion, threats, duress of any kind to achieve any of the hundreds of confessions you have developed during the time you were in homicide, did you, ever?" asked Sawyer.

"I've been accused of it, but no. I say no."

"You never so much as carried a gun when you talked to anyone, did you?"

"No, I never carried a gun."

Sawyer asked Polanco about a false confession in 1989 where a husband confessed to killing his wife and burying her body in their yard, even though he, very obviously, had not done so. An objection by prosecutor Robert Smith led to a bench conference with the judge and the two attorneys. In pretrial hearings, Judge Lynch granted two false confessions related to the yogurt shop case for the defense. Those were from Alex Briones and Shawn Smith.

"I'm not going to allow any more specific instances if they don't in any way relate to this case. I think if you ask him generally if people confess to things they didn't do . . . that's probably proper," stated Judge Lynch. "[If you] try to drag in more dead fish like this other than the dead fish I've allowed you to drag in, I think, is abusing my broad ruling."

"I'm not going to go over the dead fish limit," replied Sawyer.

Something stank to Judge Lynch. He sensed Sawyer was trying to get at the Christopher Ochoa case.

"I'm not cracking the door to Ochoa," the judge declared, referring to the Austin Pizza Hut murder case of 1988. Twenty-year-old mother and Pizza Hut employee Nancy DePriest was attacked while opening up the restaurant. She was raped and shot in the head. The crime scene was virtually evidence free. No gun. No witnesses.

Despite the lack of evidence, the case was closed quickly. Hector Polanco wrangled murder confessions from two young men, Christopher Ochoa and Richard Danzinger. Apparently, Ochoa ratted out Danzinger because he claimed Polanco threatened him with the death penalty. He believed the only way to save his own life was to implicate his friend.

Eight years after DePriest's murder, a young man by the name of Achim Josef Marino found God while in prison for robbery and sexual assault. He decided to put pen to paper and confess to another crime.

The murder of Nancy DePriest.

He mailed it to Austin police.

Marino also mailed a confession letter to Governor George W. Bush wherein he informed him, "You are legally and morally obligated to contact Danzinger and Ochoa's attorneys."

No one responded to the letters.

Finally someone did. A subsequent search of Marino's residence found the gun used to kill DePriest.

Ochoa claimed he feared for his life when questioned by Polanco. He also claimed the officer fed him the details of the DePriest crime scene.

"They're not my lies," declared Ochoa. "They're his."

The conference ended and Sawyer returned to question the witness.

"No matter what safeguards you take, people will . . . falsely confess?"

"Yes, sir."

Sawyer asked about leaks early on in the yogurt shop case. Polanco admitted there were suspicions amongst the ranks that holdback information was being leaked. As a result, Sawyer believed the majority of confessions could be considered tainted because so much information was available to the public. He mentioned that more than sixty teenagers who hung out at Northcross Mall were brought in for questioning within a week or two of the murders.

Sawyer cited one source of the leaks as possibly an emergency medical technician who worked the crime scene. He also expressed concern about the local news reporters who were in tow with Sergeant John Jones.

"Did their presence hamper and impede the investigation or did it help?" asked Sawyer.

"My personal opinion, it hampered us."

Sawyer focused on the false confessions from Smith and Briones. "Both of these men wound up confessing to this crime, didn't they?"

"Yes, sir."

"And the one thing that you and I know . . . is that neither one of them committed this crime."

"That's correct."

Sawyer also pressed Polanco on the handling of the

yogurt shop crime scene by Jones. "If that crime scene had been handled differently, this would have been a very different case, wouldn't it?"

"In my opinion, it would have."

Next up on the defense witness list was Sergeant John Jones.

"Sergeant Jones," Sawyer asked, "if you were running this crime scene today, would you handle things differently?"

"There might be certain aspects," the officer calmly replied.

"Which aspects would you handle differently, and why?"

"We have our own crime scene team now. Hopefully, they would have been out there a lot quicker." He added, "We have our own PIO now."

"What is a PIO?"

"Public information officer. When this incident went down, we didn't have a PIO. So, in addition to trying to make sure the scene got investigated, we are also charged with putting out information for the public."

"Anything else you would have handled differently?"

"I don't think so. In my opinion, a crime scene like that comes along once in a lifetime. There is really no way to prepare for it."

"If it's a once-in-a-lifetime crime, don't you think it's worth making every effort?"

"Yes, sir, and that's what we did."

"Would you try today to limit the number of people going in and out?"

"That was an unusual crime scene, sir. Everyone that was in that crime scene had a purpose."

Sawyer shifted gears and focused on the holdback information that had been leaked. He talked about how people were able to recite back supposed concealed information. "This began making a real problem in trying to solve this case, didn't it?"

"No, sir, not once we realized that. We actually turned that to our advantage," Jones stated.

"You think it was an advantage that it took ten years to solve it?"

"No, sir. Your question was about the information getting out."

After that snippy exchange, Sawyer asked about the four suspects. "You took in both Forrest Welborn and Maurice Pierce as possible suspects and you wound up clearing both in this case, didn't you?"

"No, sir, we inactivated them. We would get to a point with a potential suspect where we just couldn't go further with them and we had to inactivate them. . . . Maurice fit into that category, and so did Forrest."

"Mr. Springsteen was considered nothing but a witness?"

"Yes, sir. He was named by Maurice as being involved, so we had to check it out. But at the time, we ran into a dead end on him."

"And a dead end on Michael Scott as well?"

"Yes, sir."

Prosecutor Robert Smith focused on the holdback information during his cross. "At the time the autopsies were conducted, were certain steps taken to edit the autopsies . . . to keep certain facts from becoming public?"

"Yes, sir."

"And, in fact, there have been several court battles fought over keeping that information secret?"

"Yes, there were."

"Is it true that the police never released the caliber of a .380 to the media?"

"That's true."

"And they have never released the distance the shooter would have been from the victims?"

"That's correct."

"And they have never released what it was that the victims were bound with?"

"That's correct."

At the end of the day, the prosecution asked that Sawyer refrain from making any more on-camera interviews.

"Mr. Sawyer, have you been making on-camera interviews again?" asked Judge Lynch.

"But not about the case," responded Sawyer.

"About McDuff," interjected Darla Davis. "You told him in chambers not to give any more interviews. I just don't want my McDuff stuff walking out the door."

# CHAPTER 64

*Thursday, May 24, 2001*

The day started off on a bad note. Once again, the elevators in the Blackwell-Thurman Criminal Justice Center were experiencing difficulties. After welcoming the jurors back into the courtroom, Judge Lynch said, "I understand that our multimillion-dollar building and multimillion-dollar elevators . . . still are not working properly.

"A couple of months ago, we had a prosecutor in my court that left here one day with some witnesses and pushed the elevator button and the door opened and there was no elevator there," Judge Lynch recalled. "It was a floor or so below. We reported that to the company, of course, immediately, and the company wrote us a nice letter saying it was impossible, and she really didn't see what she said she saw. We may call on some of you as witnesses, since you have had bad experiences with the elevators as well."

It was an apt metaphor for the current stage of the trial.

The next stage reverted back to an earlier stage—fire.

The defense hoped Gerald Hurst would take a hot poker to the analyses of the origin of the yogurt shop fire as presented by Melvin Stahl and Marshall Littleton. Hurst, a scientist who worked as a consultant for the military and corporations in regard to the use of incendiary devices, came to the same conclusion originally posited by Melvin Stahl. He believed the evidence showed the fire probably started on the shelves and not on top of the girls.

Joe James Sawyer asked Hurst, "You agree with Stahl's conclusions he drew in the hours following the fire actually happening, don't you, Doctor?"

"Yes, I do."

"Do you believe that the observations he made and the conclusions that he drew on-site that day using his eyes, his nose, and his training are supported in everything that you have seen in all of the data that we have been provided?"

"Yes."

"In all probability, I take it you agree with Stahl that the fire, its ignition point, was probably one of the shelves three feet off of the ground?"

"Yes, on one of the shelves."

"And we don't know whether it was the left or the right shelf as we face the shelves, do we?"

"No, we don't."

"All that we know in looking at the evidence on the shelves is where the greatest intensity of burn happened. We can establish that, can't we?"

"Yes, we can establish that."

"But in terms of ignition point, it could have been paper goods to the right, paper goods to the left. It could have been a polystyrene cup?"

"Could have been both."

Hurst described the fire as "a very intense, short

fire." He was also certain of the fuel load that caused the fire. Hurst believed the intensity of the burn was due to the polystyrene from the little Styrofoam coffee cups.

"I would estimate that the fire burned intensely probably no longer than about three minutes," continued Hurst. "It could have reached a stage of intensity high enough to do the damage you have seen in a minute-and-a-half or less."

"Going back just a moment to Mr. Littleton's fire," posed Sawyer, "(i)f an accelerant had been used to start the fire, would you have expected there to be some physical evidence that would have been observable by someone immediately after the fire to support the notion that an accelerant, let's say lighter fluid, had been used?"

"Yes. That's the first thing an investigator looks for is evidence of a liquid accelerant."

"For example, as Stahl said, you would be able to smell the presence of the accelerant if you were there that quickly?"

"Yes. The first thing an investigator does is use his nose to see if he's getting an aroma of a hydrocarbon, a mixture of some sort."

"In this particular fire, the physical evidence supports the fuel load being in the shelves. The destruction of the shelves themselves supports the intensity of the fire, doesn't it, Doctor?"

"Yes."

On cross-examination, prosecutor Efrain de la Fuente pointed out that Hurst was not a certified arson investigator. The prosecutor also asked Hurst about the fees he charged for his services.

"What is your hourly fee?"

"Well, my hourly fee when I bill in civil cases is two hundred dollars an hour."

"And in a criminal case, sir, how much is your hourly rate?"

"It varies. Usually the defendant has no money, so I usually wind up doing it for free. If I'm ever lucky enough to get a multimillionaire, I'll charge the heck out of it."

"So, are you working for free?"

"I don't know. I haven't been paid anything and I really don't know."

De la Fuente chose to travel down a different path. "Let's assume for a minute that the fire did, in fact, start on the bodies. My question to you, sir, is, is it possible in your expert opinion that if, in fact, the fires started on the bodies that the fire—and we know that fire travels up and out—could have, in fact, hit the shelves, ignited the items on the shelves, ignited the entire thing on the shelves, gone all the way to the corner, causing some great damage over there—ignite the ceiling, go across, hit the ladder, come down, and get your lines of demarcation? Is that, in your expert opinion, possible?"

"Oh sure. It's also possible that the fire started by a meteorite strike. But if you are just going to deal in possibilities, you will get a yes out of me every time."

"Was there a strike that night? Do you know?" asked the annoyed prosecutor.

"I don't think so. It's highly improbable."

"All right. I just want to make sure we are on the same sheet of music here, Dr. Hurst."

Hurst described how he believed Marshall Littleton ascribed the origin of the fire so it would be beneficial to the prosecution. He claimed he, on the other hand, merely sought out the truth.

"And the best person to ask as to how the fire started would be the person who started the fire," claimed de la Fuente.

"That's hard to say. People who start fires tend to lie a lot."

"But that would be a good source of"—de la Fuente stopped himself—"well, yeah, I guess you would be right on that. But that would be a good source to start with, wouldn't it?"

"Maybe under Sodium Pentothal."

Hurst also testified he did not believe the fire started on top of the girls and Jennifer Harbison's body rolled off the pile, into the shelves, and ignited the items on the shelves. "I haven't seen any evidence that she rolled off anything. I think she was lying in the same position at the origin of the fire."

"Let me ask you a common-sense question here," said de la Fuente. "If I had a pile of clothes here and a pile of clothes back there and I wanted to get rid of these pile of clothes over here in front of you by burning it, where would I start my fire?"

"Well, there isn't any good way to start the fire you're talking about. A pile of clothes doesn't burn worth a damn."

# CHAPTER 65

*Friday, May 25, 2001*

For the final day of defense testimony, the Springsteen team chose to focus on the psychology behind false confessions. To guide the court through the myriad pathways as to why a person would confess to a crime they did not commit, the defense called in Dr. Richard Ofshe, a Pulitzer Prize–winning professor and an expert in coerced and false confessions. Dr. Ofshe testified in the high–profile trial of Jessie Misskelley, one of the so-called West Memphis Three, who had been profiled in the two *Paradise Lost* documentaries.

Dr. Ofshe spent most of his time testifying outside of the presence of the jury. Berkley Bettis led the direct examination of the doctor. "Please tell the court what is the major analytical method for determining the existence of a false confession."

"The existence of a false confession," the doctor responded, "would be determined ultimately by the relationship between the evidence in the case and the confession itself.

"So one is looking for a demonstration of actual knowledge of the crime, or a pattern of errors that would ultimately appear to be guesses."

"Is there a common misperception among the public about persons who confess to the commission of the crime?" asked Bettis.

"People presume that someone who did not commit a crime, who was not tortured, would not give a false confession. And knowing nothing about how interrogation works, it appears not to make any sense for someone who didn't commit the crime to give a confession.

"Interrogation is complex," continued Dr. Ofshe. "It is a system of influence that has been developed over the years for the purpose of manipulating someone's decision-making. Unless you know each and every step in that system of influence, you can't even begin to comprehend how someone would do something that foolish.

"So, police interrogation makes a great deal of sense to an ordinary individual if it is explained to them how it works step by step, because it is a logical process. But knowing the details allows one to see why it can culminate, if misused, in a false confession of someone who did not commit the crime."

Bettis asked Ofshe to provide a scientific framework for a false confession.

"I can do two things," surmised Ofshe. "One, I can explain how interrogation is built and give the jury a framework so they can evaluate the presence or absence of these techniques in the interrogation itself.

"And then I can give them a set of principles that they can use for weighing the statement to try to make their own decision about whether or not they should treat it as a true or false confession."

Bettis passed the witness.

Before Efrain de la Fuente could cross Dr. Ofshe, Judge Lynch stepped in.

"Doctor, what do you propose to testify to concerning this specific case?"

"[I] propose to testify in general about the fact that false confessions occur," answered the doctor, "about the types of false confessions that are generally recognized to occur."

"What are those?" asked Lynch.

"Those are what we call voluntary false confessions, or compliant false confessions, or what are called persuaded false confessions."

"Let's hear an (en)capsulated version of that, if you don't mind," demanded Lynch.

"Modern police interrogation depends on manipulating a person's perception of the situation in which they find themselves and their expectations for the future.

"The first major step is to convince them that their situation is hopeless. Through the use of 'evidence ploys,' which are references to claims of the existence of evidence, which, if those claims were true and the facts alleged were . . . reliable and valid, would tend to link the person to the crime.

"The object for the interrogator is to convince someone that there is such overwhelming evidence that links you to the crime that I am personally convinced that anyone else looking at this evidence will be convinced that you committed this crime.

"The purpose in doing this is to take someone who initially expects to be able to survive the interrogation and change their perception of their situation so that at a certain point it's probably reasonable to characterize them as seeing their situation as hopeless. The cost of making the admission has now been substantially reduced, which means it then gets easier to obtain the confession.

"So now the interrogator starts introducing a series of motivational tactics which are intended to get the person to take the last step to say, 'Okay, I did it.'"

Dr. Ofshe described the tactics commonly used fo. "compliant false confession" and "postadmission narrative." Of the former, he stated that, "an innocent person is not going to falsely confess simply because they are told, 'Do the right thing. Be a man about it. Make yourself out to be a better person'—[it's] simply not going to work.

"But if an interrogator is willing to go up the scale and an interrogator is willing to introduce psychologically coercive methods . . . [for example] a threat or offer of help, then the situation can break down to the point at which it appears to be rational, the best thing to do for someone who did not commit the crime to choose to make a false confession, believing that is their only way to minimize their punishment."

Dr. Ofshe stated that the postadmission narrative "can incorporate information that will demonstrate a person's actual knowledge, or can pose the questions that someone who doesn't have the actual knowledge is now obliged to answer, and in order to preserve the deal that they think they have just entered into, they are likely to guess. They are likely to try to supply answers, but they simply don't know the right answers."

Dr. Ofshe concluded by stating that "what is very likely to happen with a false confession is that the person will demonstrate a lack of actual knowledge of the crime."

The doctor spoke specifically of the Springsteen interrogation. "There are about fourteen different statements in this interrogation which worked to communicate the expectation that if you continue to maintain that you have no information, no knowledge of this crime, then you will be identified as the leader. Whereas, if you cooperate, you will be thought of as a victim and you will get through this."

Judge Lynch then spoke up. "And this modern police-interrogation technique, this and the other ones you mentioned, are used daily, I would presume, throughout the United States."

"There are certain tactics," answered Ofshe, "which . . . are prohibited: to threaten someone with beating them unless they confess, or threatening them with a guarantee of the death penalty, or offering to speak to the judge on their behalf and get them a lesser sentence. Those kinds of coercive tactics are improper, but they nevertheless appear sometimes."

Prosecutor Efrain de la Fuente cross-examined the doctor about his background. "You are not a licensed psychologist, correct?"

"Correct."

"You don't treat people?"

"That's absolutely right."

"And you've performed no test on the defendant here, Mr. Springsteen, right?"

"I'm not testifying anything about Mr. Springsteen's personality or personal characteristics. I'm testifying about methods of police interrogation."

"Now, one of your students who has also coauthored some of your material, Richard Leo—you know Richard Leo, do you not?"

"Yes."

"Richard Leo actually did a random sampling out of San Francisco, where he just took random cases and said, 'Okay, these are confessions. Let's see if we can determine whether they are false confessions or not.' And he was not able to find any one of those cases to be a false confession. Is that true?"

"No, it is not the truth," replied an agitated Ofshe, who fumbled his words. "It is, as you typically do, misstate facts. Apparently, you don't know them." Ofshe, who worked on Leo's dissertation committee, was prepared to set the prosecutor straight.

"He did not do a random sample, number one. Number two, he was not studying whether or not there were false confessions in the cases he studied. What he did was study police interrogation methods. He was doing observational study of the kind of tactics that appear in interrogation.

"He never considered the question of whether or not any of the interrogations that he studied resulted in a false confession because he never studied the cases. He only studied the interrogations. He was simply interested in what happened in the interrogations and did not evaluate whether it resulted in a true confession or a false confession."

Dr. Ofshe was asked to step down for the time being.

After a lunch break, Joe James Sawyer attempted to introduce evidence that would possibly implicate Kenneth McDuff in the murders. The attorney informed the judge of the statement McDuff gave the day before his execution in which he placed himself at the yogurt shop.

"I think given the fact that we know that McDuff was a mass murderer" (actually, a serial killer), claimed Sawyer, "who was engaged in murders throughout this time, given the fact that there was at least one eyewitness who believes she saw him at Northcross Mall, given the fact that we know in an attempt, obviously, to implicate [his partner, Hank Alva] Worley, McDuff places himself at the scene and then goes on to list certain details." Sawyer also mentioned McDuff had his parole officer's business card with a hand-drawn map on it with directions to the yogurt shop.

"For those reasons, Your Honor, we believe we meet the burden posed and would respectfully ask that we be allowed to advance that theory in the presence of the jury."

Judge Lynch addressed the issue. He first stated that the evidence to be included in regard to McDuff would not be sufficient. It was hearsay, as well as multiple hearsay. In regard to the substantive nature of the information, Judge Lynch did not believe the information met the requirements of case law to be included by Springsteen. He also believed McDuff's statement to be merely a rambling, incoherent, self-serving diatribe that was only uttered to get back at Worley, who testified against him.

The McDuff information was denied.

The jury was brought in for the first time that day. Surprisingly, Robert Burns Springsteen IV would testify on his own behalf. The parents of the girls were stunned by the revelation. It also appeared as if the prosecution was quite taken aback by the pronouncement.

Springsteen took a seat in the witness stand.

"You understand, Mr. Springsteen," asked Sawyer, "that these people up here in the jury box heard you confess to your involvement in these murders?"

"Well, allegedly confess, yes, sir," replied Springsteen in a smooth, even tone.

"Well, no, plain words," Sawyer gently admonished his own client. "You were being asked questions about your involvement and you were making admissions and you were saying that you had the .380 in your hand and that it was fired through the head of Amy Ayers. Are you here to tell these people that that is not true?"

"Yes, I am."

Sawyer asked him about December 6, 1991. "And is it true that you did sneak into *The Rocky Horror Picture Show* that evening?"

"Yes, it is."

"Did Mike wait for you?"

"Yes, he did. I believe he also tried to get in and got caught."

"After the film was over, did you go to Mike Scott's house and spend the night?"

"Yes, we did."

Sawyer asked Springsteen about September 15, 1999, the date of his confession. His client informed the jury he had not slept for three days before the interview because he worked two jobs and was making repairs on his house at the time.

Sawyer wanted to know why Springsteen did not leave the interview if he knew he was not their suspect. "Why didn't you just stop talking to them? Why didn't you just tell them to go to hell?"

"Well, to be totally honest, I was under the impression that I was not allowed to leave."

"What kept you there, hour after hour, with these policemen?"

"I thought I had invoked my right to an attorney. I don't know that much about the law. They totally ignored what it was that I asked of them or asked for them to do for me, so I was under the impression that it wasn't a valid option for me."

Sawyer asked the question everyone in Austin wanted an answer to: "How is it that you got to the point where you could admit to participating in a terrible crime like this? How did it happen?"

Springsteen hesitated. "Well, I guess I just kind of gave up on myself and said, well, what little bit I do know about the law in West Virginia, there has to be evidence matching any type of crime, whether it be a murder or a robbery or anything of that nature.

"And I thought, well, these guys keep telling me that I'm not telling them the truth. They keep telling me I'm lying to them. Well, if I just make up a bunch of stories and tell these guys what they think they want to hear, they can't do anything to me because I wasn't there. I didn't do anything. The physical proof will show that it couldn't have been me.

"I guess I got myself into a little deeper situation than I thought I was getting myself into. I thought I would be able to prove my innocence by saying, 'Hey, this is a false statement. There is no evidence, because I wasn't there.' And here we are today." The jurors sat and listened with their arms crossed.

"You understand that the words you used on the day you were interviewed could literally kill you? You could wind up on death row. Do you understand that?"

"I do now. At the time, I did not."

"How did you know any of the details about this crime?"

"Well, some of the things were quite publicized, as everyone is aware of. [With] Northcross Mall being a place to hang out . . . and the closeness of it in the area, it was something that everybody was talking about. I figure that's where I probably picked up a lot of the information that I had, and also from the newspapers and the news media."

Sawyer wanted to know what caused the dissolution of the friendships of the four boys after they were interviewed by police officers back in December 1991.

"Forrest was upset with Maurice because—I still to this day don't know what it was he said in 1991. I have no idea.

"I was not upset, because I was not implicated in anything. But Forrest had a real problem with Maurice's saying that they, or him, or whoever was involved. But I didn't have a falling-out with Maurice."

Springsteen explained he guessed at the .380 caliber of the second gun. He claimed Detective Robert Merrill asked him which large-caliber weapon was used in the murders. He claimed he once saw a .380 owned by an assistant manager at a convenience store where he worked. When Merrill asked him about a large-caliber weapon, the .380 was the only gun that came to mind.

Sawyer squared up in front of Springsteen. "Tell the

jury. Did you participate in the killing of these four girls?"

Springsteen looked at the jury; then he looked down momentarily. "No, I did not."

Prosecutor Robert Smith asked, "So, all of these facts that you knew, Mr. Springsteen, are lucky guesses on your part?"

"Well, I wouldn't exactly call them 'lucky guesses.'"

"No," stated Smith. The door was now wide open. "They are, in fact, accurate information, aren't they, Mr. Springsteen?"

"Well, I don't understand what you mean by 'accurate information.'"

"How is it you knew that Michael Scott could not get an erection at the yogurt shop? How did you know that?"

"I didn't know that."

"You said it, didn't you?"

"That is in the statement, yes."

"Yeah, you said it. And you know what? Michael Scott said it too, exactly twenty-four hours before you said it. What do you say to that?"

"There isn't anything I can say to that, sir."

"It's a fact that only you would know is true, because you were there. Right?"

"No, sir. I believe you are incorrect."

"That's just a couple of lucky guesses that crossed the universe; is [that] what you are telling the jury?"

"Well, sir, I believe I was led into that answer by the police officers."

An incredulous Smith asked, "When they said, 'What about Mike?' that led you to say, 'Mike couldn't get it up'?"

"To my recollection, yes, sir."

"You knew that Mike Scott threw up at the bridge, didn't you?"

"No, sir."

"You just said it."

"Yes, sir."

"And as a coincidence, Michael Scott said it twenty-four hours earlier in a completely different state. That's just another one of those inferential facts that crossed in the universe, you are telling the jury?" Smith asked, unable to conceal his sarcasm.

"Yes, sir. It must be."

Smith became even more disgusted with the defendant. He walked up to the witness stand and faced Springsteen. "So tell us what you did on December 6, 1991."

"Where would you like for me to start, Mr. Smith?"

"Just wherever you feel comfortable. Since you have all these different stories, pick one and tell the jury your version today."

Springsteen gave the same story he told Merrill in the beginning of his interrogation in West Virginia.

Upon completion, Smith asked, "Tell us, then, Mr. Springsteen, how is it that you know, ten years later, the exact position of Amy Ayers's body on the floor of the yogurt shop after she has been shot in the head with a .380. How do you know that?"

"I didn't—until testimony here in court—know what the position of her body was."

"Do you know that you demonstrated the exact position for the police?"

"No, sir. I don't believe that's correct."

"Have you intentionally refused to look up at the photograph of yourself?"

"No, sir. I saw the photos up on the screen, just like everyone else did."

"And you don't think that looks anything like poor, dead Amy Ayers?"

"Well, sir, I don't understand what you are asking me."

Smith glared at Springsteen. "Oh, I think you do, Mr. Springsteen. You just can't think of a good answer."

"It doesn't look like the same position to me."

"It doesn't? Well, I guess we'll let the jury make that determination. No further questions."

Judge Lynch dismissed Springsteen from the witness stand. The young man took his usual seat behind the defense table. Judge Lynch stated, "It's my understanding that the defense is preparing to rest."

"That is correct, Your Honor," agreed Sawyer.

# CHAPTER 66

*Tuesday, May 29, 2001*

Court was back in session after a three-day Memorial Day weekend. It was a much-needed break for everyone involved. Both sides were prepared to make their closing statements.

First up, the state.

Darla Davis took the lead. The prosecutor started off by saying that Robert Springsteen is "not a very good liar." She spoke of how the defendant changed his story so often he could not keep his lies straight.

Davis talked about Robert Springsteen's cockiness. In regard to his interview, Davis described Springsteen as "very arrogant with the detectives. He has gotten away with murder for ten years. He is obviously smarter than the police. He has lied to them over the years, and they have never caught on to him. He's bulletproof and also very curious. 'Why are they here? Why did they come now? What have they found out? Who is talking? Did we leave something behind that nobody noticed until now? Have they found the .380?'"

Davis believed that Springsteen agreed to be interviewed because "he wants to know what the police know." And also the defendant is "confident in his ability to beat them at their own game because he thinks he's done it before."

Davis also talked about the limited amount of physical evidence in the case. "Our ability to get meaningful scientific evidence from this crime scene went up in smoke when Mike Scott flicked on his lighter." She felt the state should not be penalized for the lack of evidence. "If we are going to bemoan the lack of physical evidence in this case, we need to give credit where credit is due," she said as she turned toward Springsteen. "The defendants in this case set out to destroy the crime scene and they succeeded."

Davis questioned the fire analysis provided by defense witness Gerald Hurst. "Why would anybody bother to take bodies that are dead and move them and stack them on each other and stack them on trash and then go off and start the fire somewhere else? That's why these girls were stacked like that. That was the whole purpose."

Davis looked directly at the jury when she mentioned Springsteen's lack of remorse. "On the videotape, he absolutely can recount the tale of these murders without a hint of it, without a hint of any sorrow, without a hint of remorse. He can sit there and light a cigarette and smoke it and have the most matter-of-fact conversation about the whole thing." Davis continued to look at the jurors. "He displayed that same eerie calmness on the stand on Friday discussing the Fifth and the Sixth Amendment, like it's no big deal, like it's the most normal thing in the world. Sitting there, sparring with the prosecutor, like he's playing some sick kind of game.

"His attitude on Friday and his attitude on the videotape was enough to turn your insides to ice. I just wanted to walk up to him and say, 'Look what you did. Was that part of your soul always missing, or did you have to carve it out so you could look at yourself in the mirror every day?'

"How could he sit there and lie so terribly," Davis pondered as she glanced at the defendant. She returned her attention to the jury. "Lie to you, to this jury, lie to the families of those girls, lie to himself, and lie to God?

"How could he?" she asked quietly.

"I told you Bob Merrill was right about at least two things. Robert Springsteen is not a good liar, and God knows. Thank you." Davis bowed her head down and returned to the prosecution table.

"Thank you, Ms. Davis," said Judge Lynch. "Mr. Bettis, you may proceed."

The skittish attorney tentatively approached the jury box. "Talk about nervous, me being here—to be honest with you, in twenty-five years of practicing law, this is the second time in my life I have ever actually gone to the trouble of writing out my remarks to a jury in a criminal case rather than just extemporizing them."

Bettis composed himself. "In its simplest terms, the case of the state of Texas against Rob Springsteen boils down to this. It's the confession, stupid!

"I want to help you understand why when you look at it closely, it's a stupid confession. It's a stupid confession because of the very fact that it was given.

"Rob, I'm sorry." Bettis shot a furtive glance toward his client. "We called one rocket scientist to the stand and it was not you. You sit here today convicted by your own words of nothing more than what could be a capital crime of stupidity."

Bettis spoke of the state's lack of physical evidence against Springsteen. "But there is the confession, argues the state of Texas, so we don't need no stinking proof. I tell you, it's a stupid confession. Not only for the reason that it was given, but more importantly, because of the way it was taken."

Bettis examined the Austin Police Department's methods of interrogation. "The relentless pursuit of this purpose of extracting confessions by the Austin Police Department not only can, but it does, and in this case it has resulted in a confession which is false, that people who did not commit any crime have nonetheless made confessions when they were compelled and coerced to do so as Rob Springsteen was in this case."

Bettis spoke about the setting of Springsteen's interrogation. He described the sense of isolation, the feeling of being trapped his client must have felt. He alluded to the possibility that Detective Lara may have had a gun inside the fanny pack he wore into the interview room.

Bettis also slammed the lack of witnesses for the prosecution. "Two years after this investigation, the best the state can come up with is poor, addled Chandra Morgan to intone the accusation in a narcotized haze like some late-blooming opium poppy of an evidence ploy."

Bettis continued down the path of evidence ploys.

"All these statements by the police are evidence ploys," he informed the jury. "Police are allowed to lie in order to break down a suspect and reduce him to a state of hopelessness. And what does the descent into hopelessness sound like? Listen over a period of hours and you will hear it. I think it sounds something like this: 'I thought we went to the movies, but I guess since you said they didn't even have it that night, I guess we didn't go to the movies,'" referring to the midnight screening of *The Rocky Horror Picture Show*.

"Police interrogators are allowed to lie," Bettis confidently informed the jurors again, "and reducing the suspect to that kind of state of hopelessness is the result they intend. But what they are not allowed to do . . .

is overbear the will of a defendant so that as a result of compulsion or coercion, the defendant makes a statement which is involuntary caused by their motivators."

Bettis argued that the detectives who interviewed Springsteen kept jerking him around from being the key to the crime to being a victim.

"Finally at this point is where Springsteen realizes what the game is and takes the carrot," Bettis explained. "Merrill has offered him a scenario at this point where falsely admitting participation is less threatening than continued truthful denial."

Bettis finished up his portion of the defense's closing argument. "I told you it was a stupid confession," he reminded the jury, "but it is more than that. It is worthless as a basis for the type of evidence that you should use to make a decision of the profoundest and the most awful significance. It is in Shakespeare's apt phrase, 'like a tale told by an idiot, full of sound and fury and signifying nothing.'"

Bettis sat down. Judge Lynch called for a fifteen-minute recess.

After the break, Joe James Sawyer stood up from behind the defense table. He broke the ice by saying, "Somehow I think it's not going to have a regretful response when I observe this is the last time I'm going to speak to you in this trial," which elicited a few smiles from the jurors.

Sawyer began his discussion by referencing Memorial Day.

"Yesterday is one of my least favorite holidays. With the exception of my two youngest brothers, every male member of my family has been a soldier, starting in World War II, going through Korea.

"What you ponder on a day like yesterday is that concept of duty. It is the cruelest and meanest four-letter word in English.

"I wish there were a universal draft. I really do, like

it or not, because I think the times we live in invite an ability to simply do what we want and believe what we want and have no concept of that word and what it means to us, duty.

"The police in this case," continued Sawyer, "the investigators in this case, had duties. And we are about to hand this case over to you, and you will have the most terrible duty I can think of—I think worse, really, than being a soldier.

"What you will have a duty to do in the long hours ahead of you is discerning the truth."

Sawyer proceeded to dissect the jobs of the parties involved at the crime scene. He castigated the DPS crime scene team for spending less time at the scene than it took for them to get there. He questioned Sergeant Jones's desire for media attention. He harangued about the lack of control at the crime scene. He bemoaned the lack of a crime scene log and spoke of contamination.

"The most terrible threat running through this case is the use of the word 'confession.' A confession only invites you to believe and not to think, to substitute emotion for reason. That is the dark adjure of a confession. It says, 'Just believe me.' It appeals to the part of you that says, 'I could never do such a thing. I could never confess to something I didn't do. Therefore, no one else can either. Therefore, I believe this thing.'"

Sawyer concluded with an appeal that the jury not be overcome by the emotional aspects of the crimes, but rather focus on the evidence, or lack thereof, in the case.

"There is no one who has touched this case that hasn't been affected by it. There is no one who has looked at the photographs of these little girls and not shed tears for them. I am the father of a daughter. I think every parent has that terrible fear that somehow their children will die before them. And I can't even begin to contemplate what it was like to have a child murdered, particularly in this way, with this kind of savagery. I can't.

"But that is not to stand in front of your duty to pursue the facts and align them and see if there is sufficient reliability here for you to undertake what the state wants.

"Be guided by your conscience," Sawyer concluded, "and your sense of duty and fairly examine this evidence. I promise you it is there if you will look, if you will do your duty, if you will perform the hard work. And I believe that reason will lead you to the only answer here, and that's not guilty. Thank you."

Prosecutor Robert Smith made the final closing argument.

"I will agree with one thing Mr. Sawyer says, and that is the evidence speaks to you. You cannot speak to it. And I firmly believe that. And I intend to tell you that this defendant right here told you the truth when he confessed to this murder. And Michael Scott told you the truth when he confessed to his participation as well."

Finally someone mentioned the girls.

"These two girls were closing. They locked the door. They start doing the dishes, thinking about fixing their car tomorrow, thinking about how much they love Sam, how much fun they are going to have with Amy tonight. They are sweeping up. They are cleaning the dishes. And men with guns come through the back door.

"Imagine what is going on in their heads. Here is the one place you should be safe. It's the back room. There [are] no windows. There [are] two metal doors that always stay locked. Men with guns come in and they want money. And you give them what is in the cash register, but it's not enough. They want more. And so you tell them, that's all there is. It's already been dropped. You can't get to it. That's not good enough. Then, what was just a robbery turns into something much, much worse. These children are forced to take off their clothes.

"I have always found it especially telling that Sarah Harbison took off that ring of her boyfriend. She knew what was coming. Then each one of them are bound and each one of them are gagged. Sexual assault. You decide.

"Then it got worse still. They executed them one at a time. My friend. My sister. Myself. Nowhere to go. Nothing to do."

Smith singled out the struggle of Amy Ayers. "We will never know exactly what happened, but I can tell you she put up a fight.

"A man took that ligature and wrapped it around her neck—so that her eyes started popping and her blood vessels started popping—and a man put that .22 at the top of her head and shot her, just as sure as you are sitting there. But that didn't kill Amy Ayers. A man pressed the muzzle of the .380 to the back of her head and killed her. That's it. She's dead.

"But those people weren't through yet. They stacked the bodies. Sarah's body has been positioned by some sick person who wants to put the ice scoop back in there."

Smith switched gears to Springsteen's confession. "You have a videotape of this defendant's confession. You get the whole story from beginning to end from Robert Springsteen.

"I swear, only lawyers could make that seem like an involuntary confession, could even argue that it's not a voluntary confession. We don't have a warrant for him. He is not under arrest. The law says you don't read them their rights. You tell them they can leave. If they want to leave, they leave. If they want a lawyer, they get a lawyer. Otherwise, they can interrogate them.

"And then the lawyers want you to penalize those cops and make it seem like there is some sinister plan."

Smith looked at Springsteen and said, "But there is something about being guilty that sticks their butt to that chair."

Smith concluded by asking the jury to remember the photograph where Robert Springsteen imitated the pose of Amy Ayers's dead body. "That's the one girl they didn't move. And if he can see that, then he can hear the terror and he can see her crawling across the ground and he can remember pressing the muzzle of the gun to her head."

Smith again approached the jury to summarize the case. "Ladies and gentlemen, you are sitting in the room with the man that killed Amy Ayers, and he'll still be here when you return your verdict."

Judge Lynch informed the jurors they would be sequestered in a local hotel if they did not complete their deliberations that day. As they exited the courtroom, the jurors passed a giant overhead projection of Robert Springsteen posing as Amy Ayers with an inset photo of the dead girl.

The poses were eerily similar.

# CHAPTER 67

*Wednesday May 30, 2001*
*3:55 P.M.*

After thirteen hours of deliberation, the panel of twelve jurors returned to the 167th District Court courtroom. Once seated, Judge Lynch addressed the jury. He complimented them on their behavior during the trial. He also admonished the gallery that there should be no demonstrative activity upon the reading of the verdicts.

"Ladies and gentlemen of the jury, speaking through your foreperson, have you arrived at a verdict in this cause?"

"Yes, Your Honor, we have," replied jury foreman Phil Rodriguez.

"If you will submit it to the bailiff, please, sir." Lynch read the verdict. He looked up toward Springsteen and asked him to rise. The young man stood up next to his attorney Berkley Bettis. Joe James Sawyer, Springsteen's number one advocate, was nowhere to be seen. He claimed he was not present because he did not believe the jury would reach a verdict until the following day.

"'The *State of Texas* versus *Robert Springsteen IV,* in the one hundred sixty-seventh District Court of Travis County, Texas, verdict of the jury: We, the jury, find the defendant, Robert Springsteen IV, guilty of the offense of capital murder.'"

Robert Springsteen showed no emotion as the judge read the verdict.

The families of the girls, on the other hand, fully expressed themselves. Tears and smiles abounded from the front row.

Maryjane Roudebush, Springsteen's grandmother, was Springsteen's only family member to attend every day of his trial. For the verdict, her hair was ensconced in black.

Several jurors shed tears as the judge read the verdict.

Judge Lynch informed the jury the penalty phase would begin the following morning.

When asked how she felt, Barbara Ayres-Wilson, through a veil of tears, responded, "It's just over. We wanted some kind of ending." She asked the seemingly impenetrable wall of reporters to part so she could leave.

Everyone quietly stepped aside.

# CHAPTER 68

**Thursday May 31, 2001**

For the state to get a death sentence for Robert Burns Springsteen IV, they had to prove that the defendant would be a continued threat. They attempted to achieve this goal by bringing up several witnesses from West Virginia, who testified about several of Springsteen's adult indiscretions. Stories of public drunkenness, violence, and disobedience toward authorities rang throughout the courtroom.

The defense, on the other hand, chose not to bring forth one single character witness on behalf of their client.

Sawyer did, at least, provide a closing argument. He asked the jury point-blank, "The unspoken question, I suppose, is: doesn't he deserve to die?"

Sawyer questioned the death penalty's ability to bring closure to anyone involved in the case. "I think it's true that there are people that believe that death somehow brings closure, that killing Robert Springsteen will somehow help. It brings no relief. It's only a Dead Sea fruit that becomes ashes in the mouth, an illusion."

Sawyer wondered aloud what it would take to spare a convicted man's life. "The New Testament offers us a story of a man who thought nothing of taking life, who reveled in it, who looked forward to taking life. And I wonder if, as he took the road to Damascus, if anyone in the world would have bet that Saul of Taurus would become Paul the Apostle.

"And I am not suggesting that Robert Springsteen is Saul of Taurus. But rather I believe that story tells us what we want is redemption for the least amongst us. I believe it takes great moral courage to spare a life."

Robert Smith took his turn before this jury one last time.

"No one in this room wants to kill Robert Springsteen. That's not the point.

"The point is, you have convicted him of capital murder, and despite the guilt trip that you just suffered"—he referred to Sawyer's closing—"he is, in fact, guilty of murder."

Smith spoke of how Springsteen committed an execution himself. "You have to realize that there are people in this world, and one of them is sitting right there"—as he pointed toward Springsteen—"who will come up close to you and press the muzzle of a gun to your head and kill you.

"You have to weigh this against this girl," Smith stated as he pointed at a photograph of Amy Ayers, "who would be twenty-three and this girl"—next, a photograph of Sarah Harbison—"who would be twenty-five"—and finally the photographs of Jennifer Harbison and Eliza Thomas—"and these girls who would be twenty-seven.

"That's what they were. You have to think about the women they would be today and the children they can't have, the veterinarian that they will never become. And you have to weigh whatever mitigation you find against this atrocious crime and then answer the question. That's all anybody wants, is an honest determination of the facts here. Thank you."

The jury was excused at 1:40 P.M. Again they had to make another tough decision. This time, it was for Robert Springsteen's life.

# CHAPTER 69

*Friday, June 1, 2001*
*3:18 P.M.*

The day's courtroom proceedings were delayed due to something rather unusual. Earlier that morning, an inmate escaped from the Travis County Jail, the same location where Robert Springsteen was being held. The entire jail had been placed under lockdown. Eventually order was restored and Springsteen was allowed to be escorted to the courtroom.

In Texas, a jury does not actually sentence a defendant. They must answer three questions posed by the court. In this particular case, the three questions were:

- Did the jury find beyond a reasonable doubt that Robert Springsteen intentionally caused the death of Amy Ayers?
- Would Robert Springsteen pose a continuing threat to society?
- Were there any mitigating circumstances that would explain Robert Springsteen's behavior?

As soon as the jury sat in their chairs, Judge Lynch asked for their verdict. As jury foreman Phil Rodriguez handed the verdict to the judge, one of the jurors began to cry. Springsteen's wife, Robin Moss, covered her eyes with her hand. Springsteen's grandmother did not show up because she knew she would cry.

The responses to the three questions were "Yes," "Yes," and "No."

"At this time, we will proceed to punishment and sentencing in this cause," stated Judge Lynch. "It is, therefore, the judgment of this court that you, Robert Springsteen, are guilty of the offense of capital murder.

"Furthermore, in conformance with the jury's verdict on special issue number one, special issue number two, and special issue number three, and in compliance with the laws of the state of Texas, I hereby assess your punishment at death."

Robert Springsteen would be sent to death row in Huntsville. Under state law, all death penalty cases receive an automatic appeal.

Juror Gunther Goetz stated that the key evidence for the jury were the confessions from Springsteen and Michael Scott. "That really struck a chord. Do people make up facts that weren't known?" Goetz also commented that the jury was surprised when the defense did not call a single character witness on Springsteen's behalf.

"We just didn't get a very clear picture of this person," he stated.

Jury foreman Phil Rodriguez expressed relief that the trial was over. "I think our whole community will appreciate this being over."

But it was far from over.

# CHAPTER 70

*Wednesday, August 14, 2002*
*167th District Court*
*Austin, Texas*

It took more than a year for Michael Scott to go to trial. He was represented by three capable attorneys: Carlos Garcia, Dexter Gilford, and Tony Diaz.

Garcia had handled several high-profile defendants such as John Brickley, who stabbed his wife and son to death, set them on fire, and severely burned and crippled himself in the process; Martin Gonzalez, who killed his wife, his lover, and another woman over the span of four years; and later, Caleb Thompson, the twin brother of Pastor Joshua Thompson, both convicted of beating a teenager during a Bible Studies program. Garcia had been appointed by the court to represent Scott.

The soon-to-be thirty-seven-year-old Gilford graduated from the University of Texas Law School in 1992. He actually worked on the other side as an assistant district attorney in nearby San Antonio from 1993 to

1995. He eventually switched sides and took up defense work. He served as the president of the Austin Criminal Defense Lawyers Association in 2001 and was also a board member of the Texas Criminal Defense Lawyers Association.

Garcia and Gilford were joined by the heavyset, salt-and-pepper–bearded, forty-five-year-old Tony Diaz, Scott's original trial lawyer. Diaz was known for his work as a member of the State Executive Board of Directors of the Texas League of United Latin American Citizens (LULAC) and as a district director of LULAC's District VII Board. He was also director of the Youth Leadership Academy at the University of Texas, a Parades Middle School mentor, and a board member of La Fuente, an education advocacy group. Diaz had much less experience in criminal cases than Garcia and relegated himself to the background as support.

The state was, once again, represented by Darla Davis, Efrain de la Fuente, and Robert Smith. Many of the same witnesses who testified before the court in the Robert Springsteen IV trial also testified in the Michael Scott case.

The opening statement by the prosecution basically mirrored the argument they gave one year earlier. The defense set about a familiar path with the tactic of attacking the police's desire to pin the crime on someone—anyone. Scott's attorneys did, however, bring a few new wrinkles to the case.

Carlos Garcia stated "It's a lot more to this case than meets the eye, not just about that confession. That's just the starting point. But go with the facts and details, strange things."

The first thing Garcia mentioned was that yogurt shop manager, Reese Price, had received death threats before the murders. Not only did Price receive death threats, Garcia explained, but Jennifer Harbison had allegedly received some as well just prior to the murders. Supposedly, someone said they would kill her and cut her up. Garcia claimed that Jennifer told her parents, a teacher, and her boyfriend. The police even got involved and placed a trace on her home phone.

Garcia also mentioned several yogurt shop employees reported they heard noises on top of the roof just days before the murders occurred.

Garcia informed the jury there was a cross scrawled on the inside of the yogurt shop the night of the murders. He wondered why none of the police officers had addressed this potentially significant clue.

After the shocking revelation of the death threats, Garcia redirected the jury's attention to the boys involved in the case. He spoke of Michael Scott's trust of law enforcement. He explained how Scott looked up to police officers. He also spoke of his client's battle with ADHD.

Garcia stressed that the case was about 1991, not 1999.

"Mike had never killed anybody until he got into that room because when they were done with him, they made that man believe he was a murderer."

Garcia believed Scott's confession was shaped by the detectives to fit the facts. "The truth about this confession is this poor man doesn't get it right the first time or the second time or the third time. He didn't get it right the last time either."

Dexter Gilford picked up on the topic of confessions.

"Friends, I have been a prosecutor down in Bexar County. I've sat on both sides of the courtroom. I know what a confession is. This ain't a confession."

Garcia closed the opening argument on a strong note. "There will be no conviction because if you are honest, and if you are an independent thinker, if you are objective, you will see, you will recognize reasonable doubt. You will see it. You will know it. We will expose it for what it is, which is the grossest miscarriage of justice this town has ever seen."

# CHAPTER 71

*Thursday, August 15, 2002*

The state started off with the parents of the girls. Much of the same testimony presented in the Robert Springsteen IV trial was repeated here. A few new tidbits, however, were introduced.

Bob Ayers spoke about how his daughter, Amy, was a "private little girl." How she literally became sick when she had to undress and shower in front of other girls in her gym class.

Barbara Ayres-Wilson spoke of how Jennifer and Sam Buchanan had wanted to get married. Ayres-Wilson also showed she would not back down from a fight. During cross-examination, for whatever reason, Carlos Garcia asked her if she knew how much Sarah Harbison weighed.

The mother glared at the attorney and said, "You can find it on the autopsy report."

The gallery also found Garcia's description of the girls' charred bodies as "roasted chickens" to be rather

unpleasant and unnecessary. He also had a penchant
for leaving pictures of the girls' dead bodies on his laptop computer screen pointing in the direction of the
girls' families. Ayres-Wilson found his behavior dis-
gusting.

"I couldn't let my mother see that." She sighed, referring to her elderly mother, who came to the trial
every day and had to stare at the graphic photos of her
granddaughters.

Garcia was not off to a smooth start.

*Wednesday August 21, 2002*

After a couple of days of identical witnesses from
the first trial, the prosecution called Reese Price to the
stand. Price, the yogurt shop manager, testified during
voir dire, outside of the presence of the jury, that she
spoke with Detective Paul Johnson in 1998.

Garcia asked her if the conversation revolved
around her being stalked in 1991.

"Correct," Price responded.

"Now, there was a report made, wasn't there, of a
burglary at your house?"

"Correct."

"And this is before the murders?"

"Correct."

"You were also getting harassing phone calls at the
yogurt shop. True?"

"I had someone that would call and hang up."

"You were also getting these calls at your house.
Right?"

"Yes, sir. That was before someone broke in."

"Your apartment was burglarized sometime before
the murders, correct?"

"I was away for Christmas. So Christmas or Christmas
Eve."

Garcia took a step back and a long pause.

Judge Lynch stepped in and asked, "Was that before or after?"

"Before," replied the diminutive Price.

"You mean a whole year before?" asked the judge.

"Yes, sir."

Garcia stepped back into the questioning. "The thing that struck you was because all your underclothes were put in a pile, and they took a knife and displayed it on top of the underclothes."

"Correct."

"One of the things that [also] struck you was that you felt that you were close in body size or petite just like Jennifer, correct?"

"Correct."

Judge Lynch was not convinced the break-in of Price's home and the phone calls warranted inclusion. "Based on what I have seen, and based on my understanding of what probative evidence is, the probative value of this evidence at this particular time is next to nil. It's like throwing stuff on the wall and seeing what might stick to the jury."

*Wednesday, August 28, 2002*

Carlos Garcia asked for a mistrial. His reason was due to a response given by Detective Ron Lara, one of the detectives who interrogated Scott. Lara's mention of Scott's "cold-blooded nature" set the attorney off.

Judge Lynch denied the request.

Throughout the trial, Judge Lynch appeared annoyed at Carlos Garcia's methods. The judge complained the attorney was "slow as molasses on things that are irrelevant." He was also annoyed by Garcia's habit of "testifying" instead of asking questions.

*Tuesday, September 3, 2002*

Dexter Gilford crossed Billy Sifuentes, a retired Austin police officer who witnessed the written statement of Scott, about the alleged cross that had been scrawled in the yogurt shop. After showing the witness a photo of the cross, Gilford asked, "Can you tell the members of the jury what that is?"

"It's usually a tattoo marked on the web of your finger," informed the officer. "Back in pachuco days. Before the gangs, before the word 'gangs' became prevalent, people that would serve time would put a little cross and how many times they served going to prison by a marking over the little cross. Texas Syndicate brought back that sign. You will see some TS members wearing it sometimes. It indicates a prison trip, that you made it by God's way; that's why you survived it."

"Texas Syndicate is a prison gang?" asked Gilford.

"Yes."

*Tuesday, September 10, 2002*

The most important cross-examination of the trial took place between Detective Robert Merrill and Carlos Garcia. The defense attorney loosened the detective up with a few basic questions regarding interrogation methods.

"You would never intentionally try and suggest to an individual how something happened so that they could then adopt it from you and give it back to you in the form of a statement?"

"I don't know about never," replied Merrill, "but I would not try to."

"Is it fair to say that the difference between an interview and an interrogation is that while the interview is fact-finding, the interrogation is accusatory in nature?"

"I would think so."

"Sometimes you lie to people, right?"

"I have," Merrill calmly replied.

"And when you lie, you have to lie without them knowing you're lying, right?"

"That's correct."

"So, basically, you're faking it. You're giving a false impression of sincerity and objectivity, right?"

Garcia honed in on the specifics of the interrogation of Michael Scott.

"What was the purpose of you guys wanting to take him to (the former location of) the yogurt shop?"

"He asked to go. We thought it might help."

"You have an operator who can operate that video camera, right?"

"Correct."

"Now you testify that he started remembering more things, right?"

"Yes, sir."

"Why didn't you tape-record him right there and then?"

"I just didn't."

"Why not?"

"I wanted to do it in the office."

"But you took a video camera to videotape him at the scene. He's remembering things. It doesn't make any sense, does it, that when he's supposedly spouting off these things you don't tape-record him?"

"Did to me at the time," replied a nonchalant Merrill.

"So all of that is undocumented, right?"

"That's right."

Garcia switched gears again to after the interview. "You tell him that he probably feels like you have beaten the hell out of him. What do you mean by that, Detective Merrill?"

"The interview process is tough," replied the stocky detective. "Everybody goes away just worn-out."

"How is it tough?"

"Because you're thinking as a detective—crime scene. What has he said? What can you use against him? Where are we going here? How do we get him to tell us what we want? And by the time I leave the room, I'm beat."

"You just said, 'How do you tell him what we want?' What did you want?"

"We wanted the truth to these murders. That's what we wanted."

Garcia wanted to find out the truth about Merrill's brandishing of the .22 revolver during the interrogation. "Why did you have to take that extreme measure of taking a gun, putting it in a person's hand, and at some point putting your finger behind their head?"

"Trying to get those sequences; getting the chain of events down."

"And you were willing to do whatever it took to get your story?"

"I don't know about whatever it took. I was willing to do what I could to try to get the story."

"And you scared him, didn't you?"

"Yeah, it did."

"It scared him. As a matter of fact, he says on that tape that you scared the shit out of him. Remember that?"

"Yes, I do."

"So the truth is that Michael Scott was aware that you put something behind his head."

"I don't believe that at all. He said when I put that gun in his hand, his mind went blank. I think that's what scared him. And then when I had him stand in that chair and accused him of killing four girls, three or four girls, I think that really scared him."

The following day, September 11, 2002, the state rested its case. It was the one-year anniversary of the terrorist attacks on the Twin Towers in New York City.

# CHAPTER 72

*Wednesday, September 11, 2002*

Michael Scott's defense team was prepared not to let their client be the second suspect in the yogurt shop murders to collapse. Again, as with the Springsteen defense team, Scott's lawyers tried to disprove the theory that the fire started on top of the girls. Several firefighters who were at the scene were brought in to testify.

Carlos Garcia also attempted to show that the door in the back of the yogurt shop was a key-lock door and not a swing-latch door as Scott had confessed to. Garcia argued how that would mean the killer had taken the key prior to the crime. Judge Lynch, however, did not believe Garcia ever proved this argument.

*Monday, September 16, 2002*

Another huge confrontation loomed on the horizon for Carlos Garcia. He was ready to take on Detective John Hardesty, the key interrogator of Michael Scott.

Garcia informed the detective that they would read through the interview of Scott.

"The transcript you've got in front of you has page numbers and line numbers and a lot of times we'll just refer to each as we go along. Okay?"

Hardesty would be difficult. "Well, I'd prefer we use the state's."

"We're going to use mine."

"I don't trust yours, Mr. Garcia."

"That's your opinion, sir. We're going to use mine."

"Well, the answers I give you I can't say are going to be one hundred percent correct."

Garcia took offense to the detective's attitude and asked Judge Lynch if he could be deemed an adverse witness. It was a rocky start.

"Would you try to change his memory," asked Garcia about Scott, "if he tells you one thing that's not quite accurate?"

"I guess in a general sense we might."

"So, you would try to change peoples' minds as to what they remember?"

"No. If Mr. Scott says he remembers something that we feel or I feel is—just totally contradicts what we know or is completely the opposite from the facts that we know, I'm not saying I would try to change his mind. But I would tell him he's on the wrong track and I think he knows more than what he's saying."

Later in the cross-examination, Garcia asked Hardesty, "Did you ever consider the fact that perhaps just he either doesn't have a good memory or he doesn't really remember?"

"Never," replied the officer. "He's extremely intelligent. He has an extremely good memory."

"But you never considered whether or not the fact that when he tells you earlier on, 'Look, I don't have a good memory,' that that could be the truth? You didn't consider that?"

"No. I don't believe that. Didn't believe it then and I don't believe it now."

*Tuesday, September 17, 2002*

Scott's lawyers brought in their own expert witness on false confessions. Dr. Richard Leo, an associate professor at the University of California, Irvine, and a student of Dr. Richard Ofshe, the expert witness who testified in Robert Springsteen's trial, broke down the parameters of false confessions for the court, outside of the presence of the jury.

"I think to understand the interrogation confession," began Dr. Leo, "one has to understand the process, how the techniques are designed, what they are meant to communicate and how they affect the decision-making and perceptions of both the guilty and the innocent."

Dexter Gilford asked Dr. Leo, "What is the basic underlying psychological principle of modern interrogation tactics?"

"Modern interrogation is premised on the notion that the person is guilty, that they will deny their guilt, and that you need to use psychological techniques to break down their denials and change their perceptions so that they come to see it as in their self-interest to make an admission."

"Are the interrogation tactics effective in eliciting confessions?"

"Yes. They are meant to affect a guilty suspect a particular way. They are not intended to be used on the innocent, but sometimes, inadvertently, they are."

"Can you go through the main techniques that are used to achieve this purpose?"

"Typically in an interrogation there is some type of isolation of the suspect. There is an attempt to remove the suspect from an environment that would support resistance. There's an attempt to build rapport to get the suspect to trust, maybe even like, the interrogator.

"And then at some point, there is the accusation, which serves as a kind of an ambush . . . where the interrogator will accuse the suspect. The suspect will deny. The interrogator, anticipating the denials, will attack the denials in multiple ways.

"The interrogator is trained to escalate pressure, to repeat the attacks, to generate a sense of hopelessness or powerlessness in the individual."

Leo spoke of a different method. "A separate set of tactics are meant to motivate the suspect to think that it's in his or her best self-interest to confess. A theme is inventing a scenario in which somebody could have committed the crime, but trying to minimize the seriousness of the crime."

"Basically, what you have described is two general parts of these interrogations," stated Gilford. "The first part is meant to break down the person's confidence and their ability to deny, correct?"

"Correct. And convince them that they are caught and there is no way out of this."

"And the second part [is] to build them back up as to, given that situation, here is the best course of action?"

"Correct. Given that your situation is hopeless—there is no way out, you are caught, no one is going to believe your denial—here are the reasons why you're better off by making an admission."

"And these techniques are effective in eliciting true confessions from guilty suspects, correct?"

"Correct."

"Are there times where a typical interrogation characterized by those techniques we've just talked about can result in an innocent person giving a false confession?"

"Yes. It typically takes a fair amount of pressure to get a false confession."

"Is it your opinion that it's the intended effect of these techniques and the interrogator to elicit a false confession from an innocent person?"

"No, absolutely not. There's numerous indisputable proven false confessions out there, but typically they result through an erroneous belief in the suspect's guilt and through a misuse or overuse of interrogation tactics. But it's not intended. The police intend to get the guilty, not the innocent."

"Is there a common myth that you are aware of concerning the notion of false confessions?"

"Yes. The common myth is that most people will not confess—well, people won't confess falsely unless they are tortured or they are mentally ill."

"Now, you have studied interrogations and confessions, and particularly you have focused on the phenomenon of false confessions, correct?"

Leo acknowledged that he had. He also mentioned three types of false confessions: voluntary, compliant, and persuaded, or internalized.

"The first category," Leo began to explain, "is known as voluntary false confessions. This is the typical example where somebody calls the police department after a high-profile crime and says, 'I did it.'

"The second category is called compliant false confession. This is where after an interrogation, the suspect is worn down and perhaps they are promised some kind of reward or suggested that they will be threatened with something harsh if they don't confess, and they knowingly confess falsely to escape the pressures of the environment, to terminate the interrogation, or to receive whatever benefit or promise that's been suggested.

"The third type is called the persuaded false confession. It's the most counterintuitive and most rare. Through the course of the interrogation, the suspect comes to doubt their memory. They come to believe, or are persuaded, that they have committed the crime, despite having no memory."

"We talked earlier about the techniques of interrogation," stated Gilford. "How would those tactics have some role in eliciting a false confession from an innocent person?"

"Well, an innocent person being accused is obviously going to deny," Leo replied, starting his explanation. "The police will not believe the denials. So when the innocent person is interrogated, typically the police will make up evidence of their guilt.

"An innocent person, who is naive or has no experience with the police, or is trusting of authority, may have no idea that police can lie and make up evidence.

"The suspect may come to doubt themselves. They may come to perceive that their denials are pointless; that they are not going to be accepted, that there is no way out of the situation. The suspect may start to think, 'Well, I am being railroaded, or maybe I did it and I just don't remember it.'"

"How does one go about developing a narrative description of the crime scene?" wondered Gilford.

"The suspect desperately tries to remember, even though they have no memory of doing this. And so they sometimes look to the interrogator and try to infer what are the correct answers. They sometimes incorporate knowledge that is publicly known. And sometimes they guess. They speculate. They try to reason from inference. It's a desperate process to search for or excavate or find memories that don't exist. The pressures of the interrogation environment and the interrogator are what caused the person to create a narrative.

"It's only the sustained pressures of the interrogator

and the interrogation environment that caused this phenomenon in the first place."

"Can you tell the court briefly, what are your criteria for qualifying a confession as false in the studies specifically related to false confessions?" asked Gilford.

"There are only four ways you can absolutely prove a confession is false. One is if you can show that it was physically impossible for the person to have committed a crime. Say, they were in another state at the time.

"A second is if you can show that the crime never occurred; murder victim shows up live after a person falsely confesses.

"A third is that scientific evidence exonerates the person. DNA—you hear a lot of cases about DNA.

"And then a fourth is where the true perpetrator comes forward, as in the Christopher Ochoa case, here in Austin, Texas."

The jury, however, would never hear Leo's testimony. Judge Lynch limited the parameters of what the doctor could discuss. The result was Leo would be limited to discussing that guilty people confess and why they confess. The doctor would not be allowed to talk about the fact that innocent people confess and why they do it. The judge cited Leo's lack of empirical scientific evidence that proved that the methods of interrogation used would lead to a persuaded false confession. As a result, the defense chose not to include Leo as a witness because he would have, in effect, become a witness for the prosecution.

# CHAPTER 73

*Wednesday, September 18, 2002*

In addition to Dr. Richard Leo, the defense for Michael Scott had another key witness, an expert on crime scene reconstruction, Ross Gardner. Gardner was a twenty-nine-year law enforcement officer and a twenty-year military veteran. He also coauthored *Bloodstain Pattern Analysis: With an Introduction to Crime Scene Reconstruction,* with Tom Bevel.

Gardner explained the purpose of crime scene reconstruction. And he was allowed to do so before the jury.

"Crime scene reconstruction is really simple logic, deduction, scientific method. That's all it is. In a criminal investigation, we have a variety of information that comes to us. Much of it is testimonial evidence, but the more significant evidence is the physical evidence, because the physical evidence never lies. It is what it is.

"Crime scene analysis is designed to look at the information in the crime scene, specifically every item of evidence, its relationship to other items of evidence, and from that define specific events that occurred."

Gardner gave an analogy to explain what he does. "Imagine it this way. Somebody walk(s) up to you with a jigsaw puzzle, five hundred pieces, reaching in the box and grabbing a couple of handfuls, throwing them down in front of your face, and then walking off with the box. They then turn to you and say, 'Okay, tell me what happened based on the pieces you have.'

"So what we do is take those pieces of physical evidence, we put them in as much order as is possible. When we're done, what we have is a skeleton, a lattice, and those pieces fit in certain orders, and then that tells us these things occurred within that scene."

In regard to the yogurt shop murders, Gardner was given the autopsy reports of all four girls, the original incident report, all scientific reports, and the fire reports from Melvin Stahl and Marshall Littleton. Gardner did not receive a copy of Michael Scott's confession.

Based on his research of the materials, Gardner came up with several conclusions that differed from the scenario divulged by the prosecution. He believed the girls died in the positions where they were discovered. He believed Eliza Thomas was raped. He also believed Sarah Harbison was anally raped. He believed the girls were lying on the floor, facedown, when they were executed.

Gardner believed Amy Ayers was next to Jennifer Harbison when the older girl was killed. He believed Amy was dragged across the floor approximately seven to nine feet with the ligature around her neck. She was repositioned on her knees and shot with the .22. She fell to the ground on her left side. She either rolled or was pulled even farther away. She was shot a second time, this time with the .380. Someone grabbed her arm and dragged her several feet away to the middle of the back room.

Gardner further testified that the evidence showed him the fire did not start on top of the girls' dead bodies. He concurred with Stahl's initial fire analysis.

"This arson investigator certainly did know his job."

Gardner stated there was no evidentiary support for the claim the fire started on top of the girls.

The defense rested its case later that afternoon.

# CHAPTER 74

*Friday, September 20, 2002*

Efrain de la Fuente stood up to make the closing argument for the state in what had been the largest trial in the history of Travis County. The prosecutor asked the jurors to take a close look at the Michael Scott confession videotape.

"You will see his demeanor on the tape. Look for it. When he's talking about shooting those two girls, it's nothing to him. 'But don't blame me for killing all four girls because I did not do that,' and then he starts crying."

De la Fuente repeated many of the same arguments presented in the Springsteen trial. He concluded his discussion while looking at Michael Scott.

"How do we know what a real killer looks like? Is there an age that we put on them? Do they have to be white, Hispanic, African-American, Asian? Do they have to have tattoos? Do they have to come from a well background or a bad background? When do you know you are looking at a killer? That's what they're going to say. Look at this face here. You think this guy was capable of doing what he did?

"Is there really a face that we can put on a killer?" de la Fuente asked as he turned toward the jury. "There is no face you can put on a killer, folks."

The prosecutor looked back toward Scott and said, "You got two options here, folks. You can award this defendant the Oscar for Best Actor and acquit him when you look at that videotape. Or, you can do what the evidence dictates you must do and convict him. Thank you."

After a ten-minute break, Dexter Gilford took his place in front of the jury box.

"It is true that guilty people confess to crimes," the thirty-seven-year-old attorney opened. "It is also true that innocent people confess to crimes. The question then, it behooves us to try to at least determine when does that happen and if we can identify when it happens, [and] how it happens."

Gilford proceeded to read through a list of details Scott provided during his confession that did not match up to the actual crime scene evidence.

"We have a confession in this case and we ought to ask for more, right? We are all citizens of this city. We deserve it. Those girls' families deserve it. We deserve something better than a slipshod, disjointed, inaccurate, incomplete, unreliable, manifest lies–filled substitute for what happened to those girls.

"Mike Scott should not be our easy way out of this. If the function of this whole thing is for us to get to the truth, then Mike deserves it. This town deserves [it]. You deserve it. The families deserve it."

Judge Lynch dismissed the jurors for deliberation.

# CHAPTER 75

After nearly two days of deliberations, the jury members returned to their seats in the courtroom.

"Good afternoon, ladies and gentlemen of the jury," greeted Judge Lynch. He did not waste any time. "Speaking through your foreperson, have you arrived at a verdict in this case?"

"We have, Your Honor," replied the foreperson.

"If you would tender that to the bailiff for presentation to the court." The bailiff, Bob Burnett, took the verdict from the foreperson and walked it over to the judge. The proverbial pin drop could be heard, it was so quiet. Judge Lynch read the sheet, folded it back up, and said, "Would the defendant please rise?"

A stoic Scott stood up from his seat.

Judge Lynch read the verdict.

"'We, the jury, find the defendant, Michael Scott, guilty of the offense of capital murder.'" The crowd was quiet. Jeannine Scott was stunned by the judge's announcement. The victims' families remained calm and quiet. "Mr. Foreperson," continued Lynch, "is this the individual, personal verdict of each of the twelve jurors in this cause?"

"Yes, Your Honor, it is."

"Ladies and gentlemen of the jury, this concludes the first phase of the trial, the guilt/innocence phase. The next phase is, of course, the punishment phase. We intend to start that tomorrow morning at ten A.M."

Afterward, Jeannine Scott was furious. Visibly upset, Michael Scott's wife stated in a clear and articulate speaking voice, "The state of Texas has succeeded in putting another innocent man in prison. God, I can only hope the jury has enough sense to realize it's not worth his life. The fight starts now. He's innocent, and I'm going to fight every day to bring him home."

# CHAPTER 76

*Tuesday, September 24, 2002*

The previous day's testimony focused on the good and bad of Michael Scott after the murders. The jury had the night to digest the information. Now they were ready to hear the final arguments in the case.

Prosecutor Efrain de la Fuente covered the same bases as in the Springsteen trial that the jury would need to decide: future dangerousness, participation in the crime, and were there any mitigating factors. He stated that the answers should be yes, yes, and no. And that Michael Scott should receive the death penalty for the murder of Amy Ayers.

"We, as a society, did not fail Michael Scott. And do not blame society for what this defendant did to those four girls. Thank you."

Dexter Gilford took his place before the jury box.

"I've had to stand before a jury one time in my career and face the kind of task that I face this morning. I'm going to ask you all to answer those questions in such a way that you give life, that you maintain life, that you all preserve life."

Gilford stood straight before the jurors. "All twelve of you, and me, Carlos, Tony, and Mike, Robert, Darla, and Efrain, and the families on both sides of the aisle, are bound together in ways that we will be appreciating years from now. If you all live a long, full life, as I hope to do, I imagine you will appreciate that as time goes on.

"I say that to you for one reason, and for one reason only, and I don't want to suggest it; I just want to be up front with you. You all stand on a precipice. And you will make a decision that, the truth is, will be very, very, very difficult to undo."

Gilford spoke of human fallibility. "We all know that everybody is much more than one day, however bad that day was, however horrible." Gilford said his client had traveled the straight-and-narrow path for the majority of the time after the murders. "Mike Scott learned how to be a father, a good father. He learned how to be a friend, a good friend. He learned how to share what he could with people that he knew and cared about. Everybody can't do that. Everybody doesn't do it.

"You never know how your daily walk affects other people. And it ought to count for something."

Again the defense team turned to the Holy Book for inspiration.

"Let me leave you with this," Gilford stated quietly. "When Paul addressed a group of citizens of the city of Corinth who had been persecuted, and when it was finally clear that at some point the persecution might stop, he had one admonition. Be careful that you do not take, retake, life for life and kind for kind.

"I listened to Mr. Ayers. He said that he was running out of things to do. I have two daughters at home, and every night I come home during this trial, I look at them both, and I don't know how these people do it. They're the most gracious people I've ever seen.

"But let me say this to you. I don't know how killing Michael is going to give anybody anything to do. Thank you for your time and your patience. Godspeed to all of you."

Carlos Garcia picked up the defense's closing argument. He struck with an additional emotional plea.

"If Martin Luther King were here today, he would choose life for Michael James Scott. If Gandhi were here today, he would choose life for Michael James Scott. If Mother Teresa were here today, she would choose life for Michael James Scott. If Jesus Christ were in human form present here in this courtroom, there is no doubt where he would stand. He would choose life. The best of us chooses life, time and time and time again, no matter who the sinner is."

The historical and evangelical angle seemed to work. A few of the jurors cried as Garcia spoke. Tears formed in Scott's eyes as well.

"The best of us," Garcia continued, "the best of humanity, chooses life. We choose life. The law is satisfied with life.

"And the best of those human beings that I just mentioned is in this courtroom today. It is. That best is in all of us.

"This case is a test for you. Sometime in the future, all of us are going to die and whoever your Maker is is going to ask for an accounting, going to ask, 'What did you do?'

"You can answer, 'Lord, that day there was a man before me who at one time was a child, and flawed as he was, I chose life, because that's what I learned from you.'"

Garcia paused and turned toward the jury.

"We're asking for a verdict, not for this man, but for a boy. A seventeen-year-old boy. Thank you."

The state had one last argument for the jury. Prosecutor Robert Smith stood before them.

"I will not be arrogant enough to tell you that I know what the answers to these questions will be," stated the soft-spoken attorney. "I will not be presumptuous enough to tell you how God will judge you for the decisions that you make in this trial."

Smith wanted to remind the jury that Scott's actions were not those of a boy, but rather a cold, calculating killer.

"They came in through those back doors, men with guns. The one place in the world that these girls should feel safe is in the back room of the yogurt shop." Smith spoke of how the girls gave them everything they had, but it was not enough.

He pointed to a photograph of Amy Ayers, "a thirteen-year-old girl who was embarrassed to even dress at school is made by these men to take off all of her clothes."

He next pointed at Eliza Thomas's photograph and said, "This beautiful young lady, on her period, is required by these men at gunpoint to take off all her clothes."

Then a photograph of Sarah Harbison. "This young lady, fifteen years old, she, too, is required to disrobe. Remember that young girl took the time and made the effort to take the ring of her boyfriend off when she took off her clothes. This young girl, who only moments earlier had been so happy because she's been with her boyfriend."

Smith reminded the jury of the brutality of the crime. He also stressed that Michael Scott was capable of making adult decisions.

"This was not an impulsive act. Choices like that are made on values, not on science."

Smith again turned his attention toward the jurors.

"I want to leave you with one last thought when you

are evaluating Michael Scott. They asked him a question on that tape. 'How were the girls shot?'

"And he said, 'In the back of the head.' And then he slipped and out of his mouth came 'quick, easy kill.' That's how he remembers that. And he's home taking care of Jasmine, and that's how he remembers it. 'Quick, easy kill,' *bang, bang*. That's who you're talking about here."

*September 24, 2002*
*3:01 p.m.*

Once again the jury returned with a verdict. Several of their faces were red from wiping away tears. Once again Judge Lynch wasted no time in reading the verdict.

"'Issue number one. Did you find from the evidence beyond a reasonable doubt that there is a probability that the defendant would commit criminal acts of violence that would constitute a continuing threat to society? Answer: No.'"

Scott stood motionless and emotionless.

A hush fell over the gallery.

"Based on the jury's answer to special issue number one," Judge Lynch stated, "the court is ready to proceed with the punishment and the sentencing at this time.

"After the required hearing on punishment, the jury today returned a verdict answering special issue number one, no. The court hereby accepts the verdict of this jury in this case." Judge Lynch glanced up toward the defendant.

"It is, therefore, the judgment of this court that you, Michael Scott, are guilty of the offense of capital murder. Further, in conformance with the jury's verdict on special issue number one and in compliance with the laws of the state of Texas, I hereby assess your punishment at confinement in the Institutional Division of the Texas Department of Criminal Justice for life."

After Judge Lynch dismissed the jury, he addressed all of the attorneys.

"I know this has been a tough trial for the lawyers as well, and contentious at some times, contentious amongst each other and with the court. But I appreciate the diligence of the lawyers on both sides. I have never had harder-working attorneys—I will say that for the record—and I appreciate it from both sides. Thank you.

"We are in recess at this time."

The reaction to the verdict was mixed. The defense was elated Scott had avoided the death penalty. Attorney Tony Diaz stated, "Today's verdict shows we are evolving into a new standard of decency. That's what this represents for the city of Austin."

Scott's wife, Jeannine, received hugs from her friends and family. She repeated, "All we have to do is bring him home now."

The parents of the girls were less than thrilled. Barbara Ayres-Wilson sat quietly. When asked if she had anything to say to the jurors, she replied, "I just couldn't say anything nice to them."

Bob Ayers briskly walked out of the courtroom past reporters without saying a word.

The jury foreman gave a quick quote: "It was a sad experience for all the family and friends of the victims and the guilty party."

Christian González, senior Web correspondent for Channel 8, a local television news station created by Time-Warner Cable, conducted an interview with the three defense attorneys after the sentence was read.

***Channel 8:*** *Is this a bittersweet victory?*

***Garcia:*** *A lot of satisfaction. We think it was the appropriate verdict, given the facts that were pre-*

*sented in the punishment phase of the trial, given the little evidence the government had, future dangerousness, I think the jury reached the only decision they could reach given what they heard.*

*Q: What caused the emotion in your final argument?*

*Gilford: When I talked about the courage, I couldn't help but think about how scared I had been in that courtroom many a days, as the evidence unfolded and as frightened I was of what might happen to our client. And just that fact that I had gotten this far is what caused the emotional outpouring in me.*

*Q: How has the case affected your faith?*

*Garcia: The only way you can do this kind of case is to have some sort of faith that the right decision is reached. My faith was shaken to some extent on Sunday, that's what I want to say there. But nonetheless, I've come to realize that things happen for a reason. But for our faith, I don't think we could have produced the kind of commentary in closing arguments we produced today. All of that material is not ours. At least I don't think it is. It comes from inspiration from God.*

*Diaz: I prayed for Dexter. And I prayed for Mike. And I prayed for Carlos.*

*Q: What did you learn from this case?*

*Garcia: You can't do it alone. There's no way that any of us individually could have done this job alone.*

*Gilford: I drew a lot of my will to kind of show up every day from Mr. Ayers, of all people, and his wife. All of the families, but particularly those two because they sat right there in the front row. More than anything a sense of grace. A sense of grace that I kind of drew on from him. I know that might sound odd but I really did because I thought that he was a very, very gracious man. But if he showed up every day, I figured I certainly could.*

*Q: Who is Michael Scott the person?*

*Garcia: He is goofy. He is patient. He is kind. I mean we didn't find one person, one person . . . you know, to say one bad thing about this kid, with the exception of this allegation.*

*Q: What did you tell Scott's wife?*

*Gilford: Mainly along the lines of not being shaken to the point that she lost all of her hope.*

*Q: What's next for Scott?*

*Garcia: Legally we file a notice of appeal and a motion for a new trial, certain things that you just do as a matter of course and it goes from there. He's got three cases pending all arising out of the same incident. We don't know what that district attorney is gonna do.*

*Q: What do you say to your critics?*

*Garcia: I got on this case a year ago this week and our job is real simple. Our job is to defend our client. That is what we get court appointed to*

*do. That is what we get paid to do. And it's to fol-
low the law and defend him. On a personal note,
I'm against the death penalty. And so no, it doesn't
matter to me one way or the other what anybody
else thinks. I'm gonna work as hard as I can to
complete that job.*

*Q: What were the costs of the case?*

***Garcia:** The cost is we don't get to see our kids.
We don't get to see our families. We miss the sum-
mers and we miss family events. There is a cost
that you cannot put a price on, that's something
that doesn't show up on a voucher. It doesn't
show up on a county budget and that kind of cost
you cannot account for.*

*Q: Compare this case to others.*

***Garcia:** It doesn't. That courtroom on a day-to-
day basis, every time we went in there you could
cut the tension with a knife. That pressure and
tension just permeated that courtroom. There was
a clear division down that aisle of the family of
the victims and the Michael Scott family and
friends. There was a clear line between the prosecution and defense. It was very contentious. It
was just different. It's just different. It didn't feel
good and it takes a toll on you. But you can feel
it. It's a weight.*

***Gilford:** There were times where it was just, you
felt like it was you, Carlos, Tony, and Mike at that
little table and everything else [was] just closing
in on you and those were the times that were most
difficult.*

*Q: What's next for you?*

**Gilford:** I gotta go back to my office and see what's left of my practice. I had a practice before this thing started.

**Garcia:** I'm gonna go build a tree house, go lay ceramic tile in my kitchen because it's been without tile for eight months. And just take some time off. And then after that I've got two other capital murder cases. Our practices are shot in terms of business. So we gotta go back and build that up again. I suspect that if we both (Gilford) continue doing death penalty work that we're going to be working together.

*Q: Describe the legal system.*

**Garcia:** We have a criminal justice system that is flawed. But in spite of its flaws, its defects, it works. It's the best that we have. Sometimes we don't agree with its results, sometimes we do. But the point is, that it is a human system, a human artifice and with all its flaws, it's the best we got. You know, we respect it.

*Q: Describe that hug you shared with Scott before they took him away.*

**Gilford:** He was trusting me with his life. And whether or not I was up for that job, realizing that at that time and also realizing that Mike's life had been spared, all of that kind of happened at once. I knew that he appreciated all that we had done, even if that jury would not have come back with the verdict that they came back with. He trusted me. When they came back with that ver-

*dict, he and I just shared in all of that. So, all of that kind of happened at the same time.*

*Q: Explain Scott's sentence.*

**Gilford:** *Thirty-five years, including the time that he spent in jail when he was arrested on Oct. 6, 1999. Which was what? Almost three years now. So, it'll be 32 more years before the board of pardon and paroles can even consider him.*

*Q: Some may call you the dream team.*

**Garcia:** *(Laughter) We did the best we could with what we had.*

**Gilford:** *Often times we just kind of felt like Laurel and Hardy. We wanted to make sure our personalities came out because we thought having some credibility at punishment was going to be very important.*

*Q: Any parting thoughts?*

**Gilford:** *None of us are unmindful of the pain and suffering that those families have to go through all the time. None of us are unmindful of that. And like I told the jury, I probably haven't seen a more gracious set of people, and that'll remain with me for the rest of my life and my career.*

# CHAPTER 77

*Tuesday, December 3, 2002*
*167th District Court*
*Austin, Texas*

There was still one suspect left. Maurice Pierce, the alleged ringleader, had been in jail, unable to make bail, since October 1999.

Pierce's attorney, Lad Slavik, filed for a change of venue. The hope was to escape the media crush that surrounded the murder case. Judge Mike Lynch stated he would probably make his decision on January 22, 2003, at Pierce's next court appearance date.

*Tuesday, January 28, 2003*

Nearly one week had passed since Pierce's scheduled court date.

At the Travis County Courthouse, District Attorney Ronnie Earle stepped up to the podium. He appeared sullen as he leaned into the microphones.

"It is without pleasure that I announce today that the

yogurt shop capital-murder cases against Maurice Pierce have been dismissed."

Earle explained that the primary witnesses against Pierce were Robert Springsteen and Michael Scott. According to the district attorney, "Both have made statements that cannot be used without violating the constitutional right of Maurice Pierce to confront the witnesses against him." Their statements, therefore, could not be entered against Pierce.

"The state is therefore unable to proceed at this time," Earle declared.

"The case against Maurice Pierce remains open and the investigation continues. Murder has no statute of limitations.

"We do not have the evidence to convict him right now, but life is long. We believe there are people who know something that would be helpful in this investigation. We urge them to come forward. They will have an attentive audience."

Earle looked up at his own attentive audience. "The murders of Amy Ayers, Jennifer and Sarah Harbison, and Eliza Thomas left a scar on Austin's soul. The convictions of Robert Springsteen and Michael Scott have helped to provide a measure of healing to that scar. But we're not through, and we won't rest until justice is done in full measure."

*January 28, 2003*
*Outside the Travis County Correctional Complex*
*Del Valle, Texas*
*3:40 P.M.*

Maurice Pierce, clad in blue jeans and a white T-shirt, which bulged from too much prison food, stepped outside the Travis County Correctional Complex in Del Valle and into the arms of his cousin Annette Castellaños.

"It is an act of God that he has been released," claimed Castellaños. "He has a daughter and he has a wife that he lost years with that they'll never be able to replace."

When asked how he felt to be released from jail, Pierce simply replied, "Happy."

Pierce was taken from the jail in an SUV to Lad Slavik's office in downtown Austin. He was greeted there by two dozen friends and family members. His wife, Kimberli, and their daughter soon reunited with him after they drove down from Dallas.

Jeannine Scott was ecstatic about the news of Pierce's release. She declared that she was "completely stunned." She stated she was riding a roller coaster of emotions. She was happy for Pierce but upset that her husband would not be coming home to his daughter that night.

"I don't believe they actually said they had no case. I never expected them to say that," she stated with a smile. "I'm glad they did."

She turned serious and said, "Based on what I'm understanding, it has done nothing but bolstered the appeal for Michael and Robert." She said of Pierce's release, "It doesn't improve my faith in the system. It does show that the innocent can go home. I continue to maintain that all of them are innocent."

Jeannine Scott also sent a personal message to District Attorney Earle.

"Stop wasting the taxpayers' time and money and find the actual perpetrators."

The parents of the girls, of course, had a different reaction to the news of Pierce's release. Barbara Ayres-Wilson, never at a loss for words when it came to her daughters' cases, was almost left speechless. She did state she was confident Pierce was guilty.

"I can't imagine why his friends would include him in that scenario if he was not," she said, referring to the confessions made by both Michael Scott and Robert Springsteen, which pegged Pierce as the leader.

Bob and Pam Ayers refused to comment on the decision.

*Thursday, January 30, 2003*

Maurice Pierce, flanked by his wife and daughter, legal team, and additional family members, stepped in front of a passel of microphones. He removed a sheet of paper from his pocket, opened it, and read a prepared statement.

Pierce thanked the media for showing up. He thanked his wife, daughter, and family for sticking behind him. He thanked his lawyers for their tireless efforts. He also thanked God for giving him strength.

"As for my incarceration, it has been a very difficult and painful period of time. For three-and-a-half years, I was separated from my wife and daughter, my family, and my friends, and those years I will never be able to regain. When I was detained and arrested, I proclaimed my innocence of all the charges that were filed against me, and I am standing here today with that same proclamation. I am innocent of any and all charges pertaining to the yogurt shop case."

Pierce said he needed to move on. He wanted to make a new life with his family. He also declared he would not sue the city of Austin.

He asked the media to give him space.

"I am sure that this has been a very emotional time for my family and I," Pierce concluded, "and we would like the opportunity to move on with our lives. I thank you very much and Godspeed to you all."

# EPILOGUE

*Wednesday, October 8, 2003*
*United States District Court—West Eighth Street*
*Austin, Texas*

The yogurt shop murders cases were far from over. Patric Davidson, Michael Scott's "longtime best friend," stood before United States magistrate judge Andrew Austin. The thirty-seven-year-old man had been arrested as an accessory after the fact.

Additional charges against Davidson included failing to report a felony, making a false statement, and obstruction of justice. Davidson's statements specifically revolved around the .380 pistol that Scott supposedly hid after the murders. He claimed he gave a bag to Davidson to hide. After he confessed in 1999, Scott allegedly called Davidson and told him to tell the police about the gun.

If they asked.

The gun has never been located.

Davidson faced up to twenty-years in federal prison and as much as $1 million in fines. It only took $5,000, however, to bail him out. Upon his release, he said he was "not surprised" by his arrest.

"They are out to blame somebody," Davidson claimed, insisting Scott's conviction was bogus.

Barbara Ayres-Wilson stated, "Anything they can do to put an end to this, to find out who is involved, is wonderful. Until we know the whole truth about how my girls died and those other two died, it's always going to be unresolved.

"The pain continues."

*Tuesday, March 9, 2004*
*United States District Court—West Eighth Street*
*Austin, Texas*

"Guilty, Your Honor," stated Patric Davidson to United States district judge Sam Sparks. Davidson admitted he told authorities several different stories regarding the whereabouts of the bag Michael Scott had given him, which allegedly contained the .380 semiautomatic pistol used in the yogurt shop killings.

On May 21, 2004, Davidson was sentenced to one year in federal prison, the maximum amount, by Judge Sparks. Chris Davidson, Davidson's brother, believed there was an ulterior motive behind the sentence.

"It's someone's political agenda. Someone wants resolution to this case and a mark in their belt."

Judge Sparks, on the other hand, claimed the imposition of the sentence was the direct result of Davidson's actions. Sparks believed Davidson had detectives "trying to shimmy up flagpoles, where there's no flag."

*Present Day, 2005*

Michael Scott is currently imprisoned in Ramsey Unit II in Rosharon, Texas, located about thirty miles southwest of Houston. Ramsey houses almost twelve hundred male inmates, who range in custody levels from G1 to G4. They are observed by more than 230 security employees. Scott is allowed weekend visitors. He usually spends time with his wife and daughter. According to his mother, Lisa Scott McClain, Michael enjoys playing basketball, exercising, and reading books.

"I can't even keep up with how many books I send him," McClain recalled. "He is a voracious reader."

Scott's mother also talked about the problems her son encountered at Ramsey. She said Scott was only one test shy from earning his high-school-equivalency diploma, or General Educational Development (GED) test, before his 1999 arrest. She claims prison officials have refused to allow her son to complete the test.

"He still receives death threats," McClain also claimed.

Michael Scott's appellate attorney, Ariel Payan, filed an appeal on his behalf that alleged his client's conviction should be overturned: "Because another man's confession was used against him illegally." Payan used the March 2004 Supreme Court decision in *Crawford* v. *Washington* as the backbone of Scott's argument.

*Crawford* v. *Washington* focused on the trial of Michael Crawford, who assaulted and attempted to kill Kenneth Lee on August 5, 1999, in Olympia, Washington. Crawford, at first, denied the attack, but he eventually confessed to stabbing the man. Crawford claimed Lee had attempted to rape Crawford's wife, Sylvia, at an earlier date. Sylvia also testified her husband intended to kill Lee. At trial, Sylvia did not testify against her husband because of the state of Washington's marital privilege, which usually prevents one spouse from testifying against another spouse without the other's consent. Such a privilege, however, "does not extend to a spouse's out-of-court statements admissible under a hearsay exception." The prosecution sought to enter the audiotapes wherein Sylvia admitted she led her husband to Lee's apartment, thus facilitating the assault and disproving Crawford's self-defense theory. Crawford argued that admitting the evidence would violate his federal constitutional right to be "confronted with the witnesses against him." The tape was played and Crawford was convicted of assault.

The Washington Court of Appeals overturned Crawford's conviction. The Washington Supreme Court, however, reversed the court of appeals and claimed that Sylvia's statement "bore guarantees of trustworthiness."

The United States Supreme Court agreed to hear the case. It ruled in favor of Crawford by a unanimous vote of 9–0, citing the defendant's Sixth Amendment right to confrontation.

Payan argued Scott's case before the Texas Third Court of Appeals on June 9, 2004, just four days after one of the toughest presidents on crime, Ronald Reagan, passed away.


Robert Springsteen currently sits on death row in the Polunsky Unit in Livingston, Texas, waiting to hear the status of his appeal filed by his attorney, Mary Kay Sicola. The appeal was filed on his behalf on October 16, 2002.

Sicola alleged several points of error:

- The trial court should not have allowed excerpts of Mike Scott's written confession, since he was a non-testifying codefendant and, therefore, did not give Springsteen a chance to confront him.
- Amanda Statham's (and her mother's) testimony, about Mike Scott's confession should not have been allowed in.
- Springsteen's confession to the police was a violation of the Due Process Clause of the Four-

teenth Amendment and should not have been allowed in.

- Irrelevant testimony which should not have been included, was allowed in,
- The execution of a minor is unconstitutional and a violation of international law.

# AUTHOR'S NOTE

The complex case presented here touches so many facets that almost overwhelmed me during the writing of this book. Many people believe the yogurt shop murders is a case of out-of-control Texas justice. Others believe it is an open-and-shut case.

The reality, however, is so much more.

Those facets are severalfold: senseless murders, innocence lost, police corruption, potential judicial failure, politics and crime, wayward youth gone wrong, and so on. It would be a disservice to the readers, however, for me to tell them how to think in regard to this case.

My goal has been to present a most unique and difficult case in a straightforward fashion and let you, the reader, decide how you feel about the outcome.

I believe I have achieved this goal.

As a result, I hope you come away with a better understanding of this tragic story, but I also hope you have even more questions.

Remember. Don't ever be afraid to ask questions.

One of the best discussions I had concerning possible preventative measures in this case took place with Barbara Ayres-Wilson, mother of Jennifer and Sarah Harbison. We spoke for five hours on May 25, 2004, in her SAJE offices, in Austin, Texas.

"Do you want to talk about the boys at all?" I asked.

"What I would like to know," Ayres-Wilson replied, "is what we could have done different? I don't mean helping them. Don't let me miscommunicate what I'm trying to say. I don't mean helping the little bastards. But, as a society, how, as parents, what did we do wrong raising them that they didn't have a soul?

"Of course, I have an opinion about it. Bonding comes in the first few weeks and if you are not bonding early on, then you can't give a damn later. Were they given too much? Were they not given enough? Obviously, as teenagers, they were thrown out in all kinds of ways, emotionally, physically.

"I would like to know what we did wrong raising those boys. Where we made those mistakes.

"Two days after the girls were murdered, I had the basketball team over at my house and I told them, 'Somebody didn't love these people (the killers) enough.' Now, that's a dumb statement for someone who doesn't know anything. This is probably way-out for the time. I'm sure those girls were like, 'What is this woman talking about?' I said, 'This is why you need to be so careful and not have any children that you don't want.'

"I'm talking about safe sex here and my kids are being murdered, but that was my first thought. I mean, I didn't know they were children, but even adults, whoever it was, they didn't have any love in them that they could do something like that. And that's still my premise.

"We have learned so much about the brain and how it works and kids aren't getting enough attention. We've learned that it takes twenty-one hundred words an hour spoken directly to a child to make their brains develop properly. And it's not yelling at them or putting them in front of the TV; it's directly speaking to them. You have to bond with your child. You can't ignore them; you can't put them off; you can't neglect them, in all kinds of ways. You can't give them too much; you can't dote on them; you have to be present in their life. You have to have them on a good schedule; you have to put them into bed every night; you have to feed them; you have to care. Those are real simple things that I'd like to know: What part of that scenario those four boys didn't get? When did it start falling apart for them? When their families divorced? When did that happen? Because we have to decide, when is a divorce a good thing for children?

"That's why we have to say, 'What happened to Robert Springsteen?' I met his father. I know what happened. His father's a loser. He got thrown away. When his parents divorced, he became very unimportant. Now, before then, I don't know, but after then, he was overstimulated. Too much TV, didn't bond with anybody, there was . . . I don't know all the details. I'd like to know all the details from all four of these boys.

"This isn't about blaming his parents. It's about understanding what we did wrong as parents. I mean, I know what I did wrong. We have to know what the system did wrong. We have to know that if we own a business, what is our responsibility to keep it safe for the people that work there and the customers that come in. It's not enough to buy a franchise and invest in it and just want to know what the bottom line is. We ought to know as bankers what we invest in, and if we loan out money to a company that is not taking care of their employees and customers.

"These are common-sense questions that we ought to be gathering from these problems that we go through. 'Maybe, we shouldn't let kids work? Maybe we should?' These are the kinds of questions that need to be talked about. We need to have a dialogue about these issues. 'When is it a good thing for kids to work alone at night? When is it a good thing for other kids to supervise a younger kid?' Probably not very often, because there is a lot of abuse that goes on at work, because they don't know how to deal with the responsibility that they have. They are working with people that they don't know what their backgrounds are. There are just so many questions that we don't have the answers to, but we need to be asking the questions.

"You have to ask yourself as a parent, 'How much of this is my fault?' 'How much of this as a parent of two little girls that got murdered, how much could I have prevented?' And then you have to ask yourself as a business owner, 'How much of this could I have prevented?' As an insurance company that insured that business, you have to ask yourself, 'How much of this could I have prevented?' As a community, we have to ask ourselves, 'How much of this could we have prevented?'

"I know some people think you shouldn't connect anything, but you should. It's not enough to say, 'Well, you can't do this.' Yeah, you can and you should. That's our responsibility. That's being a grown-up. You're a grown-up now and you have the responsibility of connecting all the dots. We have to have enough information. It's not enough to say, 'I don't want to do it.' Well, I don't want to do it either. I don't want to do any of it. But I know I have to keep asking the questions until somebody says, 'What is it that you want?'

"And then there's a part of me that's like, 'I don't know why I should care if your children are safe? It doesn't make any difference to me.' And then I remind myself that Jennifer and Sarah want me to."

Tears welled up in her eyes as she tried to smile.

"I miss my girls."

For case updates, additional photographs, and more,
please go to:
*www.coreymitchell.com*

For more information, go to:
*www.saje.org*
*www.texas-justice.com*

A portion of the royalties from *Murdered Innocents*
will be donated to SAJE by the author.

# IN MEMORY

Dana Holliday—long live Astrowoman

# ACKNOWLEDGMENTS

Thank you Barbara Ayres-Wilson, Jeannine Scott, and Lisa Scott McClain—three inspirational women who carry themselves impeccably despite such horrendous circumstances.

Many special thanks go out to Travis County court reporter Jim King for holding the door open for me. Also to Judge Mike Lynch, Sal Hernandez, Melissa Ann Moreno, and Steve Goetz.

Thanks to former sergeant Mike Huckabay, Sergeant John Jones, Irma Rios, and Lieutenant Troy Gay. Also to: Berkley Bettis, Joe James Sawyer, Dexter Gilford, Ariel Payan, and Robert Icenhauer-Ramirez. William Pierce, Andrew "Brett" Thompson, Meredith Skipper, Lynn Arnold, and Michael Scott. Reverend Kirby Garner, Judy Bonham, Ramona Ramos, Renee Gately, and the lovely ladies of the St. Louis Catholic School and the Diocese of Austin. Cynthia Smith and Burnet Middle School, the librarians at Lanier, McCallum, and Anderson High Schools, and the Lanier High School Agricultural Department. The hardworking staff of Cash In Advance. Russell Porter and the Fuckemos. Rene Pavia and Memorial Cemetery and Evelyn Williams and Johanna Gravesmill of Cook-Walden Capital Parks.

Also to my sources who wish to remain anonymous.

Multiple thanks go out to the incredible staff at Kensington, including Michaela Hamilton, Stephanie Finnegan, my "Red Pencil Rescuer," and everyone who worked so hard on this book and *Dead and Buried*. Also to Paul Dinas, aka "Dr. Death."

To Richard Curtis, for assistance on all fronts. Hopefully, it will all be worthwhile.

Thank you to Poppy Z. Brite and Aphrodite Jones, two of the greatest women I have ever met. Also to Joyce King, Sue Russell, Dennis Etchison, and Diane Fanning.

Thank you to all of the wonderful booksellers and media outlets who have continually welcomed me with open arms for each of my books. See you on the road.

Musical inspiration included Stars of the Lid, Explosions in the Sky, Plaid, Plastikman, Boards of Canada, Shadows Fall, Poison the Well, 36 Crazyfists, Watchtower, God Forbid, Atreyu, Iron Maiden, Lamb of God, Slipknot, Every Time I Die, System of a Down, Otep, seefeel, Phylr, Aphex Twin, Loscil, Labradford, Vapourspace, The Black Dog, John Mayer, P. J. Harvey, and Radio@AOL.

Special thanks to three personal friends for their help with this book—David Schafer, for carrying me over the abyss; Ray Seggern, for food and shelter; and Mike Sheppard, for keeping an eye out for me.

Also to my other good friends and supporters, including Peter and Kathryn Soria, my godson, Matthew Soria, and his brothers, Andrew and Ryan Soria, Dennis and Sharon McDougal, Chris Goldrup and Beverly Rubin-Goldrup, Phil and Karen Savoie, Clint and Cathy Stephen, Knox and Heather Williams, Trey and Missy Chase, Rick Butler, Kirk and Teresa Morris, Kevin and Shana Fowler, Lupe Garcia, Lynette Sheppard and the Sheppard kids, Kelly Nugent, Cassidy and Stevie Seggern, Marti Cochran, Chris Soria, Joe and Frances Soria, Bob and Sandra Price, Sue and Mike Armstrong, and the women of Randolph Air Force Base Elementary School.

To Dana Holliday—thanks for the laughs. See you in the "Crime Lab."

I have been blessed with a new family. I want to thank my sister-in-law Denise Burke, my niece, Leah, and my parents-in-law, Dennis and Margaret Burke, for bringing me into their lives with open arms.

As always, my wonderful family, who have hopefully resigned themselves to the fact that this is my career. Mom and Dad, aka Carol and Don, thank you, as always, for your unwavering support and belief in my chosen path. Mom, you are the anchor for this family. Be strong. Hang in there, Dad. Kyle and Ramona, for believing in me even though what I do may seem strange to y'all. Also to Darrin and DeDe, Ronnie and Madison. Much love to Renee and Bill Runyan, Todd Solomon, Tracy, Jeremy Frey, and Barbara and Mickey Rehak. I cannot forget Max, Dallas, and Lucas. I love you all.

For my late wife, Lisa, I think of you every day and miss you more and more. Thank you for all your love you gave to me and continue to give. I miss you.

To my wife, Audra, I cannot begin to thank you for everything. Your grace, wit, and humor keep me going. I have been so blessed to meet you and to share my life with you. None of this would have been possible without you. I look forward to a long, healthy, happy life together. You will have all my love, forever.

# BOOK YOUR PLACE ON OUR WEBSITE AND MAKE THE READING CONNECTION!

We've created a customized website just for our very special readers, where you can get the inside scoop on everything that's going on with Zebra, Pinnacle and Kensington books.

When you come online, you'll have the exciting opportunity to:

- View covers of upcoming books
- Read sample chapters
- Learn about our future publishing schedule (listed by publication month *and author*)
- Find out when your favorite authors will be visiting a city near you
- Search for and order backlist books from our online catalog
- Check out author bios and background information
- Send e-mail to your favorite authors
- Meet the Kensington staff online
- Join us in weekly chats with authors, readers and other guests
- Get writing guidelines
- AND MUCH MORE!

Visit our website at
http://www.kensingtonbooks.com